Debi Marshall is an investigative journalist, associate producer for Channel 7's *Sunday Night* program and author, based in Tasmania. Winner of the Ned Kelly Award for Best True Crime (*Killing for Pleasure: The Definitive Story of the Snowtown Serial Murders* which inspired the *Snowtown* movie), she has written several biographies and true crime titles. Her most recent book, *Lambs to the Slaughter*, was long-listed for the Walkley Award.

Also by Debi Marshall

The Devil's Garden: The Claremont Serial Killings

Her Father's Daughter: The Bonnie Henderson Story

*Justice in Jeopardy: The Unresolved Murder of
Baby Deidre Kennedy*

*Killing for Pleasure: The Definitive Story of the
Snowtown Serial Murders*

*Lambs to the Slaughter: Inside the Depraved Mind of
Child-Killer Derek Ernest Percy*

Lang Hancock

DEBI MARSHALL

The House of Hancock

The Rise and Rise of
Gina Rinehart

WILLIAM HEINEMANN

A William Heinemann book
Published by Random House Australia Pty Ltd
Level 3, 100 Pacific Highway, North Sydney NSW 2060
www.randomhouse.com.au

First published by William Heinemann in 2012
Parts of this work were previously published in *Lang Hancock*
(Allen & Unwin, 2001)

Addresses for companies within the Random House Group can be found at www.randomhouse.com.au/offices

National Library of Australia
Cataloguing-in-Publication Entry

Marshall, Debi.
The House of Hancock: the rise and rise of Gina Rinehart / Debi Marshall.

ISBN 978 1 74275 674 5 (pbk)

Rinehart, Gina.
Businesspeople – Western Australia – Biography.
Mineral industries – Western Australia – Pilbara.

338.2092

Cover photograph © Christian Uhrig, iStockphoto
Cover design by Christabella Designs
Internal design by Midland Typesetters, Australia
Typeset in 11/15 pt Sabon by Midland Typesetters, Australia
Printed in Australia by Griffin Press, an accredited ISO AS/NZS 14001:2004
Environmental Management System printer

A house divided against itself cannot stand.
Abraham Lincoln, 'A House Divided' speech, Illinois, 1858

'Whatever I do, *whatever* I do, the House of Hancock comes first. Nothing will stand in the way of that. Nothing.'

Gina Rinehart, 1979

'I wish I'd been a boy. I'm not ashamed of being a girl, and since I'm a girl I will do what a boy would have done had I been a boy.'

Gina Rinehart to Lang's biographer,
Robert Duffield, 1979

'I believe, bad and all as it is, that the greed of capitalism is the only driving force there is.'

Lang Hancock, 1971

'. . . in order to fit herself for her coming roles as matriarch and priestess of the Hancock dynasty, she has perforce erected around herself a series of armour-plated defence barriers, lest anybody see a little girl inside who could be taken down by the brutal admirals of industry . . .'

Robert Duffield, on Gina Rinehart

'The most powerful motivational factor in his character is ambition. Nothing that he says or does is superfluous. All is directed towards the business of furthering his power, his assets, his influence and his empire.'

Neill Phillipson, author of Man of Iron, *on Lang Hancock*

'I once asked him: "Have you ever sat by a stream in the outback, watched insects and flowers and wondered what was the meaning of life in general?" He replied he would be considering how to dam the stream for power.'

Dr Neil Scrimgeour, Lang Hancock's GP

'John, we are about to go into war – it is going to be tough and I don't know how long it will last.'

Gina Rinehart to her son, John, following
Lang Hancock's death

'I think he would probably have preferred a son. But anyway, he ended up with a daughter.'

Gina Rinehart, commenting on her father's wish for a boy

'I have genuinely looked after my family for their lifetimes, without leaving the mess and debts and liabilities I was left with . . . but what about Australia's future?'

Gina Rinehart, 2012

'Money shouldn't buy access to justice.'

Former Attorney-General Jim McGinty, on Gina being
granted an inquest into her father's death

AS THE BIOGRAPHER OF a book on Gina Rinehart's father, entitled *Lang Hancock*, I have over the years repeatedly been asked to provide background information to journalists about the man and his family. Almost without exception, I obliged. But in the latest battle in the House of Hancock – the sensational feud between Gina and her adult children – I lost count of the number of journalists who called asking questions.

I hadn't looked at *Lang Hancock* for more than a decade, but as I flicked through the book's pages on a squally January afternoon I was mesmerised all over again by the magic of the story: the great vastness of the unforgiving Pilbara; the grit and determination of Lang Hancock and his discovery of iron ore; the *Dynasty*-style, real-life drama between Lang's daughter, Gina, and his third wife, Filipina-born Rose Lacson; the twists and turns in a story that is so quintessentially Australian. And I was struck by something else: how contemporary this story is; how the mighty Pilbara, with her extremes of heat, her cyclones, her hard, unrelenting earth takes centre stage against today's mining boom and how Gina Rinehart – right wing, conservative, obsessively private, poised to become the richest woman on the planet but who reportedly loathes the title 'Iron Ore Heiress' – appears to be a carbon copy of her father.

Lang Hancock was long out of print and by the end of the day, I was granted its reversion rights. It now belonged solely to me, to do with as I wished. The trouble was, I didn't know what I wanted to do.

I had a sleepless night. Did I really want to revisit a story that had been so difficult to research the first time? A story where, time and again, people who had worked for Gina had refused to talk to me because they had signed confidentiality agreements or who had remained silent because they were wary of her wealth and influence; where Gina had made it patently clear that she would not give me any help unless she had editorial control; a book I was warned off writing by, among others, Gina's son, John, whom I had got to know when he was working at Iscor in South Africa. Did I really want to revisit all this?

I made numerous attempts to engage Gina's help when I was writing *Lang Hancock*. After all, I reasoned, she knew him better than anyone else alive. While my faxes to her were always met with a polite and speedy response, from the outset Gina indicated that she would look forward to reading an 'excellent' biography of her late father, but she was not in a position to help. I came to understand, very quickly, that Gina is zealously devoted to preserving her father's legacy and that her definition of an 'excellent' biography meant one that was favourable to his memory and not sullied by his third marriage to the woman Gina had once disparagingly referred to in a letter to Lang as a 'Filipina prostitute'.

In early May 1999 I received a facsimile from Gina's personal assistant, Peta Wright, writing on Gina's behalf. 'It is very difficult to write a book about Lang Hancock without a good understanding of the events and complicated matters involved,' it began. 'Mrs Rinehart has a great deal of knowledge of her father's life and business dealings and probably more so than anyone still alive; however, the time commitment she would need to give for such a book to be done adequately would be immense. Unfortunately she would not have the time to do this, this year. She would, however, like to see an excellent book written on her father and would like to see the book you have already written [my first book, *Her Father's Daughter – The Bonnie Henderson Story*] to get an understanding of your writing. She would not be prepared to assist in a publication re the stressful end of her father's life that got too much publicity and was something her father did not want in the latter period of his life.' In short, it appeared, Gina wanted me to excise Rose from the manuscript; to edit history.

Another facsimile to me from Peta Wright, dated 26 July, made it clear what Mrs Rinehart meant by the 'stressful end of her father's life'. 'Mrs Rinehart noted that your division of the "3 periods" of Mr Hancock's life included 1 of the 3 for his marriage to Mrs Porteous,' it reads. 'This period of 6 years, July '85 to March '92, is not the 9 years of marriage to which you referred [in earlier correspondence]. You may or may not be aware that they were separated at the end of their lives and a divorce was planned . . .'. Rose strenuously denied that she and Lang had planned to divorce when interviewed at a later date.

In August 1999 Gina's daughter, Bianca Rinehart – then Gina's right-hand girl – led my brother and research assistant, Wayne, and me into the cavernous Hancock Prospecting boardroom where, after polite preliminaries, we were shown hours of documentaries – some excruciatingly dull – celebrating Hancock's achievements. According to Bianca, Gina was in the next office, but she did not have time for introductions. Not then, nor at any other time did I meet with her, or talk to her by telephone. She had no interest, it appeared, in meeting a woman who was writing a book about her father.

As the head of HPPL, Gina's time is extremely limited, but there was another issue at play. Without permission to view the entire completed manuscript, with editorial input from her lawyers and herself, she would not talk to me. I denied that request on the grounds that while any input on her behalf would be welcomed, the biography had to remain critical and unbiased. I did, however, offer for her to read the manuscript in my presence so that she could provide the balance she was concerned was lacking. She declined to do that, and undertakings from her son John to provide documentation did not materialise. All attempts to negotiate were met with a stone wall: it was all or nothing. The request to see the manuscript was reinforced by a letter from Gina's (then) solicitors Corrs Chambers Westgarth sent to the publishers in February 2000. In part, they wrote: '. . . We would thus like to include a review by ourselves of the text as Mrs Rinehart's and her companies' lawyers prior to publication. The purpose of such a review would be to point out to you matters that are *sub judice* and/or in which there are factual inaccuracies.'

Employees at Hancock Prospecting claim that despite Gina's long-held policy of not speaking to journalists, she nevertheless cares a great deal about her public image, proven by her long-standing contract with Media Monitors to deliver daily all media coverage of stories with phrases including her own name, her father's, iron ore and Rose Porteous.

John Rinehart, then something of a mouthpiece for his mother, also offered a perspective as to why Gina would not talk: over the years, he said, she had often been misrepresented by the media.

Disappointed as I was that Hancock's daughter would not help present a personal and professional perspective of her father, I was never tempted to abandon the project. In this, I was encouraged by other writers who have forged ahead with unauthorised biographies. Kitty Kelley's biography of the late

Frank Sinatra, for example, quoted an article in the *Baltimore Sun* applauding her determination to continue to research and write that book despite Sinatra's threat of legal action. 'If all the public can learn of a person is what the person himself wants it to learn, then ours will become a very closed and ignorant society, unable to correct its ills . . .' the article stated. I was also encouraged by the late Lang Hancock himself, who was a great believer in the freedom of the press to express an opinion, and who expressed his own at every opportunity. Indeed, in the preface to the revised edition of the book *Hancock and Wright*, which he and his partner, Peter Wright, commissioned in 1972, he wrote: '. . . it was a condition of the contract that [author] Mr Moyes had complete freedom to write the facts as he saw them. This he has done, and we do not necessarily agree with everything. Such a publication, we believe, was necessary because we felt it important that the book should be completely independent . . .'

If only Gina felt the same way. It is a catch 22. If she doesn't see the manuscript, she has no way of knowing what it is she may wish to add. If she does see it, then with that go her demands for editorial control.

Around early 2000, John and I met for a meeting in Perth. Ever the negotiator, he was there on behalf of his mother to find out what my plans were regarding the publication of *Lang Hancock*. He didn't mince words. 'Look, Mama doesn't want you to write this book,' he started, stirring his coffee. 'She isn't happy that you won't allow her to read it and to offer input about her father and the company. Would you consider going on the payroll for the duration of the research? Mama will organise your travel and accommodation, plus access to Hancock Prospecting documents so that you get your facts right.'

'And in return?' I asked. 'What does Gina want in return?'

He sighed. 'She wants to be able to edit the story. Take things out, put things in.'

'You mean, she will have full control?'

'Yes, that's one way of looking at it. But your book will benefit from her knowledge of grandfather and the company.'

I gave him a wry smile. 'Nice try, John! But no, thanks. If I give away control, I have nothing left.'

He grimaced. 'Mama doesn't like people saying no to her. You should give it some consideration.'

'No, John. No way. I have to keep editorial independence, otherwise I've got nothing.'

He tried again. 'Be reasonable. It would be helpful.' He repeated what he had said. 'She doesn't like people saying no to her.'

I stood to leave. 'Give your mama a message, John. Tell her thanks for the offer, but the answer is no.'

Prologue

GINA RINEHART. WHO IS this enigmatic woman behind the media hype? What makes her tick? Is she a 'chip off the old block', as is commonly suggested, or has she long stepped outside her father, Lang Hancock's, shadow? Was she simply in the right place at the right time to turn her millions to billions on the back of the staggering resources boom or is she a genius businesswoman driven by ruthless rat cunning and a determination to win at all costs?

Was she, in her protracted and often tawdry court battles with her father's third wife, Rose Porteous, driven by an obsessive desire to bring Rose undone or by a strongly held determination to fight for justice? How much of Gina's life today was shaped by her childhood, out there in the Pilbara on lonely, remote Mulga Downs station where, as her father said, her 'only companions were kangaroos and lizards' and where she absorbed like a sponge the lessons he taught her? And what of her father's influence? How strongly does the ghost of the cantankerous, complex Lang Hancock shape Gina's psyche and decision-making today? Was she moulded by her father like playdough?

The metaphorical guards around the Rinehart company palace – her staff – ensure she is well insulated from media calls. All requests to interview Gina must be put in writing. Getting to the woman herself is, it seems, a near impossibility.

With Gina now wielding more power than the Prime Minister (she ranks at number 19, four places ahead of Julia Gillard, on *Forbes* magazine's list of the most powerful women in the world), wealthier than the Queen and poised to leapfrog Microsoft founder Bill Gates' fortune of $55 billion, or Mexican industrialist Carlos Slim's pile of $73 billion, her first name alone gains instant recognition. So, too, does her reputation: not as a Pilbara Princess but as Queen of Litigation; a woman who is, by turns, charming and churlish, a conservative loner whose wealth ensures the ear of those in power; an uncompromising entrepreneur and workaholic and, now, a serious media player with her escalation to an almost 13 per cent share in Fairfax Media – publisher of *The Age*, *The Sydney Morning Herald* and *The Australian Financial Review* and owner of multiple radio stations – and her recent $166 million plunge for a 10 per cent stake in Network Ten. Armed with the sure knowledge that media does not return the profits of mining, what prompted these moves that got Australia talking?

Much mythology surrounds the Hancock legacy. What *is* indisputably true is that from the moment of Lang Hancock's chance discovery of iron ore his life – and everyone else's close to him – irrevocably changed forever. Vast wealth would bring its own vast problems.

Nicknamed 'Rogue Bull', Lang Hancock had the face of a boxer, a mind like a computer and the tongue of a viper. In many ways, he had much in common with the Pilbara he so loved: like it, he was solid, earthy and imposing, as hard as rock. And he was isolated: indifferent to public opinion, political correctness, bureaucrats and anybody else whose views differed from his own. He is remembered either with fondness as being a maverick Aussie who refused to bow to authority, or as more right wing than Genghis Khan; a man who did not temper his attitudes or criticisms with tolerance. How will his daughter be remembered?

To his supporters, he was a visionary genius, imposing in the boardroom and yet happiest in the bush. To his opponents, he was an arch-capitalist, a fractious and flinty self-serving opportunist known for his support of extreme right-wing political parties. But Lang cared not one whit what people thought of him. 'I'm not in public life,' he famously stated. 'I don't have to have an image; I don't have to get votes. People are quite free to call me what they like.' Gina does not take the same sanguine approach. Known to inspire equal parts fear and loyalty in her employees, she does not take kindly to criticism. Hancock bellowed; Gina whispers. Hancock bullied; Gina sues.

For all Hancock's clout and enormous wealth, his holy grail – to own and operate his own mine – eluded him. Significantly, it was a holy grail that shadowed Gina too, but which is now within reach. 'I don't care what Gina does when I die,' Lang once commented. 'She can go and spend it all in Monte Carlo.' While it was always a safe bet that this young woman with the will of iron would not squander her inheritance on a frivolous, party lifestyle, many argue that she has squandered a great deal more than she needed on vengeful litigation.

Prior to his death in 1992, Hancock had become a household name. His legacy has become equally well known for the bitter and protracted court cases between Gina and his third wife, Rose. His role in developing the Pilbara has been overshadowed by the high glitz that came to be synonymous with his third marriage – parties, fashion shows and extravagant dinners – which made the couple's lifestyle legendary in Perth during the 1980s, where they stood out even in a town known for its profligate spending. It is an image that Gina is determined to erase. She is nothing if not complex: on the one hand, lionising her father as King of the Pilbara and on the other, condemning that his empirical coffers were empty, looted by generosity to his third wife and laid barren through his own errors.

Gina's recent forays into Fairfax and Network Ten have changed her public persona as much as has her battle of the billions with her children. Journalists reason that a woman who wants privacy but who buys into the media has to expect – and accept – scrutiny. From the moment the press learned that Gina's wealth was tipped to increase beyond $100 billion in the next few years, it started a media meltdown. Suddenly, this elusive, notoriously media-shy woman was everywhere – her business acumen dominating front pages across the nation and making news around the globe and the latest scandal, the war between Gina and her children, dissected by a salivating press. The infinite wealth of this girl from the bush is mind-boggling. As Perth-based business journalist Tim Treadgold commented: 'If Rinehart were listed on the stock exchange, she would be valued at more than Fairfax, Ten, the Seven network, David Jones and Qantas. Combined.'

When writing *Lang Hancock*, finding people who were willing – or able – to talk was one of the most difficult tasks. A newcomer to the nuances of Perth and its people, I realised quickly that while it is a city which can well hold its own among other Australian capitals, essentially it is still small enough for everyone to know everyone else. That, in part, explains why some people were so guarded. From the time I started researching the biography of her father I quickly learned firsthand that Gina Rinehart was a tough and demanding businesswoman, fiercely protective of her family name. Gina was also concerned that the events following her father's death, in which she plays such a critical role, not colour his lifetime achievements. But a study of Hancock's life would not have been complete without detailing the intrigue that followed his death. As the respected Caroline Jones said in her preface to the ABC TV program *Australian Story* entitled 'House of Hancock': '. . . the aftermath of [Hancock's] death was nothing short of a media circus and even today litigation continues over his estate.' That circus, it appears, has now rolled on to the next generations.

For my research into *Lang Hancock*, Gina, through her company Hancock Prospecting, provided a list of names of people I could speak to who had known Lang in both a business and personal capacity. All but one refused to participate. With the exception of two people I could not locate, some returned my calls with polite refusals, but most ignored them. 'I'd love to be able to talk, but my lips are sealed because I have signed an agreement,' one person commented. It was a common refrain, and one I would encounter time and again. Gina was, however, happy to allow me to talk with her son John, then working in South Africa, and her daughter Bianca, in Perth. Eleven years on, in the wake of the bitter family feud between herself and three of her adult children, I wonder if Gina would still furnish their names to me.

Even in 1999, Gina inspired that curious mixture of fear and loyalty in people who worked for her or knew her. Many people were happy to share reminiscences of Lang as a great Australian but beyond that they wanted permission from his daughter to talk further. Despite the difficulties faced in eliciting informa-tion from some people, all were, however, quick to agree that Hancock was a charismatic character. It is not an adjective that is readily used to describe Gina. She is known as enigmatic. Secretive. Driven. But driven by what?

Sir Valston Hancock, a relative and lifelong friend of Lang, knew him particularly well. 'The image which seems to emerge from the media predominantly is that of a ruthless, uncouth, greedy, intolerant, obstinate character softened somewhat by a keen sense of humour and a capacity for friendliness,' he said before he died. 'This is not the real Lang Hancock.' If her father, then, was not what he appeared, can the same be said of Gina?

So to 2012. Little has changed since 2000.

Some of the people named as 'sources' herein were reluctant, for legal or other reasons, to have their name used. One, who worked very closely with the Hancock and Wright Partnership and who has known Gina for 20 years, was particularly helpful in providing material and insights into the Rinehart family. His personal, firsthand knowledge, combined with his intelligent understanding of legal, mining and other issues, was invaluable to me in my research.

Much of the material in this book is taken from my own dealings with John Rinehart (who changed his name to Hancock); Bianca Rinehart; their father, Greg Milton; the son of Lang's business partner Peter, Michael Wright; and Rose and Willie Porteous. From my past experience with approaching Gina, I chose not to do so again.

When researching this book, I came to realise one thing with absolute clarity: that to understand Gina Rinehart, you first have to understand Lang Hancock.

Like father, like daughter.

1

AFTER SEVEN YEARS OF marriage, Lang Hancock and his second wife, Hope Margaret, had abandoned all dreams of having children. Lang was almost 45 years old; Hope 38. Even by outback standards, their isolation at Mulga Downs station, nestled in the shadow of the Hamersley foothills to the south and the Chichester Ranges to the north, was intimidating. A man could ride all day without reaching a fence line; the 1,600,000-hectare property under a vast, velvet sky stretches to the horizon.

Like her husband, Hope was a child of the Pilbara, used to the loneliness and seclusion and with only employees to talk to. But now, a beautiful surprise: a telltale baby bump is showing and Lang – gruff, cantankerous Lang – is beaming with delight.

He is going to be a father.

He is going to have a son and heir. He is sure of it.

Hope told friends that Lang was convinced their little bundle, who arrived on a steaming-hot early February morning in 1954 at Perth's St John's Hospital, was going to be a boy. 'He was sure of it,' she said. 'He was going to be called George, after his own father. Even when it was born, he wouldn't believe it was a girl. It looked just like him.'

But 'it' wasn't the expected boy. 'It' was a girl they christened Georgina Hope, known from early childhood simply as Gina.

Gina Hope Hancock.

2

LANG HANCOCK'S HOUR HAD come. Some say they heard him scream in the seconds before he died, a desolate, primal scream which carried through his bedroom walls and was airborne by his tormented spirit back to the ancient, ochre mountains of his beloved Pilbara; the haunting, mournful cry of a man who cannot keep death at bay. His once stocky body had withered, racked by sickness and despair.

He was not ready, but no amount of money could buy him more time.

He was not afraid of dying. They breed them tough in the vast isolation that is Western Australia's Pilbara, tough and hard as the baked earth. If God were to exist – which Hancock doubted – he believed his spirit would move up there in the north-west of Australia, in the dark cinnamon dust and moonscaped mountains, the weeping gorges and mustard-coloured riverbeds, the vermilion sunsets and luminous stars of the southern skies which light the empty darkness. Death is inevitable, it comes to us all, and he had no time for poignant goodbyes, no intention of changing his atheist position. God had not revealed Himself to Lang Hancock through his lifetime and he was doubtful He would do so after his death. Hancock trusted few people, and if he couldn't see Him, touch Him, buy, barter or sell Him, then He surely could not exist. He had 'died' once before from a heart attack and the experience was uneventful. No bright lights, no white tunnel and no one waiting on the other side with open arms. God was mythical, an invented fantasy, and Lang had no time for fantasies – particularly as death drew near.

The press, sensing that a major story was about to break, jostled for position like crows at a feast outside the *Gone with the Wind*-style mansion, Prix d'Amour, in the ritzy suburb of Mosman Park. They were primed for action in the blistering heat of this March 1992 Perth morning, one collective eye trained for movement through the massive electronic gates and the other on their watches, now ticking towards 10 am. They couldn't miss their deadlines. The man on whom they had bestowed the nicknames 'King of the Pilbara' and 'Maverick Millionaire' might be 82, with gangrenous legs, pulmonary heart disease and renal failure, but that was immaterial. If their sources were correct, if the old man of mining was indeed dying, it would dominate headlines. In death, as in life, Hancock was a good story.

Lang is in the guest house behind the main pile, christened the 'Rose Mahal', which he had built for his third wife, Rose. The room, decked out in medical equipment, emulates a hospital ward. Next to him, his daughter, Gina, sits quietly. Also there to give comfort in his final moments is his long-time chauffeur and friend, Reg Browne, and his doctor, Barry Hopkins. Rose is asleep in the main house. Lang's grandson, John, is upstairs in the guest house. His other grandchildren are not present.

By Hancock's own admission he'd had a good innings, but none of that mattered now. His affairs were in disarray, the lawyers circling in a feeding frenzy, and the two women in his life – Gina and Rose – were poised to begin a bitter fight which he was now powerless to stop. To the victor, the spoils.

Hancock, bushman, knew that the darkest hour is just before the dawn. More than at any other time in his life, he needed to get his house in order.

But at 10.12 am his time ran out.

His hour had come. There were no goodbyes.

Lang Hancock's lifetime achievements had changed the face of Australia, but the battle for the legacy he had left behind was only just beginning. The once immensely private House of Hancock was about to start splitting at the seams.

3

GINA RINEHART'S FOREBEARS WERE made of stern stuff. Disembarking at the Swan River Colony on the ship *Warrior* in early March 1830, after a long and treacherous sea journey from England, they must surely have thought they had arrived in hell.

Their destination, Perth – established only five years before their arrival – was the most isolated settlement in the world, and the vast Indian and Southern oceans reinforced the state's isolation from the world's thriving trade centres. The Nullarbor Plain and Simpson Desert acted as sandy moats, separating the colony from the east coast of Australia, and the Arafura Sea formed a natural boundary to the north. The Hancocks' first impressions of Fremantle, a wild, raw and uncouth port in its infancy, was that it was no match for the village at Coldridge they had left behind. Only seagulls, with their unmistakable shrill call, would have provided a brief illusion of familiarity as the ship finally lay at anchor in an alien land.

Fifty-nine-year-old Grace Hancock, sheltering from the

searing heat under a parasol and blocking her ears to the seamen's profane language, no doubt wondered why she had ventured to this godforsaken continent on the other side of the world with her husband, John, and sons George, 22, and James, 20. She must have wondered, too, whether she would ever again see her two daughters, who had remained in England.

The light was blindingly intense here, more luminous than the dappled sunshine that fell gentle on English fields, and the air pure as crystal – sharp, hot and still. The distinctive scent of the eucalypt pervaded all. Here, there were no lush, green hills to break the eye's journey; the horizon seemed limitless, stretching to the Never-Never. But if Grace wanted to turn back for home, that was not the Hancock way. John, a carpenter five years her junior, had visions of making his mark in this new country; they were free settlers, in a land of opportunity. But even he was alarmed at its apparent barrenness. 'We will starve to death,' he reputedly groaned when he first set foot ashore.

The family applied for a land grant at the fledgling town of Perth, and established one of the state's first timber industries at Belmont Farm. Starting from scratch, they laboured at the gruelling task of sawmilling through all seasons, their advertisements for timber appearing frequently in the local gazette. For a short time, the farm also doubled as a tavern, but John did not have the heart of a publican and showed little enthusiasm for the thirsty strangers who sought relief from the scorching summers with a cool ale. His requests for additional land to the Surveyor General became increasingly relentless.

He was granted 640 acres at York. But, less than a year later, it became clear all was not well within the family. A private dispute over money was laid out in the *Perth Gazette* for all to read – a public airing of dirty linen that was to become synonymous with the Hancock/Rinehart name, echoed more than 140 years later.

CAUTION

WHEREAS JAMES HANCOCK has absconded and left his Business, this is to give notice that the Undersigned will not be answerable for any Debts, Bargains or Contracts, he may incur after this Notice; and further, any Persons indebted to the Undersigned, are requested not to pay the said JAMES HANCOCK any monies, as he has no authority to collect any debts.

JOHN HANCOCK
GEORGE HANCOCK

History does not record the reasons for the falling-out which occurred a year after Grace's death at the age of 63, just three years after her arrival in the colony. What is clear is that on John's death at 62, five years later, the animosity between father and son still prevailed. In his will, John Hancock left the bulk of his worldly possessions to George, including sole ownership of the timber business.

Lonely at Belmont Farm following the death of his parents and no longer in contact with his only brother, George spent what little spare time he had wooing Sophia Gregory, a young housemaid. Their respective families had met on the sea journey from England, although it is doubtful that the seeds of George's infatuation with the slip of a girl were sown at that time. At their marriage in 1839 – nine years after settling in Western Australia – Sophia was just 16 and George almost twice her age. The couple continued to manage the timber business but, by 1842, they had fallen on hard times. George, austere and dour by nature, faced debtors' summonses in the civil court, and the business was forced under the hammer at auction. They later purchased a property near Beverley where they remained until the end of their days, George working at various jobs to keep his burgeoning family afloat. Sophia was constantly with child, and life was unremittingly tough. From 1841 until 1868 she bore 13 children. At 59, George suddenly passed away, leaving Sophia to raise the surviving children on her own, the youngest of whom was only three. Photographs taken of her in middle age show a stern-faced woman with thin, tight lips and unsmiling eyes, but her tough exterior belied her sensitive nature.

She died a well-respected pillar of the community in 1906 at the ripe old age of 83, and left her adult children to make their mark on history. Their second-born, Emma, would become known as the Mother of the North. Their first-born, John, was Gina Rinehart's great-grandfather.

The Pilbara. A vast area covering 457,238 square kilometres, almost twice the size of Victoria – geologically, one of the most ancient places on earth. The formation of the monoliths, spinifex-covered plains, valleys and narrow deep gorges was by turns gentle and turbulent. For millions of years, mother nature sang a lullaby to embryonic life forms which were cradled under a warm sea, followed by huge upheavals, when the rocks were broken by fissures and smothered by molten lava. When nature's painting was finally complete, the colours on its canvas, which had taken more than 1500 million years to prepare, were spectacular. The deep rusts and muted greens of the earth stand out against a lavender sky which fades to velvet damask in the dying of the day. Then the light is gone, suddenly, and all is plunged into darkness until the stars light the way. Ghost gums, with their entwined limbs outstretched as if in prayer, dot the landscape – the signature of the outback. In summer, the earth is incinerated; temperatures soar into the high forties, a sweltering heat so intense that only the brave or the insane enter its furnace ill-equipped. Dust, fine as talc, encases everything, and perspiration encrusts bodies and soaks clothing. Eyes blur, lips crack and lungs gasp as the dry air burns throats. At dusk, the heat of the day yields to the cool of night and the Milky Way forms a belt of light from horizon to horizon. In the monsoon season, clouds roll in pregnant with rain, heralded by a chorus of thunder. Lightning emblazes the sky and spears the ground, igniting spinifex. Wind whips the flames, as fire spreads unchecked, scorching the landscape. The heavens unleash a violent fury, deluging the land with water; parched, sandy riverbeds and gorges swell and dusty bowls become boggy mires. During cyclones, an eerie silence precedes the gale, then winds tear trees from their roots, animals take shelter and man cowers from the fury. If the summers are often marked by heartbreaking drought which can last for years, the monsoons are moody and unpredictable.

It is a land where solitude can send a man mad, and often has. And it is to here that the young John Hancock, with his sister Emma Withnell and her husband, John, ventured in 1864 in a 187-ton three-masted schooner, the *Sea Ripple*.

4

THE SEA JOURNEY WAS perilous enough: for Emma Withnell, heavily pregnant with her third child and caring for her two young sons, it was doubly uncomfortable. At the tender age of 16 and against her father's wishes, she had married John Withnell, 16 years her senior, in 1859. By 1861, word was spreading about the opportunities for pastoral leases in the largely uncharted and virtually empty north-west. Emma's cousin, Surveyor Francis Gregory, had recently returned from the north and regaled the couple with colourful stories of his adventures. Within three years, Emma and John had sold their holdings and finalised arrangements to venture into the unknown and start a new life. Their destination was the region surrounding the De Grey River. Emma would have had some comfort in the knowledge that her 15-year-old sister, Fanny, and three house servants were on board the *Sea Ripple* in the event she went into early labour. Her brother, John Hancock, now 22, and brother-in-law, Robert Withnell, completed the party. Below the decks, cattle, sheep, horses and fowls shared the stifling air of this late March 1864. The atmosphere was moist and cloying as they sailed towards their destination, 1800 kilometres from Perth. As the days stretched into weeks and the schooner went further north, the clouds became increasingly dark and threatening. Two days out of Cossack (then Port Tien Tsin) and by now 1000 kilometres from Perth, the storm broke. The weather, unpredictable at the best of times, was in an ugly mood. Before the party had time to set anchor, the ship was tossed into the path of the storm, which flung it 120 miles past its destination. The ship was holed when she finally ran aground on a reef, and the cost to the livestock was huge. Many of the sheep were smothered when the ship listed to a sickening 40 degrees and cattle died when they drank seawater. It was a heartbreaking beginning to their new life, a warning to the pioneers that the Pilbara did not welcome strangers – a warning noted by many today who venture into her blazing heat seeking big money from mining exploration.

The ship was refloated and turned back to Cossack, the hole repaired with a piece of canvas. Leaving his wife and children, John negotiated the river in search of a site to build a homestead. He chose an isolated spot at the base of a hill overlooking the river, to where the entire party later decamped. Emma, undoubtedly relieved to finally be able to rest, named it 'Mount Welcome', which today overlooks the town of Roeburne. Explorer William Dampier, who had sailed into this coastal region some 300 years earlier, did not share her enthusiasm. He did not, he recorded, think it fit for human habitation. His notes also recall that he was irritated with the erratic movement of his compass, which, he wrote, 'did describe a most powerful attraction to the mountains of the south'.

Emma did not rest for long. Within weeks of settling, she went into labour in the tent they had erected at the riverbank. While her sister Fanny held her hand and the servants scurried to heat water, their third son, now celebrated as the first white child born in the north-west and who they named Robert Harding De Witt, finally made his entrance. In all, Emma would bear 11 children.

For the Withnells, life was raw and rudimentary and only courage and perseverance sustained their spirit to conquer the empty landscape and call it home. Emma's courage in the face of fear is now legendary in the Hancock family. The early years were marked by a torturous run of bad luck. Starvation beckoned when ships carrying supplies failed to negotiate the savage coastline, and fresh water was dangerously low. The seasons, with their floods and droughts, mocked their efforts; for every good crop, there were three bad. Smallpox raged through the area in 1866, an unwelcome gift from Malay pearl divers that threatened to wipe out the Aboriginal population, hitherto unexposed to white man's diseases. With virtually no medicines, an exhausted Emma spent weeks nursing the sick natives; her efforts earned her the nickname 'medicine woman'. The Withnells were determined to overcome the hardships, and in doing so they became the first white settlers to establish a homestead in the area. Even if they had wanted to leave, however, return to a civilised life was almost impossible. To reach Perth overland took months, and the sea journey was even more hazardous. Hundreds of ships lying in watery graves were proof of that.

Having ensured the party was established at Mount Welcome, John Hancock returned to Perth in 1864 to apply for land for himself and the Withnells. He secured 30,000 acres near Roeburne, a property which he later named Woodbrook, and, for the Withnells, made successful application for some acreage at Mount Welcome and a further 100,000 acres on the Sherlock River. John was married in 1867 to Mary Strange, a farmer's daughter, and the young couple returned to the north-west with their two infant daughters in tow four years later. John managed

Andover station, where two further children were born, until the family moved to their own property at Woodbrook in 1877. Two more daughters followed and it was here, on 6 May 1882, in a stone hut lacking electricity, running water or medical help, that Lang Hancock's father, George, made his debut into the world.

The following year, the Hancocks returned south where they bought a farm near Northam and where Mary's last child was born. She did not have long to enjoy her son: with no warning, she died, aged 37.

Lured by the prospect of gold at Halls Creek, John Hancock quickly found, as would his grandson and others in their turn, that the earth did not readily give up its treasures. He abandoned prospecting and, after buying a share of the lush Ashburton Downs station, which boasted more than one million acres of prime land 200 miles from Onslow, he returned to Northam to gather his family. By 1889 he had gained sole ownership of the property.

The Pilbara was ripe for exploration, and from the early 1860s adventurous men began to expedition into its heart to discover its mysteries. One expeditioner, Francis Gregory, undertook the challenge, traversing hundreds of kilometres in the worst possible conditions. His journal offered a colourful account of the flora and fauna, but his description of the minerals he found is simplicity itself.

'Minerals. I was unable to discover any traces,' he wrote. 'Except iron.'

Emma and John Withnell spent 25 years in the north-west, eventually moving to their property at Sherlock River. Age and increasing frailty forced the couple's reluctant return south, where John Withnell died in 1898 at the age of 73. His death was followed four years later by that of John Hancock, who died in Perth at the age of 61. In his will, John Hancock left

18,000 pounds sterling to be divided equally among his three sons, Richard, George and John.

Historian J.S. Battye wrote about him: 'He may be described as one of Australia's grandest sons, a man with integrity, high courage, truthful as the light who never made an enemy and never lost a friend, and his claim to honourable mention among the band of pioneer heroes who opened up the country for those who followed them will readily be accorded and always remembered.'

The men and women who still work in the heat and isolation of the Pilbara mining camps recognise that their working conditions today are far removed from the conditions of last century. Air-conditioning and an attractive income are seductive lures, but the lifestyle is still a far cry from that enjoyed by city dwellers in their plush offices. Although civilisation has now come to the Pilbara, the conditions are still exacting. Port Hedland resident John Love, who has lived and worked in the region for many years, described it as a test of mettle.

Not everyone was as tough as the Hancocks and Withnells. The untended graves of men, women and children litter the hostile land; heartache and homesickness preyed on many, some of whom drowned in their despair. Time has preserved the poignant reminders of their past. Jerry-built meat safes hoisted in the naked limb of a tree, rusting cutthroat razors, tin pannikins and plates and pitted picks and shovels, the simple tools of their labours against an unyielding earth.

5

THE HANCOCK BOYS, RICHARD, George and John, were known in the district as the 'H3B'– the cattle brand of the family station, Ashburton. But their father's generous estate, left to them in his will, came with a price tag. Each son had to manage the station for three years, starting with the eldest, Richard. Neither he nor John showed any interest in station life, and it was left to George to clean up the mess when it was finally his turn to take over.

George spent his early childhood in the outback, moving with his parents between Roeburne and Onslow before attending college in Perth, which he left at the age of nine. At 26, while still in partnership with his brothers, his attention was caught by the fair-headed and bespectacled Lilian Mabel Prior. Her sister, Olive, had married his elder brother, Richard, in 1906; two years later Lilian and George walked down the same aisle at the Anglican Church in Onslow to take their vows. After their honeymoon, the couple set up house at Ashburton but, by the conclusion of his three-year stint, George had to face the harsh reality that the station was not salvageable. Industrious, hard and uncompromising, he had visions for the future. The timing was perfect: he had been offered a position to manage a sheep station owned by one of the wealthiest men in Australia, and he intended to take it.

Mulga Downs station is more than 60 kilometres from the living quarters to the out-camp, and double that distance from the east to west boundaries. Through its belly snakes the Fortescue River. George and Lilian set up house at the dilapidated homestead. Their work was cut out for them: beyond the usual vagaries of nature, there was the distance to the marketplace. Meat and vegetables were plentiful in this scrub grazing land, but camel wagons had to haul in food they could not grow and flour was inevitably infested with weevils by the time it arrived.

Using his resourcefulness and endless capacity for hard work, George turned the station's fortunes around within a few years. During a drought he chopped down all the mulga trees on the property, leaving them lying where they fell so that the hungry sheep could eat the leaves.

Lilian coped with her husband's long absences from the homestead when he was out mustering with the Aboriginal stockmen by presenting an outwardly indomitable spirit, and never complaining. Raised in the north-west, she was accustomed to loneliness, but George's acerbic tongue, for which he was well known, wounded her deeply. The Aboriginal house-girls were little company for her, and the station so remote that very few visitors had the time to make the journey. But Lilian would soon have someone to talk to, for she was with child for the first time. There were few other options but to travel to Perth for the delivery.

George stayed at the station while Lilian, accompanied by two house-girls, made the lengthy overland journey to Perth. On 10 June 1909, Lilian gave birth to a son. George was relieved;

he now had someone to whom he could pass the baton when the time was right.

They named the child Langley George Hancock.

Lang would later laugh that he was such an ugly baby, he wondered why his parents didn't drown him at birth.

6

LANG HANCOCK WAS BORN into a world which was holding its breath. The first years of the twentieth century had been joyously ushered in with prayers for ongoing stability and peace, but by the end of the decade, rumblings of disquiet were beginning to stir in international politics.

Within five years the world would be plunged into unprecedented darkness by the Great War. By its close, the 'war to end all wars' would have claimed the lives of almost ten million men, women and children. But Mulga Downs station remained a rarefied world immune from strife. With no aeroplanes, newspapers or television, it was remote from the mainstream. Life moved slowly, in tune with the seasons. When news of the outside world did get through, it was months out of date.

History does not record the birth date of Lang's younger brother Jack. Nor does it record the reason for his early death, sometime before 1913, nor the heartache Lilian and George must have felt. Until the birth of his two sisters, Lily Kathleen, 'Kay' to the family, in April 1914, and Sheila Laura, 'Peg', in

March 1917, the young Lang had no white companions. The nearest neighbour to the west was 80 kilometres away, and to the east, 200 kilometres. An independent and outspoken child, he was unexceptional looking, with a short, thick neck, bulbous nose and a serious expression. His playmates were the local Aborigines, and he was naturally drawn to the outdoors, exploring every inch of his Pilbara playground. Through his mates, he learned survival skills which would stand him in good stead throughout his adult life: tracking the savage dingoes that lurked on the homestead's fringes, the kangaroos that bounded across the plains and the wild turkeys whose gamey flesh was roasted over hot coals. Fat, juicy lizards, boiled, skewered and seared on a bush oven were served as an entree to snake, with its distinctive flavour between fish and chicken. Witchetty grubs, the bush tucker delicacy that tastes like scrambled eggs with lashings of butter, were relished, as were the juniper berries and nuts they picked up on their travels. As soon as he could walk, Lang learned to ride a horse, though he had little affection for the animals, and by the age of four he could handle a rifle, if not shoot one. He was five years old when Britain entered the First World War, his sister, Kay, just four months, but the family endured little hardship. The station was self-sufficient, and the war a long way away.

His first cousin and childhood friend, Sir Valston Hancock, had exceptionally close ties with Lang's family: his mother and Lilian were sisters, and they married two brothers. Sir Valston recalled the young Lang as a larrikin. 'He was quite a colourful personality, even as a young bloke. A lot of his life had been spent in the presence of shearers and he picked up some of the colourful language of the labourers in his father's station. So much so that he used to swear as a matter of course and couldn't be taken out publicly in trams and conveyances for some time because he used to create a storm.'

The two boys spent their formative years together at boarding school and Lang often visited his Aunt Ollie, Val's mother, at weekends and holidays. Val recalls that his mother, like Lilian, was sensitive by nature and, after an abrupt argument with her nephew, asked him if he had forgiven her. Lang replied, 'Yes, Aunt Ollie, but you're still a bit of a bugger.'

When his sisters were old enough, they rode with Lang to Wittenoom Gorge, 14 kilometres from the station. The gorge was named after Frank Wittenoom, from whom Lang's father had bought the station. Over the years, Lang often noticed blue fibre floaters on the floor of the gorge, but George dashed his hopes when he identified a piece Lang took home as blue asbestos. The Hamersley Range was laden with the mineral, but it was white, not blue, asbestos which was worth money.

When I met Aboriginal Wobby Parker in 2000, he didn't know how old he was, but he guessed his age at around 80, 85. But he had vivid memories of moving to Mulga Downs with his parents when he was six years old. A gentle old man who could not read or write, he lived at an Aboriginal community close to Mount Tom Price, a hot and dry place of mangy dogs and small children. But despite his advanced age, he well remembered George and the young Lang, and life in those far-off days at Mulga Downs.

'I never went to school at all, I started work when I was 13, mustering sheep and cattle,' he said. 'My people didn't work for dollars – we got clothes, bakky, flour, tea and sugar. Them days was hard times; we lived in a spinifex bough shed. We started work at 4 am, knock off in the afternoon, work all day riding and mustering, work seven days a week. It was dirty work, and they didn't want to pay us blackfellas.'

Wobby had a high regard for George, much higher than for Lang. 'Old George used to love a fight – he loved boxing – and when he make our boys jump fences and go to work, there'd be fisticuffs. But in the morning he would talk again, and work next to us. Lang didn't work like that; he gave us orders and then sat back, let us do all the work. Hancock wasn't one of them blokes who would have a joke. He was a tough man, a tough boss.'

Lilian may have turned a blind eye to George's drinking, which over the years increased to half a bottle of whisky a day, but his son noticed. Throughout his life, Lang never touched anything harder than raspberry cordial. Lang liked to stay focused, crystal sharp, and alcohol blurred the edges. In his later life, many people would come to rue just how focused he was.

7

EDUCATED ON THE STATION until the age of eight, Lang
reluctantly packed his prized personal possessions – his football
and cricket bat – when the time came to move to boarding
school in Perth. He did not want to go: school held no fascina-
tion for him, and he could not see its relevance to his life at
Mulga Downs. He wanted to be a pastoralist, like his father,
and he reasoned he couldn't learn that from history books and
mathematics class. It was not an idea shared by George. While
work was his raison d'être, and he believed the best man for
the job was one with common sense, he had high aspirations
for his son to become a mathematics professor. In his short
pants and starched shirt, the young Lang cut a mournful figure
as he waved goodbye to his mother and was left standing in
the imposing grounds of the exclusive Hale boarding school.
The school was tough and competitive, and prided itself on its
high level of academic and sporting achievements. Better than
average in his academic grades – he was second only to the dux
by the time he left – Hancock tried hard to make the first teams

at cricket and Aussie Rules football, which he proudly achieved. Throughout his life, he maintained an enduring passion for a great game of cricket, and he kept fit with tennis.

At Hale, Lang formed a friendship with another student who was later to become his business partner and lifelong friend. The two men could not have been more different in temperament or personality: Lang, a larrikin intolerant of social conventions, was impatient, aggressive and outspoken; Peter Wright was diplomatic, cautious and precise. The young friends were the Yin and the Yang, two sides of the coin, but it was a balance which was to prove devastatingly effective.

Like Hancock, Wright's family had settled in Australia in the mid-nineteenth century. Peter Wright's grandfather, Frederick Thomas Wright, arrived from Liverpool in 1854 and moved to Maldon in Victoria. His grandmother arrived with her family from Scotland in the 1860s and settled in the same district; soon after, she met and married Frederick. He died in 1885 and during the Depression that followed, the family lost their farm. Peter Wright's father, Frederick William, left school at 13 and gained employment cracking stones on the roads, but he had dreams for a better future. Just before Federation, he headed west to the Kalgoorlie goldfields, where he saved money from his job as an engine driver. With his stash firmly in his pocket, he returned to Maldon to help his brother and family move to Kalgoorlie; on that trip, he met and married a girl from the village next door. Peter Wright was christened Ernest Archibald Maynard Wright in Kalgoorlie in 1907 and married Pauline McClemmens in 1932. Pauline loathed his name and bequeathed him with another: Peter, by which he was known for the remainder of his life. Lang would simply call him 'Ern'.

While they spent holidays together, neither teenager could foresee their later business partnership. Wright, brilliant with figures and with a cool head, was the scholar; Lang was more interested in the practicalities. After leaving school, Wright took a lowly position in a bank before joining a firm of chartered accountants. Lang always knew where he was going: back to Mulga Downs, to his beloved Pilbara.

At 18, Lang finally got his wish to return to the station. It was a decision he never regretted, and he recalled why with typical bluntness. 'My father wanted me to go on to university and become a mathematics professor, but luckily I elected to go back to the bush. For a few packets of lollies you can buy a professor to work for you, so I'm very glad I didn't waste my time at university.' Like many other of Lang's ideas, it was a sentiment that Gina would later echo.

Ken McCamey, who, like Peter Wright, was later to play a pivotal role in Lang's business life, grew up on a sheep and cattle station south of Whim Creek, over the Chichester Range from the Hancock property. Although he was much younger than Lang, his parents, Stella and Loris, were good friends with George and Lilian, and Ken would see their son at the infrequent bush gatherings – cricket matches, Christmas and bachelors' balls. Australia was in the grip of the Great Depression; city streets and bush towns echoed with the despair of men begging for work and with the cries of women who could not feed their children. But Ken recalls that station owners were luckier than most.

'None of the stations really suffered during the Depression, because there was food there. But we used to get the old swaggies looking for work, or food; they'd do a couple of days and then they'd be on their way again, the poor brutes. They were hard times. I don't remember much of Lang's mother but I met his father many times; he was an old scallywag. George Hancock was a pretty gruff customer, he used to really drive his workers, and Lang was being primed to take over. He had a different management style than George and he never expected a man to do anything he couldn't, or wouldn't, do himself. He used to say, "Don't skimp on anything, we've got plenty of money." But he wouldn't put up with a bloke who wouldn't work; he was tough in that respect, very tough.'

Lang learned his lessons in station management well, and the years slipped by, one shearing season to the next. By 1930, his interest in minerals was increasing, and he sent a sample of the blue asbestos he had found near the family's property to the Mines Department in Perth. Their opinion – that it was virtually worthless – dashed any hopes he may have had to capitalise on it. The freight cost was 30 pounds a ton, and its net value for tonnage only half that price. 'You couldn't make much money that way,' he recalled. 'I used a block of it as a doorstop at Mulga Downs and forgot about the idea, even though I knew there were huge deposits in the gorges right through the Hamersley Ranges.'

Nineteen thirty was also the year in which the first alarm bells started ringing about the shocking effects on workers of exposure to asbestos dust. A health report published in England pulled no punches: the 'magic mineral', as it was known, was deadly. Compensation claims had already been on foot in America for the past three years; a victim of asbestosis who had worked at an asbestos factory successfully sued his employers for the debilitating disease he had contracted at his workplace, the first win of its kind in the world.

Despite his isolation at Mulga Downs, it is highly unlikely that Lang Hancock, who was in contact with the Mines Department and businessmen who stayed at the station, would not have heard of the dangers.

Years later, the men and women who suffered torturous deaths from asbestosis and mesothelioma after a stint at the hellhole that was Wittenoom, would curse him for pursuing his dream to mine the fragile, deadly mineral.

8

ISOLATED MULGA DOWNS WAS no place to be alone for a strapping young man with fire in his loins. In 1935 Lang, then 26, married a pretty, vivacious girl from the city. Her friends were puzzled as to why 21-year-old Susette Maley, an attractive blonde with laughing eyes, chose a man whose facial features were ripe for caricature. Even Hancock's redeeming physical feature – soft, cornflower-blue eyes which smiled when his mouth did not – were hidden behind heavy, dark-rimmed glasses, a blight which he wore all his life and which became his signature and stigma. But Susette knew what her friends did not: behind the rugged, misshapen face and belligerent exterior, Hancock was a charmer, a ladies' man who could talk his way into any bedroom. His way with women earned him the guernsey 'Town Bull', a reputation which he neither confirmed nor denied. Peter Wright's son, Michael, recalls his father mentioned Lang's reputation with women.

'He was quite the ladies' man. My father told me he used to have strings of girlfriends before he married Susette, and he was very good at getting them into bed. He had a reputation as being a stud, but a very careful one. Lang could be exceptionally charming when he wanted to be.'

Nineteen thirty-five was memorable for Hancock in another way: it was the year he took over management of the station, which by now had up to 40,000 sheep. His stockman's hat, offering shade from the savage sun but little protection against the bush flies, suited Hancock and gave him an impressive air. An excellent rider, he drove himself as hard as he did the sheep and the men. By average Australian standards the family was well-off and Hancock, a healthy and ambitious young man, embraced his new responsibilities with relish. His needs were few; he neither drank nor smoked and he had no affectations. Like his workers he drank his coffee – strong, bitter and black without sugar – out of a dirty plastic mug, a habit which was to stay with him throughout his life.

In his typically laconic fashion, when retelling the story years later, Hancock could not remember why the stranger from an English asbestos company made his way to Mulga Downs in 1934. But the outcome of their meeting was indelibly etched in his memory.

'This fellow, Izzy Walters, was a manager of a British-based company and he expressed great interest in the asbestos doorstop. I told him my sad story about it being next to worthless. He shook his head and said, "It's worth 70 pounds a ton." I suggested to him that he was talking rubbish, and then he said that he'd pay me 70 pounds a ton!'

Where there are minerals, there are men to mine them, and within a short time, prospectors were pegging their leases in the Yampire Gorge area, close to Wittenoom. They were a mangy crew: with the bum out of their pants and barely a horse between them, they laboured from dawn to dusk chipping the asbestos which would reap them rewards. Hancock remembered them as a rough lot. 'They'd gamble and pay their debts in fibre, and booze came in by the truckload. One day a fellow was almost hanged. Another day a throat-cutting attempt was given up only because the knife was too blunt.'

Walters joined forces with another Western Australian mining legend, Claude de Bernales, and opened a plant at Yampire. The mine eventually closed not because the asbestos ran out, but because the partners, each with an eye to operating solo, embarked on long and expensive litigation against each other in England. Unlike his daughter, litigation was not Lang's way; he watched the prospectors with great interest, and did not intend missing out. 'Of course, I pegged out the best area at Wittenoom Gorge and went into asbestos mining,' he boasted. The original leases were in his sister's name; during the last years of her life she lived at Wittenoom, dying in her eighties an eccentric, lonely recluse.

Despite his belief that drinking alcohol was the pastime of fools, who would go the way of all fools – nowhere – Hancock was canny enough to realise that empty trucks equalled unprofitability. When his operation was in full swing, he made extra money on the side by bringing alcohol back in the same vehicles which had transported the asbestos to port.

Hancock's rudimentary mining techniques consisted of open-cut blasting and 'cobbing' the host rocks to extract blue asbestos fibre, which was hand-picked and packed into hessian bags. From Wittenoom, it was transported to Cossack or Point Samson for overseas and domestic markets. The bulk of his mining labour force was made up of Aborigines, including women; packing of the bags was usually carried out by the elders and young children. The few surviving Aboriginal miners remembered that for their efforts, they received no wages other than their 'tucker' and tobacco.

Hancock quickly realised that the road to riches was not paved by the laboriously slow process of chipping the asbestos away with hammers and collecting it in bags. He sensed that there was big money to be made from the mineral; worldwide, only Russia and South Africa had commercial deposits.

Using his native intelligence, Lang improvised a machine in his station workshop which could do the work of ten men – crush, screen and bag the asbestos. Elsewhere the practice of hand-picking and packing into bags continued. Hancock's invention succeeded where others had failed; the machine was designed to split the rock without eroding the fibre, and it also graded the fibre into strengths. For the overseas companies exporting the asbestos, it was manna from heaven.

His old schoolfriend Peter Wright was holidaying at Mulga Downs, and with his keen eye and attention to detail, he could see that although Lang was on a winner, he lacked the necessary business acumen to put it together. He also needed a financial boost to develop the plant. Wright had already earned his stripes in business circles and was looking for expansion. He could work on the administrative side of the business, and Lang could maintain his hands-on approach. It was a perfect, simple solution.

A partnership was born – Hanwright.

For decades, neither Hancock nor Wright committed the terms of their partnership to paper. It was a gentleman's agreement, and Hancock recognised Wright's qualities. 'He has an outstanding brain,' he said. 'And he is a man of immense courage . . . a very strong character with an immense capacity for detail. A very honest chap, and lionhearted.' Lang failed to mention other facets of Wright's character – his patience and ability to hold his tongue. They were qualities that over the coming years he would be required to exercise time and again, after his partner had offended yet another person. Hancock needed Wright.

The economic returns from his primitive operation – almost 960 pounds a month – were lucrative, but Hancock was impatient

36

to achieve more. Impatience was his stock-in-trade, the over-riding personality trait which he displayed in all his business dealings, and for which he would pay the price time and again. But if his leapfrog into bed in 1943 with a company which could provide a greater capital turnover was to give him his first taste of corporate disillusionment, he learned little in the way of patience.

'CSR, the sugar company, came in and formed a new company called Australian Blue Asbestos [ABA], of which they owned 51 per cent,' Hancock said. 'I was foolish enough to believe that gave them 51 per cent of the say and me 49 per cent, but of course, they had 100 per cent.' For the first five years, he continued operating the mine for ABA, but a former CSR manager recalls that his operational methods were so crude that they were desperate to part company with him. 'The whole operation was so filthy we got rid of him and managed the mine ourselves,' he said.

To his dismay, Hancock soon realised that his illustrious title of District Superintendent was in name only: in reality, he had no voice. Peter Wright, too, was disenchanted: as a director of ABA, he confidently expected that when he spoke, the other board members would listen. They didn't. Instead, their directors' meetings, held on the eastern seaboard, were a virtual closed shop. Despite his title, Wright found that he had to pay his own airfares to attend and that even then, the cards were stacked against him. All six board members were CSR employees, and his was a lone voice in the corporate wilderness. The tone of the Hanwright/CSR partnership started to sour, exacerbated by CSR's failure to show increased profitability in a short time. The Western Australian Government recognised that Wittenoom was ripe for expansion, and threw its weight behind the company, building symbols to expected success: a courthouse, government offices, roads and a post office. But Hancock was miffed. As a major shareholder, he at first expected, and then demanded, that the bean-counters and backroom boys at CSR take note of what he was saying. When he was virtually ignored at that level, he made himself known to the workers, strutting around the mine and peering over their shoulders. They, too, ignored him. Hancock was among them, but not of them.

Like Wright, Hancock was not comfortable being a ventriloquist's dummy, and by 1948, they relinquished their shareholding back to CSR for around $8000. If Hancock's leaving was celebrated by CSR, he did not admit it. 'I was disillusioned, so I got out,' he later commented.

But although Hancock had retired hurt from his experience with CSR, he wasn't down for the count. He had not finished with Wittenoom yet.

9

THE PARTNERS DIVERSIFIED, USING a white asbestos mine as their headquarters and overseeing a lead mine and copper operation, hundreds of kilometres apart. The oppressive heat and fine dust which pervaded everything made driving between the mine sites a nightmare, and ensured valuable time was wasted. On one desperate trip Hancock's vehicle suffered 17 punctures, the gearbox fell apart and the starter motor got stuck when he was 200 kilometres from the next waterhole.

He made the decision that he would use an aircraft to fly between the sites, but first he needed to learn how to fly. Years before, driving from Mulga Downs to Perth, he had shaded his eyes to the sun and watched, fascinated, as the third aircraft in Western Australia flew overhead.

'That's the bloody way I'm going to go!' he stated. 'The old fellow who founded WA Airlines had a single-engine plane for sale, so I made a deal to buy it provided he taught me how to fly.' One of the first men to use aircraft for pastoral purposes,

Hancock was on his way to earning the nickname 'the Flying Prospector'.

'Since then I've owned more aeroplanes than motor cars,' he said. 'Flying changed everything around.' A natural pilot, Hancock recognised the expediency of aircraft against the tyranny of distance. Managers were placed into the white asbestos, copper and lead operations, and he flew around to supervise them.

Hancock's personal life was changing. His seven-year marriage to Susette was destined to failure; both she and Lang recognised she was not cut out for an isolated, lonely existence, and nor was she impressed to find, shortly after her arrival at Mulga Downs station, that her new husband had earned his reputation as Rogue Bull. But Susette remained loyal to his memory throughout her life. Speaking with author Robert Duffield years after their marriage had ended, Susette Flanagan, as she later became, recalled with fondness the time she spent with Hancock. Their lifestyle was simple, bordering on austere; Hancock, pastoralist, was yet to discover the massive wealth he would later accrue. Lang, showing the determination and grit that characterised his future business dealings, made a success of Mulga Downs station, riding high where other pastoralists failed, and his reputation went before him. Treated like celebrities when they escaped the Pilbara summer for the less severe climate of Perth, Susette remembered a plane waiting for them for more than half an hour when she overslept. It was not a courtesy Lang would return. Punctual to the second, he was known to become infuriated when he was kept waiting and the person responsible would be decimated by an icy, abusive blast, the tongue-lashing delivered in deep resonant tones as flat as the Pilbara plains and heavily laced with ockerisms.

When Susette left Mulga Downs and returned to the city, Hancock was heartbroken, but he never denigrated his first

40

wife. Loyalty to his women was to prove a major dichotomy in his character. Tough and unbending around men, he spoiled his women and was unusually gentle with them.

Prior to her death, Susette spoke of her innate understanding that the bushie she had married had a big future. 'He was a very intelligent young man,' she said, 'a kind man and a gentle man. I could see then that minerals were his destiny, and that he would become much richer.'

Just how much richer, no one could have foreseen.

10

HOPE NICHOLAS WAS A perfect match for Hancock –
gracious where he was gruff, tolerant where he was impatient,
and temperate in attitude. Born and bred in the Pilbara, her
family was one of the largest landowners in Western Australia
and introduced Cobb and Co. coaches to the region.

In 1947, Hope and Lang married in a quiet ceremony attended
by close friends and family. Mulga Downs suited Hope; unlike
Susette, she was used to the isolation and happy to cater to
Lang's plain tastes. In the early days, the couple rarely entertained and lived a homely existence. But Hope was a civilising
influence, and knew when it was appropriate to turn on the
charm. Photos of Hope show a smiling, slim woman who knew
how to laugh, and did so often.

If the bushwhacker with the will of steel who only ever
wanted one way – his own – had so far been lucky with the
asbestos doorstop and his decision to buy his first aircraft, he
was soon to realise what real luck is. Hancock was just 43 years
old. He was about to discover iron ore, and join the select ranks

of Australians whose finds have propelled them into legendary status. The story of how he made that discovery is now
embedded in Australian folklore, but if most people believe that
the flight took place, not everyone was to believe that Hancock
should take credit for the legacy which followed.

Each wet season, Lang and Hope flew to Perth, via his sister
Peg Sharpe's station at Woolleen. But this year – November
1952 – he had left his run too late to fly out over the Hamersley
Range. The monsoon was in full force; the clouds hanging over
the tough terrain, thunderous, threatening and low. Most pilots
knew that this weather was a dangerous adversary, and kept
their aircraft safely on the tarmac. Hancock's small aircraft
did not possess either the power or the instruments to fly over
the top of the cloud. To attempt it could be fatal – but get out,
they must. The road was now swollen with flood, and would
be impassable for the next few months. Buffeted wildly on
take-off, the Auster went in its usual direction. Hancock made
the decision to follow the clouds down, less than eight metres
above the treetops but safely below the walls of the gorge. He
had little choice: he could neither fly through the cloud nor
above it. He knew he needed to keep his wits about him: even
for a pilot far more experienced than him, the logistics of
negotiating through this area without hitting a solid wall were
extremely tricky. Noticing a creek flowing through one of the
gorges, he turned to Hope and made the droll statement that
if water could get out, so could they. Flying lower, Hancock
made a remarkable discovery – the walls looked to be solid
iron ore. 'I knew that Australia was supposed to have very little
worthwhile iron, so I assumed it was low grade and of no use,'
he later said.

Over the coming seasons doubt niggled at him about what he
had seen, and the following winter, following the same route,
he returned for another look. Yet again, the gut instinct which
had been his guide until now did not fail him. Following the ore

for about 112 kilometres, he realised that even if it was very low grade, it could be upgraded with metallurgy. Ken McCamey, now Lang's trusted sidekick, helped him with his aerial prospecting. While Hancock piloted the aircraft, McCamey charted in coloured pencil the geological map, signalling to him where to fly. Later, McCamey would return to the area in a bush vehicle and check the finds at a closer range. Between them they were a formidable team, but a federal and state ban on the export of iron ore meant no security of tenure over the finds, and there was little point pegging the claims. Landing the aircraft in the rough spinifex, Hancock wandered around at his leisure taking samples to have assayed in Perth. 'To my great surprise, the stuff was 2 per cent higher than the standard blast furnace feed of the greatest industrial nation on earth, the United States. I thought, if it's good enough for them, it's good enough for me. I knew then that the find was not only big, but also very valuable.'

Lang Hancock – pastoralist, bush pilot and prospector – was about to become a multimillionaire, whose massive wealth would be coined 'the rivers of gold'. He had happened upon the most important discovery of his life – an exposed, brilliant ochre-red rock layer holding a billion tonnes of high-grade ore. The find was at least three times the size of Australia's official estimated iron ore reserves and would ultimately lead to the development of the world's greatest iron field.

Years later, Hancock reflected on the journey to find those rivers of gold.

'I had a very happy childhood because my devoted mother spoiled me, and I had a father who I could look up to as a great example,' he said. 'He always wanted me to get what he didn't have and nothing would have pleased him better than if I'd gone on to become a Professor of Mathematics, but I'm afraid I disappointed him, because the moment I got away from school I went straight to the land where I used to be, because everything comes out of the earth, you either mine it or you grow it . . . Here was I, a boy from the bush, with no education, no letters after my name or anything, trying to tell them that I was on by far the world's largest iron ore deposits, or field actually.'

Hancock was not the first person to discover iron ore in the Pilbara. Geologists H.P. Woodward and Gibb Maitland had noted its existence in the 1880s, but their discovery was met with little enthusiasm. There was no great demand for iron ore at that time and the Pilbara was regarded as too harsh and inaccessible for mining. Hancock's brilliance lay in his ability to tap the market and advertise its commercial viability at just the right time in 1960, eight years after he made the discovery.

Iron ore export had been banned in Australia since 1938, a decision made by Sir Robert Menzies' Federal Government. It was based largely on the perceived need to safeguard Australia's existing reserves and to keep out the Japanese, who had keenly eyed Yampi Sound in the north-west as a potential base for their operations. Japan's war of attrition with China ensured that the country needed to maintain a continuous supply of iron ore; that it existed at Yampi Sound was proven beyond doubt. So was the opinion of the average punter that the Japanese should stay out of their country; for the government to ignore that would have ensured political kamikaze. Menzies later earned the dubious nickname 'Pig-Iron Bob' when he signed off a sale of scrap metal to the Japanese in a diplomatic gesture to appease them for Yampi Sound. It was a decision that was to resound bitterly in his ears, as the catchcry went up on the wharves and in the factories that he had sold out. The Japanese resourcefully used the scrap metal to build warships and to make bullets, which were turned against Australian servicemen in World War II.

The Western Australian Government also had its own ban in place: regardless of who found the iron ore – whether a lone prospector or a major company – it belonged to the Crown. Agreements to circumvent this ban were negotiated

45

on a case-by-case basis. The floodgates opened in 1960 when the announcement was made that the Griffin Coal Mining Company, through its subsidiary Mineral Mining and Exports, had discovered more than a hundred million tons of high-grade iron ore at Scott River. The Japanese immediately wanted in, and the Federal Government was forced, again, to re-examine the export ban. Hancock had kept the location of his massive find secret, which proved to be a two-edged sword. American steel companies might be interested, but without knowing where the iron ore was – nor able to have it exported – it was useless to them. One by one, more than 30 companies he approached responded to Lang's carefully worded business letters, and their answers were all the same: Thank you, sir, but no. Hancock's contempt for white-collar decision-makers, which had until now bubbled on the surface, took root. Increasingly, he would make well known his opinions that they were fools in glass castles.

Charles Court, later to become Premier of Western Australia, was Hancock's nemesis. On his return to Australia following World War II, he was alarmed to find that the Communist Party had swelled dramatically in numbers, and his strong Liberalism took root. Here, finally, was a man who appeared to share the same dreams as Hancock and who had the power and the ear of internationalists. Hungry for political power, Court chaired the North West Rehabilitation Committee, to which Lang closely allied himself. It was the beginning of a relationship between the two men that would turn full circle over the following years. Both believed in the same principle – development of Australia's north-west – but their approaches were vastly different. Court, the consummate politician who would become premier and be knighted, wanted expansion which would work for the majority. He could not risk a loner like Hancock, with his individual-istic approach, rampaging through the Pilbara and knocking down all in his path. Hancock didn't believe in the majority voice, the nitpicking of committees and forums. He wanted to

forge ahead in his inimitable gung-ho fashion, and when seduc-
tion of the new government failed to achieve what he wanted,
he quickly proved to be an antagonistic opponent. In the new
line-up, Court gained the portfolio of Industrial Development,
and increasingly came to dissociate himself and his government
from the brash, opinionated ideas of Hancock. He had the
power which walked hand in hand with his political nous. No
amount of Hancock's wealth could match that.

In many respects, the two men did have much in common.
Court's character was forged as a child of strict, Calvinist work-
ing-class parents in the bleak Depression years; Hancock too
was moulded by a strong work ethic and a driving ambition
to succeed. Both despised the press, yet cultivated it to suit
their own ends. Court bemoaned the new breed of journalists
as '. . . people who are more interested in slanting the story to
their convenience than they are in reflecting your personal and
genuine approach to the thing'; Hancock, like Gina to follow,
regarded them as pariahs. Court was often linked in the public
psyche with the other premier of his day, the arch-conservative
who railed against Canberra, Sir Joh Bjelke-Petersen, whom
Hancock openly revered as an exemplary Australian and ideal
candidate for prime minister. But despite their similarities, there
was never a question that the ideologies of the two men would
meet. Until the end of Hancock's life, he clawed and scratched
at Court's political decisions, and blamed him above anyone
else for blocking his way.

In January 1954, a Pilbara neighbour of Lang and Hope was
on holidays in Perth and present when a heavily pregnant Hope
spoke to her mother about the imminent birth of her baby. 'My
mother and Hope were great friends,' the woman, who asked to
remain anonymous, tells me. 'She said to Mum, "I don't know
what I'm going to call this baby if it's a girl. Lang is so sure it's
a boy and he's going to call it George." I was only about ten

years old then, but I piped up and said, "Hopie, you'd have to call her Georgina Hope," – and so they did! The baby was such a pleasant surprise for them.'

News of the pending birth also set Aboriginal tongues wagging at Mulga Downs station. They rolled their rations of bakki in the cool of early evening and spoke in huddled whispers.

'Old Lang', as they called him, was going to be a father.

Again.

Georgina's birth changed Hancock. 'The fact is, Hope and I didn't think we'd have any family at all, and so we were delighted to have her,' he admitted. Suddenly, this lone ranger had someone in whom to invest his dreams. From the time she could walk, Gina shadowed her father around the vast Pilbara. Theirs was a shared passion, for the gorges, the gum trees, the tranquil outback silence, and the treasures the hard earth harboured. As Gina became older, she grew to appreciate the minerals that lay beneath the ground; onlookers would listen, astonished, as she detailed the finer points of mining gleaned from hours spent with her father. She would recite, parrot-fashion, the names of minerals; recite, parrot-fashion, Lang's ideologies.

Gina's was a simple childhood, reminiscent of Lang's own. If she was lonely without brothers or sisters or neighbours' children to play with, she did not vocalise it. As an only child, she did not have to bid for her parents' time or company, and that suited her. Hancock associates recall that Gina was possessive of her father, who made a terse, but loving parent. And another factor came into play: when Gina was a year old, her mother developed breast cancer and from that time on, was frequently ill. It made Gina's relationship with Lang closer; it was her father who shaped her thinking, her father who shaped her psyche.

A source, who knew Gina as a child described her as a 'princess'. 'The bottom line was, Gina could do no wrong in

Lang's eyes,' she recalled. 'She was groomed from a very early age to be the heir-apparent and she was more than happy to go back up to the station on her own with Lang if Hope had to stay in Perth for whatever reason, possibly because she was ill, which she increasingly was. She would ride horses up there or play tennis; isolation didn't bother her one bit. Hope adored Gina, too, and called her "my little Ginie" but Gina leaned towards her father, no doubt about that. Ever since she was a child, it's always been about Gina. She had her parents at her feet and grew up expecting the world to treat her the same way.'

Always reluctant to discuss his private life, Lang kept his wife and daughter under close wraps, only allowing the world to see rare glimpses of his feelings. Asked once if he thought it was foolhardy to carry them as passengers over the perilous Pilbara terrain in his light aircraft, he replied that if the plane crashed, he would like his family to be with him. 'I would not like to think that my daughter would be left behind at the mercy of the world without me there to protect her.' It was a sentiment that was to become particularly poignant at the end of his life.

Gina was later to admit that while she loved being a woman, she had sometimes wished in her younger days that she was born a boy. 'I think he [Dad] would probably have preferred a son,' she candidly admitted. 'But anyway, he ended up with a daughter.'

A woman who knew Gina as a child recalls she was not a sociable girl. 'She would prefer to sit on her own and watch other kids at play, rather than participate. She was like a cardboard cut-out at her own birthday parties – not in the slightest spontaneous or outgoing.'

Lang did not mollycoddle Gina with overt sentiment. She was his 'right-hand man' and he openly addressed her in company as 'young fella'. He was well aware of the responsibilities which lay in store for Gina, and determined that she would receive the best education that money could buy, 'so that she can learn to live with and handle other people'.

When she was old enough, Lang and Hope made the decision to send Gina to the elite St Hilda's boarding school in Perth. But like her father before her, Gina lived for the school holidays, when she could return to station life. She had no yen for academia; school, she later lamented, was a time to be endured. In 1967, the BBC compiled a documentary on Hancock entitled *Man of Iron*. In it, Gina's headmistress, the formidable Miss Mitchell, noted that her young student had a will of iron, a trait she carries today. 'Gina won't be overruled on things she thinks are right,' she said. 'And that is good since everything will devolve upon her.' She added, 'Her parents give her everything she wants, and this can embarrass her.' Former St Hilda's students recall Lang turning up at the school before dinner and sitting in the car, talking to Gina for hours. They were very close; inseparable, one said. But if Gina was close to her father, other sources claim the shy young girl would sit alone from other students while she ate lunch.

In the same BBC documentary, Gina, then 12, gushed with prepubescent innocence about her father. 'I think [he] is nearly perfect,' she smiled. 'He's awfully good at sport, namely table tennis; he's good at swimming and the rest of them too. He's not very good in the house though; he hates washing up, and he never makes his bed, he always leaves it for us. He's awfully untidy. He doesn't like animals much, especially horses. I think he's quite handsome, except a bit fat.'

Years later, when she had taken over the reins of the Hancock empire, she gave a rare interview on the ABC's *Australian Story*, for a documentary titled 'House of Hancock'.

'I don't think I was wrong when I said what I said, and that was he was a very excellent father,' she reiterated. 'I guess what I shouldn't have said was how he was fat because I can just imagine my children saying that about me.'

Gina knew from a very early age that she was one of Australia's wealthiest heiresses. The knowledge gave her a degree of self-awareness rare in a young woman. Commonly regarded as a chip off the old block, fierce independence, stubbornness and pride were the hallmarks of her character. But if she was also a quiet child, painfully shy around people she did not know, she had the necessary ingredients to make it in the corporate world.

She was tough, and needed to be. 'She's a lot tougher than me,' Lang conceded when Gina was in her teens. 'But she's not ruthless; I think you'll find she's very fair.'

In 1976, journalist Robert Duffield was commissioned by *The Australian* newspaper to write a three-part series on Gina, the angle being the 'richest little girl in the world'. But to Duffield's dismay, all Gina wanted to talk about was minerals, and she parroted her father's opinions on everything. Phrase by phrase, sentence by sentence, she knew it by rote, the lessons learned at her father's knee. A conversation with Gina, many noted, was like having a conversation with Lang. The only difference was that where his voice was gruff, Gina's was St Hilda's modulated, and the words delivered in barely more than a whisper. Duffield devoted so much time to Lang and Gina that his story morphed into a book, which he aptly titled *Rogue Bull*. He cuts to the essence of why Lang had such a way with the women in his life. 'The secret of this great, bluff man was that somehow he exudes to a woman a sense of love,' he said. 'I mean that in both the heterosexual and father–daughter relationships, and not to confuse the two. Gina loved him because he loved Gina . . .'

Duffield noted the tough streak in Gina's character in her early twenties. 'She tries to be nice to everybody. If they disappoint her, or annoy her, or in any way seem to threaten her, the friendly filter on the opal-clear eyes drops to reveal a more steely blue, of the sort which is likely to awe lesser millionaires

20 years from now . . . It is not anger, for anger is an uncontrolled emotion, and Gina despises people who lose control of themselves, for whatever reason.'

11

TIME AND AGAIN, AUSTRALIAN firms politely but firmly closed their doors to Hancock's proposal that they financially back a mining project. Hancock would not be defeated: he now turned to Rio Tinto, a London-based mining company which had made its name in uranium mines, the most well known of which was Mary Kathleen in north-west Queensland. He kept his cards close to his chest concerning the Hamersley find (which some dispute was his discovery); he had an ace he would use when the political climate was on his side.

Hancock's belief that the federal ban on the export of iron ore was soon to be lifted would prove correct. But his biggest challenge was still before him, one which would bear all the hallmarks of the Hancock/Wright partnership's brilliance and irrevocably set Lang apart from bureaucracy. Hancock did not take no for an answer, but first he had to find someone with the vision to believe in him. That would prove harder than he could imagine.

For Hancock and Wright, the brakes were off. Now, finally they could start finding capital for the discovery Hancock had made in 1952. 'This wasn't easy,' he would recall later. 'I still didn't have title to the site. You'd approach big international companies like the United States Steel Corporation and they'd say, "Well, where is it?" I couldn't tell them because I didn't have title. They all thought it was fairy-tale stuff.' The Federal Government's ban on export of iron ore was lifted in 1960, partly because of pressure from Western Australia where a Liberal Government had won office in April 1959. Hancock and Wright assumed that the State Government's blanket ban on the issue of iron ore tenements would also be lifted in 1960. But the Western Australian Government, led by Premier David Brand and with Charles Court as Minister for Industrial Development and the North-West, had other ideas, and did not lift the pegging ban until 1961.

'The delay in WA's lifting of the pegging ban was related to the emerging clash between Hancock and Court,' a source comments. 'The latter was hatching a plan for orderly development of the Pilbara's iron ore resources and he would have been aware that Hancock and Wright wanted to peg tenements covering a huge area of ground prospective for iron ore. So the Western Australian Government came up with three categories of ground and prospectors were only allowed to apply for iron ore tenements over ground in category "C".'

The Brand–Court line-up would remain unchanged until 1971, when the Liberal Government was finally defeated at the polls by the ALP's John Tonkin. Court, having served a 12-year apprenticeship, finally became Premier of Western Australia by defeating the Tonkin Government in 1974, holding that position continuously until his retirement early in 1982. If Hancock could have known the tussles he would have with Court, he may not have been so enthusiastic in his support for Brand prior to the

1959 election. Hancock had figured that any change emanating from the State Parliament would carry through to the north-west. He wanted change, and he wanted it fast; for the past eight years he had loudly grumbled that bureaucrats and bloody politicians were holding up his dream to open the Pilbara for exploration and export.

By early January 1961, Lang finally persuaded Rio Tinto to inspect his Hamersley findings. The man they selected for the job – Swiss geologist Dr Bruno Campana – played right into the partnership's hands. Like Hancock, Campana had a healthy ego and runs on the board; he also had the habit of leapfrog-ging bureaucrats and landing fair in the face of top-level men. This was Lang's type of man: bugger the niceties, let's get on with the job. Campana flew to Wittenoom on 7 January 1961, and eyed Hancock's samples of the iron ore he had found with growing excitement. Before the night was out, the two men were allies. Campana recalled that Hancock naively allowed him to study the find on his own the next day when they flew out to the site at dawn. Below them, a major body of iron ore stretched for a hundred kilometres. Satisfied that it was worth taking a closer look, he instructed Hancock to put the plane down. While the canny geologist took samples, Lang whipped up a bush breakfast, washed down by the mandatory cup of tea. Swinging the billy can over his head like a fan, he waited for the stray tea leaves to settle before pouring the amber brew into tin cups.

Campana was glowing in his praise of the deposit he had seen: this, he told Rio Tinto management, was iron ore worth securing. But management, stymied by the Western Australian ban that was not lifted until 1961, were not prepared to rush in. Hancock was not as dilatory. In the field, he had secreted three trusted men who would make their final mark on the lease boundaries as soon as he gave them the nod. It was a covert operation, Hancock slowly and systematically directing the traffic from his aircraft.

The exercise had a touch of high-noon theatrics: at the appointed hour, a spinifex fire was to be lit, and the pall of smoke which would stream over the valleys would be a signal to the men to date their claim forms and attach them to the pegs they had already placed in the ground. Wright could not see the smoke from his vantage point but, as prearranged, Hancock would fly overhead and wave the aircraft wings. The men waited, and waited, as high noon turned to high farce. The government directive had come through, but it fell far short of the hopeful prospectors' expectations. The Brand–Court Government was again one step ahead, and their three-point plan was meticulously designed to ensure the government kept their hands on the steering wheel.

Category A covered major deposits not yet secured by leases; these were reserved by the Crown. Category B was the known medium- to low-grade deposits, and category C – the clincher – covered the unknown deposits which undoubtedly existed. Companies and small prospectors could apply for temporary reserves in categories B and C, which would allow them the opportunity to explore their area but no rights to mine it. The reserves also offered no security of tenure over the find. Hancock and Wright had little option but to take it, even if the directive fell far short of what they had hoped for.

With feverish enthusiasm, Campana continued to climb over the mountain of ore to assess its value. His hands, swollen to double their size with the intense heat of the ore, worked from sun-up to sun-down, and his determination paid off. Rio Tinto's head boys – the recently appointed managing director, John Hohnen, and vice-chairman, John Rodd – made a flying visit to the region to put their stamp of approval on the project. Satisfied, they made application for four reserves. For Hancock, this decision was tantamount to short-sightedness and lack of vision; he had wanted Rio Tinto to tie up 40 temporary reserves, an area equalling 520,000 hectares, and their application for 52,000 hectares was nowhere near large enough. The rogue bull was on the rampage, and in no mood to mess with middle management.

Campana had picked Hancock's brains about what else he had seen in the Hamersley region; in particular, he was hoping to find hematite ore, which had an iron content of up to 68 per cent. Hancock had seen it, and armed with a budget of 7000 pounds to cover three months' exploratory work and with two sidekicks to assist him, Campana set about proving that hematite ore was in the region. Flying on a reconnaissance trip with Hancock, he noticed a thick, dark charcoal-coloured line through the mountains. This was the clue he had been looking for, and with growing excitement he began mapping the line. It appeared to stretch forever, onwards to the horizon. The line was more than a thousand miles long, and was the road to riches. In deference to the geologist, Hancock bestowed the iron formation running above the band with the name 'Campana Horizon' and the line 'Bruno's Band', by which name it is now better known. Hancock could no longer cool his heels; Rio Tinto management in Melbourne were about to find out that this bloke from the bush did not have any patience with those who had to work their way up the food chain until decisions were made.

He flatly refused to listen to any government argument about diminishing reserves if iron ore was mined. 'The whole idea is absolutely absurd,' he told anyone who would listen. 'We've gone from the position of now having sufficient ore to last say 35 to 40 years, to being in a position where we can supply the world for centuries.' But Court would not be swayed. 'If you take out the best, the high grade local tenement ores and ship all that, you would get rid of it all in 30 years. And this is what they [Hanwright] were aiming to do. In the final analysis, all

Debi Marshall

the development is for the people, not people for development. We had some very serious differences with Hancock and Wright because they wanted to make the rules themselves.'

58

12

RIO TINTO'S AUSTRALIAN MANAGEMENT team was furious when they heard that Hancock had bypassed them and was frantically trying to seduce their London-based chairman, Sir Val Duncan, to come to Australia and inspect the finds. In a cantankerous mood, Hancock wrote to Deputy Premier Arthur Watts in early 1961 warning him that it was in the interest of Western Australia to treat Duncan with respect.

Sir Val Duncan had established a reputation as a gentleman who fought for what he believed in. And he believed in Rio Tinto, becoming its MD in 1951. The Australian arm of Rio Tinto was established in 1954, and the astute company seized the opportunity to pick up the rights to the Mary Kathleen uranium reserves in north-west Queensland.

Hancock would not take no for an answer. He hammered away at the man who had the respect of all his industry peers and who moved in illustrious circles, until he finally gave in. It was a triumphant moment for Hancock, who met Duncan when he landed at the airport and regaled him with facts and figures.

Time was of the essence, and while Hancock had Duncan's ear, he intended to bend it. He was at his obdurate, acerbic best when describing his frustrations.

Hancock failed to understand that this bullying approach and contempt for middle management, which he made no attempt to hide, alienated those people he later may have needed. Sir Valston Hancock, who knew Lang as well as anyone, understood his mate's eccentricities.

'His virtual isolation in the great empty north-west during his early manhood is a factor which shaped his character and bred intolerance of prevarication,' he said. 'He is essentially a man of action who wants to get things done speedily. This obsessive drive may lead him into error, but it is also the source of his achievements . . .'

In 1971, Hancock spoke about the Hanwright initiative to get Duncan to come to Western Australia.

'When I heard that he was coming, I went to Charles Court and I said: "What is it you want that will do the most good for Western Australia in your eyes?" He said, "Oh, a steel mill." Hancock recalled that Duncan's reaction to his opinion that the best way to win over the government was to offer them a steel mill was met with incredulity. 'Don't be a bloody fool, we are not in the steel business,' Duncan had responded.

'I told him it could be done quite simply, by forming two companies – an iron-exporting company and a steel-making company,' Hancock continued. 'I told him that if he did as I said and got a title to it, and then put a levy of about 0.001 of a penny for every ton of iron ore exported, he could build a bloody steel mill and it would never matter a bugger if it never turned a wheel; he'd still come out on the right side of the ledger.'

If Duncan was firmly on Hancock's side, the government was not. Attempts to have a meeting with the Premier were stonewalled, but he would not be deterred. Next in line for a hearing was Deputy Premier Watts. This time, Duncan and Hancock received a positive response, and agreement was reached that the formal offer of a steel mill would be put on paper. Years later, Hancock told Robert Duffield that he was amazed at Sir Val Duncan's powerful international connections, displayed when he directly contacted Edgar Kaiser, the son of the president of Kaiser Steel, to sound him out about a steel mill.

For Hancock, it was to prove a valuable lesson: if you want something done, go to the real powerbrokers. For Charles Court and Hancock, the question of whether the government accepted Duncan's offer of a steel mill became the linchpin of their future animosity. On this, the two men were diametrically opposed. Court knew that there were votes in opening up a steel mill in the north-west, but was disinclined to be seen to favour any Rio Tinto-led proposal, which effectively equalled a mill in return for titles to their temporary reserves. Hancock loudly vocalised that the government had accepted the offer but that Court ultimately rejected it to stop the Hanwright push in the Pilbara. From Hancock's point of view, the men would never again operate on a civil level; the lines were firmly drawn.

While the politicking raged around them, Hancock and Duncan sought partners for their venture. Duncan, whose excellent reputation preceded him in the industry, put his money where his mouth was and quickly engaged the interest of Henry Kaiser, President of Kaiser Steel Corporation.

By now the company's vice-president, Tom Price, had been lured out of semi-retirement in March 1962 to make the journey to Australia and inspect the discoveries. If anyone knew the mining game, it was this grizzled, 71-year-old American who, like Hancock, did not suffer fools and was impatient to get results. Using the tools of his trade – sunburned hands, a small hammer and a keen eye – Price quizzed Campana about the grade and quality of the ore. Sweeping his arms in an arc, he demanded rapid-fire answers.

'What is the mountain over there made of?' he asked.

Campana was reluctant to be too expansive. 'Low-grade iron formation, sir.'

'Who is the Sir of the party?' Price responded. 'I am only Tom. Now let's get back to the mountain: what do you mean by low-grade iron formation?'

'Well, Tom, the formation is a pile of rock layers about a thousand feet thick, on the average containing between 25 to 40 per cent iron and occupying 2000 square miles.'

'Which means some 10 million-million tons of ore?'

'That would be right, Tom, but it's low-grade.'

'Never mind the grade; upgrading methods are well established by now. Now what about the limonitic tables down there?'

'These contain over 1000 million tons of iron ore, quite clean but unfortunately a little low in grade, only 53 to 56 per cent,' replied Campana.

Price couldn't believe what he was hearing. 'Which is a few units higher than the average grade of the high-grade iron ore mined in America! In Australia you seem rather hard to please! What about the bedded hematitic ore on which we are sitting? What grade would you guess it has?'

'It leaves a little to be desired, Tom. It averages only 60 per cent, or thereabouts.'

'Hard to please is an understatement! You Australian boys are only satisfied with bonanzas!'

Campana grinned. 'Indeed, we are looking for one, Tom!'

'Good for you, boys, and good luck to you. But remember that God made men out of a bit of dust, and if you cannot make some money out of the mountains of iron ore I have seen so far, then our very God would have wasted his time!'

Price reported back to the board that the Rio Tinto minefields were of inestimable value and, within months of his inspection of the discovery, Kaiser Steel Corporation had come in with a 40 per cent interest.

Consolidated Zinc had also come on board, and a new London company – Rio Tinto Zinc – was established. The Australian progeny of that company was to become Conzinc Rio Tinto of Australia – CRA – established in July 1962. Tom Price did not mince words with the company.

'Quit crappin' about!' he instructed them. 'We're sitting on a gold mine!'

For Hancock and Wright, the fruits of their early work were to become their rivers of gold.

13

IN JUNE 1963, THE Hamersley Iron Ore Agreement with the Western Australian government was signed under the auspices of Hamersley Holdings, the operating company for Kaiser and CRA. Hancock, having alienated the big boys with his refusal to massage their egos with political compliance, now found himself out in the cold. CRA had done what he would not – talked to Court – and had found allies in the Japanese for future markets. Tom Price, who had kickstarted Kaiser Steel's interest in the Australian operation, did not live to see it grow past its infancy.

Hancock and Wright, using their combined strengths, entered into negotiations with the company. In reality, they did not have the working capital to invest in equity; instead, they worked on a royalty method. Between them, they would receive a 2.5 per cent cut of the value of each ton of exported iron ore from many of Hamersley Iron's deposits. And they went further: those royalties would cover not only the deposits which they had found, but also those which would be mined by the company later from within specified areas.

The negotiation made them rich beyond their dreams, the ore providing ongoing royalties of $30,000 per day. Hancock didn't give a damn about the outraged splutterings from the company executives, who were incensed that he and Wright had not only built their own nest but had also feathered it. He would not be silenced.

'That's a problem in this country,' he retorted. 'Australia is not a land of entrepreneurs. Socialism is embedded right through the school system and there seems to be an attitude that "the world owes me a living". When people talk about things they believe are wrong in our society, they always say, "the government ought to do this or that". They don't seem to realise that they're the ones who have to make things happen.' They were sentiments that Lang drummed into his 'young fella'. They were sentiments Gina would later repeat.

Following the successful sign-off of the Hamersley Iron agreement, Hancock and Wright looked at expanding their net. Daniel Ludwig, a self-made American who, by the early 1960s, boasted a personal fortune in excess of US$450 million, caught their attention.

But Ludwig's biggest plan for the Pilbara was far-sighted in the extreme: to finance and build a super-port at Cape Keraudren to handle 166,000-ton carriers, and lead the way in backing and building roads and railways.

Hancock was impressed with Ludwig in more ways than one, especially his courage as a passenger while Lang flew his little aircraft through turbulent weather. 'I flew him [Ludwig] around and sold him on the idea of one central railway and one giant port,' Hancock said after the proposal collapsed.

'He took this up with the Western Australian Government and put a proposal to them [4 June 1964]. The deal was that he would build and finance one railway and a port which was capable of servicing ships three times the size of the iron ships in existence at that time. In fact, he had on order the *Iron Trader*, which could move 166,000 tons, whereas the next biggest capacity was 50,000 tons. That would have lowered transport costs to such an extent that Europe and America would have been able to import iron ore at much the same price as Japan. So, instead of just having 47 per cent of the Japanese market, we could have had 40 to 50 per cent of the world market, which is about eight times the size of what we had.'

The concept itself was brilliant and it was enthusiastically backed by Hancock, who realised that centralisation was the key to opening up the inaccessible Pilbara and would bring him a step closer to his dream. For Ludwig, it would ensure that he could mine, treat and carry the ore in his own ships to established markets in Europe, as well as charging other operators for the use of his facilities. But for Australian companies such as BHP and CRA it had a central flaw: it offered too much power to Ludwig. Charles Court rejected the plan for the same reasons, and coined the term 'The Ludwig Benefit Plan' to explain why. The Pilbara would not be opened up under the auspices of one man – it had to work for everyone. There were other concerns: a centralised Pilbara with one port facility would leave operators at the mercy of the elements. If a cyclone came through, as it periodically does in the region, the port would have to be temporarily closed. By 1970, Ludwig had turned his back on the Pilbara, selling out his temporary reserves to the Mount Goldsworthy Consortium. Hancock was incensed.

'Well, the West Australian Government turned him down. We've never known why – due to Cabinet solidarity – and, in my opinion, that was the greatest opportunity this country has ever had. Ludwig's money went into Brazil, which became the world's leading exporter of iron ore.'

From the mid-1960s, Hancock maintained and modified Ludwig's idea for a centralised Pilbara, and continually pushed for its evolution. He never forgave those who stood in the way of the Ludwig scheme, and it was an issue which he railed about until the end of his days.

For all his royalties, Hancock was still no closer to achieving what he most wanted – his own mine. But he had arrived, and the Who's Who of Australia's corporate and political worlds were about to find out that no amount of money would silence his acid tongue. As he would later comment, with the intriguing mix of ego and pragmatism that marked his personality: 'Most of my life people have regarded me as an idiot. Whether that's a good or a bad thing, I don't know. But more than anything, success has meant that people now have to listen to me.'

By 1966, Hamersley Iron had completed the project of building a railway from Mount Tom Price to the port they had also established at Dampier, at a massive cost. The opening of Hamersley Iron was a $200,000 gala affair, described by one journalist as the most 'expensive bun-fight the West has ever seen', and attended by hundreds of Australian and international guests. A dinner in Perth, where guests were fêted with French wines and champagne, lobster thermidor and smoked salmon, was followed by their being flown to Dampier where the celebrations continued. The esteemed *Wall Street Journal* had sent reporter John Lawrence to cover the opening, and he wrote about his impressions.

'Thanks largely to his own negotiating ability and a good sense of timing, he'll clear some $10 million or so in royalties, possibly much more, in the next 16 years. His long-time business partner, Peter Wright, will get an equal share. But despite the fact that he may be responsible for Australia's most important industrial development to date, hefty, muscular Lang Hancock is ignored, even despised, by many of the Australians now involved in the mining venture. It will be surprising if his name survives in the history books.'

Hancock's name did not appear on the guest list of those who had attended the opening; worse, Premier (later Sir) David

Brand, in a glowing and lengthy speech, did not mention him
once. The Establishment had turned its back on Hancock, a
rebuff he would neither forget nor forgive.

James Barber, an executive at Kaiser Steel based in California,
responded to an invitation to comment on Hancock's contribution to the iron ore development of Western Australia in 1966.
His summary was vastly different from those of Hamersley
officials.

'More than any one man, Lang Hancock is responsible
for the Hamersley Iron development,' he wrote. 'Australia is
fortunate to have such a man able to contribute to the development of its natural resources . . . He thought in world
terms, rather than in just national. It is this early comprehension of the order of magnitude of the scene yet to unfold that
set him apart . . . Without Lang Hancock there would be no
Hamersley Iron.'

14

BY 1966, CSR WAS floundering at Wittenoom. The township was a far cry from the days when Hancock had first seen it; the government had invested capital in a hospital, police station and housing, and 1100 people had employment at the town and mine. But it was not enough to keep the Australian Blue Asbestos company afloat and, at the end of the year, CSR made the decision to close the mine. The decision to do so was not based on health reasons. The mine had simply become uneconomic. The future, CSR believed, was not in asbestos but in iron ore, and they were supported in their decision by Charles Court, then Industrial Development Minister, who had been consistently outspoken about the need for health reform at Wittenoom.

CSR had cast covetous eyes towards the iron ore deposits at Mount Newman, and to gain entry they had to complete a fast backout at Wittenoom. The miners were furious, their anger fuelled by the very real concern that in this parched desert township, isolated from civilisation by its furnace-like heat and distance, jobs were not easy to find. Their voices were raised loudly in discontent as they sank a few beers in the town's pub and digested the bitter reality that with only four weeks to Christmas, they would be out of a job. *The West Australian* newspaper joined the miners in the outcry, and the public took up the cause with gusto. Hancock watched the fracas with increasing interest. The public outrage had Court, now gearing up for election and with his eyes on the state's top job, firmly on the back foot. It was an opportunity to hold Court up for disgrace, and Hancock took it, demanding to know why the workers had not been notified earlier of the mine's impending closure and why the government had committed so much capital to a township for which they knew the bells would soon be tolling. Court, using the calm self-possession for which he was renowned, replied that he did not want to risk a chaotic mass exodus of people from Wittenoom by an earlier notification of the closure.

Charles Court's critics – and Hancock was one of the loudest – suggested there was another reason the government had kept the impending closure of the mine secret for a month – the forthcoming federal election.

An article in *The West Australian* concluded: 'Long term Wittenoom residents who would like to stay on believe that he [Hancock] is a realist rather than an optimist and that his efforts to keep the blue asbestos industry alive are likely to be more successful than any efforts by the Government.'

After conferring with Peter Wright and organising finance, the partners made a fateful decision.

They bought the town.

On 4 January 1967, the TVW News reported the purchase.

'Mr Hancock said today that . . . [it] was the first step in establishing a huge industrial complex in the Pilbara – a complex which would include four ore-pelletising plants, an oil refinery, an asbestos cement industry and a tripling of Wittenoom blue asbestos production . . .'

Hancock and Wright's purchase included the mine and treatment mill, and the power station. What was not for sale were the government-owned hospital, school, post office, houses, airport, hotel and shops. For Hancock, it was an investment in his dreams, the kick-start he had been waiting for to finally begin to realise his own operational mine. If the partners could effectively package the deal by floating the company and accessing the hematite that was available at nearby Koodaideri, they were sitting on a bonanza worth untold millions of dollars. Hancock explained the decision to buy back the town as a means of avoiding scattering to the four winds the equipment that was there, and an opportunity to re-establish the mine. Central to his argument, though not expressly vocalised, was that CSR had failed, and that Hanwright would do better. The miners and their families who had decided to stay at Wittenoom instead of joining the desperate itinerants who had bailed out in search of other work, hailed the partners as their eleventh-hour saviours, a reprieve from the hangman's noose. But true to his oft-repeated credo to business associates, Lang attempted to water down the optimism.

'We believe that, given time, we will be able to re-establish the mine on a much bigger scale, but we don't want to raise any false hopes of an immediate reprieve for Wittenoom,' he warned. 'Any re-establishment of it on a proper basis is a long-range plan. However, we do have some schemes that may create activity around Wittenoom in the near future.'

In 1969, Hancock ruffled environmentalists' feathers with the announcement that he and Wright planned to use nuclear explosives to mine iron ore about 12 kilometres from Wittenoom, an idea later also embraced by Gina. The idea was simple, safe and foolproof, he claimed, and would cut about 80 per cent off conventional mining costs.

Hancock's views were greeted with a mixture of derision and hysteria; naively, he explained that he thought by having an

71

underground inland explosion most objections would be over-ruled. 'The only people who really stood to lose were Hancock and Wright because of our investment in the nearby town-site and in the proving and drilling of the ore-body,' he stated. Convinced that his idea was workable as well as safe, he went on the record to say that he had considered erecting an obser-vation tower about 5 kilometres from the site, and charging an entrance fee for people to watch the explosion. But his grand plans to ignite the big one came to naught.

As she grew older, Gina spent an increasing amount of time learning about minerals from her father, who was clear-cut about her future role. 'She'll inherit it [the company] eventually, and it's just as well she has a look at it now rather than have the whole lot piled in her face later on when she might make a mess of it. But if she wants to blow the lot at Monte Carlo, that will be her business.'

There is little chance of that. Gina eschews a frivolous life-style.

15

IN JULY 1970, HANDSOME, dark-haired 19-year-old Greg Milton emigrated to Australia from his native England. Greg Milton had no idea when he said goodbye to his father and travelled to outback Australia, to the desolate Pilbara, that he would meet and marry Australia's leading heiress.

Anxious to find work in his new country, Milton answered an ad for a surveyor's assistant in Perth. Interviewed by Hancock's accountant, he was sent to Rhodes Ridge where he worked for a year before turning his hand to geologist's assistant and truck driver. He was moved to Wittenoom to work at the company store. He found himself offering advice on paint to a young, attractive woman with a shy smile and an approachable manner. The paint that Gina Hancock needed was only available in the town, and he offered her a lift on the back of his moped to pick it up.

Years later, when we met in Perth, Greg told me about their first meeting. 'I was attracted to her from the start,' he said. 'From the beginning I treated her as an ordinary person. I didn't realise she was an heiress who would inherit a fortune. I took her down into the town on the back of my motorbike – much to her father's horror! – and she was very down to earth, pretty and vibrant. She was only 17, I was 19, and the feeling was mutual.' Then still at boarding school, it is easy to see why the shy young woman fell for Greg – he was handsome and articulate, with an infectious warmth – and that first meeting was the start of a passionate 18-month courtship. The couple spent as much time together as her studies would allow. 'I was her first love . . . and I guess it would be fair to say I swept her off her feet,' Greg ventured.

Greg could not recall the details of how he proposed to Gina, but he remembers asking Lang for her hand in marriage. 'I was very frightened,' he laughed. 'But he was gracious and didn't attempt to oppose it. He did ask me if I could handle Gina, and at the time I didn't think that would be a problem as we felt so strongly about each other.' It was, he later realised, a naive response. 'Lang knew that Gina was destined to take over the Hancock empire, as well as the enormous wealth and pressures that went with that. It was always going to be a tough one.'

The couple moved to Sydney for a year, where Gina started an economics degree and Greg studied to be a pilot. Lang recalled Gina's time at university in Sydney. 'When she got over there she came under a fellow called Professor Wheelwright, I think, who was an ardent socialist, and there's no way that she was ever going to progress under this fellow. So one day I found her in my office. She'd given up the university and set herself down in the office, and from then on she was all part and parcel of it . . .'

Gina herself recalls why she left university. 'They were teaching all the wrong things,' she asserted. 'I came back home and Dad taught me more than anything I learned in university.'

Lang and Hope did not want Gina to marry Greg. 'They thought she was far too young to get married,' a woman who knew them well recalled. 'But she married him in spite of their feelings. It was what she wanted to do, and what Gina wanted, Gina got.' Greg and Gina's wedding, on 8 January 1972, was held at St George's Church in Sydney, far from the prying eyes of Perth's social set. The family did not want this special event turning into a media circus and only 30 guests attended, including Greg's parents, whom Lang flew out from England. But from the beginning, control was exercised: Gina didn't change her name; he changed his. Milton, Greg's surname, was deemed incompatible with the name Hancock and he was told to change it. The groom, genial and naive, complied with the request and metamorphosed, by deed poll, into Greg Hayward. If there was a more basic reason his name was changed – so that Hancock's workers did not become privy to the fact that the boss's daughter had married a storeman – Greg remained silent on the subject. Considering the fiasco that followed when Lang later married his housekeeper, it is a bitter irony.

Around her twenty-first birthday, Gina was interviewed for a story in *The Australian Women's Weekly*, 19 February 1975 edition. Looking happy in photographs, she said she started to realise at the age of 11 or 12 that people were aware of who her father was, and that as she was constantly with adults, she matured very quickly as a result. Softly-spoken, with blue-grey eyes set in a 'youthfully rounded face', she, Greg Milton and her parents had flown to Sydney in the company Learjet for the launch of a new political party. The reporter, Gloria Newton, recognised within minutes of talking to Gina that she was a chip off the old block. 'It takes only a while with Gina to realise she is very much her father's daughter,' she observed. 'Facts and figures are no problem as she quotes the awe-inspiring number of millions of tons of ore being mined annually from each of his vast holdings.' Describing helping Lang as 'my first responsibility', she spoke of their shared love of the bush and the family properties – Hamersley, a half-million-acre cattle station, and Mulga Downs, which ran sheep. Gushing that Lang was a 'wonderful father. Strict, when he wants to be . . . but we've always been very close friends', she learned to drive at ten and Lang allowed her to roam all over the properties in a vehicle. Going camping for the first time with Lang when she was ten years old, she said her education about minerals started in earnest immediately after. Asked if the prospect of taking over her father's company frightened her, she said it would have, if she hadn't been prepared, but she would be okay as she would have Greg beside her.

Gina admitted that she didn't enjoy a great relationship with the 'left-wing students' at her university, who felt 'jealousy and resentment' towards her. Showing then the distrust of people that would increase as she grew older, she observed: 'Some people try to use you. But I can cope.'

Gina talked about what she liked best: having friends to dinner, going to the theatre, and clothes. And, of course, Lang. 'As my father's daughter – and he's a very exciting man – I love being beside him all the way.'

Gina's twenty-first birthday party, held on the marquee of the front lawn of the Dalkeith house her parents owned, was a grand affair. Gina looked stunning in a halter-neck frock. One of the guests was then-Prime Minister, John Gorton.

Five years after they married, their son, John Langley, was born, and a year later, daughter Bianca Hope. But all was not always well. 'When Gina is angry or upset with someone, her eyes ice over and the shutters go up,' Greg later told me. 'That's it. End of conversation. End of story.'

Proving that she put her babies before all else, when asked about the hordes of reporters who had been impatiently waiting outside to see her while she breastfed John, Gina appeared flabbergasted by the question: Of course she would feed her baby first, she replied. 'What else could a nursing mother do?'

In 1978 Gina Rinehart gave one of the few interviews she has ever granted. In her soft, whispery voice, the then 24-year-old spoke about her young children, John and Bianca, and her plans for them. Perhaps she was thinking of her own burdens when she told biographer Robert Duffield: 'I started a family early because I wanted my kids to know my father. I may have more, so that no single one of them has to bear the full burden of being heir or heiress.'

Hancock accepted his new son-in-law into the fold with the same single-mindedness with which he embraced everything else. Greg learned to fly and quickly became Lang's pilot, ferrying him and his guests around and looking after the aircraft when Hancock was in the bush. He recalls that while Lang was a polite but abrupt man, he was also home-loving and sentimental. 'When we moved back to the west, I had the job of flying Hancock and other dignitaries around, being chauffeur and doing odd jobs,' he says. 'Gina and I were very happy and had some wonderful adventures travelling overseas on our own. They were great years.'

The legendary Hancock grit that lay beneath the surface was becoming more evident as Gina took on increasing responsibility in her father's company. 'Gina's destiny was beyond our control. We began to grow apart, which manifested itself in arguments, or worse, protracted silences. As she became more engrossed in business pressures, many of which I was not privy to, I felt increasingly like an ancillary to her, rather than a husband. There was little room for personal relationships. And she is not good at vocalising her feelings. I felt that she had left the marriage behind and we no longer had the loving relationship we'd once shared. As she got older, she leaned increasingly towards her predestination: to fill her father's shoes.

'She could be very charming, particularly early in our relationship, but a lot of the time she seemed detached,' Greg mused. 'She is not a sentimental woman. When a relationship is over, it's over. She doesn't look back.'

The end of the marriage was swift and painful. 'I went to Queensland for six months to establish an exploration camp for Hancock and I returned to Perth on the eve of Gina, Lang and the children going overseas on a business trip. Gina told me I wasn't going on the trip and gave me no explanation why. I felt snubbed, used and discarded. I'd had enough. I told her not to expect me to be there when she got back from the trip, and she shrugged and said, "OK." That was the end of it – whether she was emotionally hurt I had no way of knowing. I just packed up what small possessions I had after they left and moved out. I was very emotional, as well as traumatised and confused, but there was a sense of relief as well.

'I didn't know where I was going to go, what I was going to do or how I was going to handle life afterwards.' Greg decided to cut his ties completely with the Perth business environment. 'It would have been too difficult to remain within the Hancock company. I just decided to make a clean break.'

Gina's wishes that she would have Greg beside her when she took over her father's company were not going to come to pass.

Following his marriage breakdown, Greg Milton moved into a small flat – a far cry from the home he had shared with Gina, with housemaids and nannies – and his world started to fall apart. 'Divorce proceedings started through the lawyers and they dragged on for years,' he says. The divorce was made final in 1981 and, still circumspect about the terms of the settlement, Greg gives a wry shrug. 'Suffice to say I ended up with very little.'

Greg recalled the shame of seeing his beloved children, John and Bianca, then four and three years old respectively, for a very short time each week after the separation. 'We were given a blanket to sit on in the garage or the garden at Gina's home,' he says. 'I felt really degraded to be seeing them under those circumstances. It was emotionally a very painful time for the children and for me, but to save fighting in front of them it was a better option just to go along with it.'

Greg considered fighting for custody, but realised it was impossible. 'Gina was a good mother, and the reality was I couldn't fight her or an organisation of that size, with all the power and money they had at their disposal. I was doing it tough just feeding myself, and my first job was driving a truck hauling meat carcasses.' At the same time, he agonised over John and Bianca's future. 'They were destined for the same life as Gina, with enormous wealth, and I thought it would be too confusing for them to see the way I lived. I made the painful decision to stop seeing them three years after we had separated because it was simply too confusing for them.' He pondered the Hancock legacy and the personal fallout for himself. 'If you're not a Hancock, born of the blood, you're not in,' he said. 'Other people have noticed it, as I did. You're not in, and you'll never be in. You're an outsider.'

Greg's last moment with John and Bianca is indelibly etched in his memory. 'It was a very emotional time. We all cried, and I said goodbye. I didn't know when I would see them again.'

It would be 20 years.

16

WHAT HANCOCK NEEDED AT Wittenoom – and the over-riding reason for CSR's major financial loss at the site – was transport. He had factored the problem in when making the decision to buy Wittenoom, and his proposal, on paper, was sound. A railway line would be built along the Fortescue Valley, ending at Cape Lambert where a huge port facility would be erected. It was a modification of the old Ludwig plan, but Hancock believed it could work.

The Capricorn plan, as it became known, was based on the concept of a railway running some 259 kilometres down to the sea at Ronsard Island. The downhill route would ensure it was cost effective, and it would ultimately be linked up with other railways in the region. At Ronsard, a deep-water port would be constructed which would accommodate 250,000-ton super carriers.

What the partners hadn't factored in was the Brand–Court Government's objections. Protracted negotiations between them and the government resulted in the signing, in mid-1967, of the

Iron Ore Agreement Act, later ratified in parliament. It appeared to be workable: Hanwright would be given 34 temporary reserves, including Marandoo, near Wittenoom, and temporary security of tenure over them. For the government, the trade-off was that within a year, the partners agreed to find markets for iron ore pellets – 10 million tons of it – and to raise $70 million. It was a massive commitment and one in which there was no in-built safety net: if they failed, it was on their heads.

As they had done in the past, they looked to overseas investors, naming the concept Hamersley Iron No. 2. Peter Wright, superb in his role as diplomatic negotiator, travelled to Japan in an attempt to interest the Japanese in investing in a new iron ore source. Hanwright's ultimate goal was an export licence from the Australian Government, but Wright's persuasion failed to interest the Japanese; their steel industry was on the decline and they erred on the side of caution.

The breakdown of the proposal was that Kaiser Steel would provide 36 per cent of the capital, Rio Tinto 14 per cent and the partners the remaining 50 per cent. To find their half, they proposed to open up shares to all Australian investors by the floating of a public company, Hanwright Minerals Ltd. As a conciliatory gesture, the idea for a public float was a stroke of genius, designed to fall in line with the political thinking of the day and as a salve to the general public who were concerned to keep out foreign ownership of Australian companies and to protect natural resources.

Hancock, not content to sit on his hands, committed a faux pas that Court would not forget: he invited then Prime Minister John Gorton to overview the Hanwright deposits, well aware that he would talk them up to the press. It was an action guaranteed to upset Court, and to precipitate another confrontation between the two men.

In 1969, Hancock and Wright started their own newspaper, *The Sunday Independent*. Fed up with the criticism he was receiving through the daily newspaper, *The West Australian*, and alarmed when the Herald and Weekly Times group – who represented, for Hancock, the hated Establishment – took over that paper, he decided to fight back. Finally, he had a vehicle through which to air his grievances, and to have his voice heard. After what he perceived as more than two decades of misgovernment, he figured it was time. *The Independent* became the means by which Hancock could raise his objections to Court, his government ministers and anyone else in general he didn't agree with.

The concept of committing his ideas to paper was not new to Hancock. From his earliest business dealings, he had proved himself to be an obsessive writer, his pen the pulpit from which he rained criticisms on his opponents. He was identified as much by his tireless pamphleteering as he was by the sentiments he expressed in them. Not for Hancock the formalities of long epistles, clothed in officialese and served with syrupy obsequiousness, his pamphlets and telexes were as blunt as the man himself, whether addressed to prime ministers or the public. If he had a message to get across, he simply did not care how it was delivered. To those who were opposed to his ideas, he generally signed off 'Best Wishes, Lang Hancock'; to soul-mates such as Sir Joh Bjelke-Petersen or prime ministers with whom he felt a political affinity, it was simply 'Cheerio, Lang'.

From its inception, Hancock found it necessary to explain why the partners had started the newspaper.

'This is not a propaganda sheet for Hancock and Wright,' he wrote in an editorial. 'If propaganda was our aim the logical course would be to employ a professional public relations firm at much less cost in money than the anticipated cost of establishing a newspaper from scratch.'

The partners hired Maxwell Newton, former editor of the *Financial Review* and *The Australian*, to head up the newspaper. Newton had his work cut out for him: while *The Independent* did not attempt to compete with *The West Australian*, its role was to bring to the attention of its readers the ills afflicting the state. In this, Newton and Hancock were at odds: the former wanted a newspaper that appealed to the masses; Hancock did not. The reading public deemed the newspaper too highfalutin, and within 12 months, parting of the ways was inevitable. Next in line for the job was hard-nosed editor Patrick Niland, who attempted to pummel the newspaper into shape with a mix of feature stories and hard news. Niland died of a heart attack at 42, and the paper carried on, though Hancock got out.

At the end of Hancock's life, journalist John McGlue noted that he regarded journalists, along with trade unionists and public servants, as the 'lowest form of life', and spoke to him about his ideas of getting more balanced reporting through the establishment of *The Sunday Independent*.

'That was the idea,' Hancock said, 'but all you could get hold of were socialist bloody journalists who did more harm than good. I said to Wright, "Look, we're losing a hell of a lot of money here feeding a lot of useless bastards and all they're preaching is socialism. That's not doing us any good." So I said, "For God's sake, chuck it up," and he said, "No, I'll carry on."'

Peter Wright's son Michael recalled that Hancock's decision to quit *The Independent* was typical of his pig-headedness. 'That was the way he behaved about many things – we'll go ahead, we'll do this, we'll do that – but his fuse was very short; he was too impatient to wait for long-term results. If things didn't fit his concept of how the world ought to be, then everybody else was a bloody idiot and wasting Hancock's time.' No amount of discussion would dissuade Hancock to change his mind about the newspaper.

For John Tonkin, running for office in the state election campaign of 1971, the occasional opinions expressed by Hancock in the newspaper were publicity that money couldn't buy. He stroked and massaged Hancock's ego, recognising, as a consummate politician, that honey catches more flies than vinegar. He was right. When Court was defeated at the polls, he was scathing about Hancock's role in his downfall and would not ignore the rogue bull's switching of political horses for his own benefit.

'He certainly worked as hard as he could, and from what one has surmised from various people he assisted the Labor Party considerably and he obviously had a good strong arrangement with them, because as soon as they got into office they set out to try and implement what they had promised in so far as concessions to him were concerned,' Court said. 'If he wants to support the Communists, the DLP, the ALP, or the Liberal Party or the Country Party that's his business; the only thing is I hope he doesn't get too closely identified with us for the next election, or it will be the kiss of death.'

Hancock could not resist gloating over Labor's victory. There was no doubt, he claimed, that it was his manoeuvrings which led to the Liberals being tossed out, and it was clear that Court had the full support of his party on the subject of mining rights. 'This left a golden opportunity for the Labor Party and Mr Tonkin to come in and point out how illegal it was what they were proposing to do, and he in very cogent terms expressed it as straight out bushranging.'

Hancock was on a roll, and he would not be stopped.

His next foray into the newspaper business was with the *National Miner*, a weekly that looked at the industry in detail.

Hancock had a complete disregard for those less fortunate than himself who held out the begging bowl to the government asking that it be filled with unemployment benefits. He was no philanthropist; according to him, social security benefits robbed a man of his dignity and created a society that bred lazy loafers. He made no bones about the fact that he was the ultimate archetypal capitalist, and that hard work was the only way to make a quid. 'I believe, bad and all as it is, that the greed of capitalism is the only driving force there is,' he boasted in 1971.

His aversion to giving to charities that he didn't believe in extended to his own health. One of America's leading heart specialists was in Perth on holiday and agreed to operate to fix a minor heart condition Hancock suffered. He offered to undertake the operation free of charge if Lang donated to a neurological foundation that the specialist was interested in. Incensed at what he regarded as a 'put-on' to raise funds for an organisation he didn't believe in, Hancock instead flew to another specialist in London, where he paid the full cost of the operation.

He had always shied away from displays of his wealth, as much for security reasons as any other, but when tourist buses started pulling up outside his Perth home, he deemed it necessary to erect a six-foot-high fence and security gates.

17

IF HANCOCK HAD HOPED the Tonkin Government would favour his interests when they took power, he was in for a bitter disappointment. The grand plans, in which the partners had invested so much, fell apart despite the electioneering promises of the new government.

Installed in office, Tonkin and his ministers confirmed the partners' rights to McCamey's, Rhodes Ridge and the Marandoo areas but declined to allocate the 'Angelas' temporary reserves to Hanwright. Lang had named the Angelas, which had several ore bodies in this group, after Peter Wright's daughter, Angela. Combined with the fall of the share market, the decision spelled the death of the public float. Unable to excite overseas interest or to borrow money from Australian brokers, who Hancock insisted had a vested financial interest in the four mining companies already in operation, the dream of starting their own mine again collapsed.

The system of temporary reserves was hated by the miners, who found it not only limiting, but offering them no protection.

It covered the miner's right to prospect only for the mineral put forward in the application form; they could not use the land for any other purpose nor transfer the temporary reserve to a third party unless there was ministerial approval. The most feared section of the system, and one that the prospectors believed was wide open for abuse, was the mine minister's right to cancel a temporary reserve at his discretion if he felt any of the conditions were not complied with.

Devastated by the rejection, Hancock resorted to other tactics, but not before taking another swipe at those who had chosen a career in the public service.

'Politicians,' he seethed, 'are mostly a bunch of hairy-arsed bastards.'

Armed with injured pride and self-righteous indignation, Hancock and Wright sought justice through the Supreme Court against executive council members, the Minister for Mines and the state of Western Australia to stop confiscation of the Angelas. They had been ordered to pack up and remove any mining equipment from the area by 12 August.

Greg Milton, Hancock's son-in-law who was working in the area at the time, recalls the urgency of getting out. 'Lang sent out a message, which was flown over and dropped by a car inner tube filled with water into the drill rig. The attached note read: 'Pull rods – get off Temporary Reserve by 3 pm. Hancock'. The American steel corporation Armco had, in turn, been given an option to move into some of the reserve areas and had three working weeks to respond. Hancock had the financial power to back a showdown in the courts, and the government knew it. Insisting an injunction be granted on the grounds that what the government had done was illegal, he came away with a victory: the judge agreed that until the legal issues were settled, they had sufficient grounds to request the injunction.

The government, faced with the unpleasant reality that Hancock was in a position to fund a continuing fight through the courts, executed yet another about-face. Casting aside normal business, emergency legislation was rushed through both houses of parliament which put the government back in a controlling position. Control of all temporary reserves, unless already ratified by parliament, was to be returned to the government. The bill went further still, enabling the Minister for Mines to certify that any person who held temporary reserves prior to 15 August 1971 had failed to satisfy him that payable quantities of iron ore had been found during the term of the right of occupancy. Pre-empting any challenge to the legislation, the government made it clear it was not liable 'to be challenged, appealed against, reviewed, quashed, or called into question by any court'.

The unparalleled legislation immediately engendered harsh criticism from legal and political quarters. Those against it were fierce in their opposition. The Western Australian Law Society President fired off a missive to the Attorney-General postulating his opinion that the state had no right to interfere in the court's determination of a dispute already before it. A minister who was later to join the Court Government described the Mining Act Amendment Bill as 'infamous', another as 'immoral'.

Upholding the government's claim that the action Hancock had brought should be dismissed, the judge made null and void the injunction he had granted to prevent the reserves being handed over to another party. Hancock had lost, but he would not be cowed. An appeal to the State Full Court was dismissed and costs awarded against the partners; following this loss, Hancock and Wright decided against pursuing a planned appeal to the Privy Council.

It became Hancock's cause célèbre, the argument to which he continually returned to prove that he had been victimised in the mining industry. In highly emotive language, he vented that anger. 'These two groups of deposits – the East and West Angelas – mark I believe the most shameful chapter of Australian history. In the whole of the Western Australian Parliament, both Houses, there were only three people who stood up and said: "This is wrong!" Yet it was the crime to end all crimes, this Great Claim Robbery. It showed that Watergate's got nothing on what can happen in Australia.'

If Court thought Hancock was perceived in the press as a little Aussie battler who was given a hard time, Lang used it to his own advantage. At an address by him in Sydney in 1971, he accused the government of changing the rules once the ball had bounced.

Time and again, Hancock believed he had cause to agree with Sidney Hillman, who noted at the turn of the twentieth century: 'Politics is the science of who gets what, when and why.'

18

THE EARLY 1970s SAW Hancock embrace a new cause, when his extreme disaffection for what he saw as the petty bureaucratic decisions that emanated from Canberra and the minions who administered them took root in his founding and funding of the Westralian Secessionist Movement. The idea was not new: it was first raised in parliament five years after Federation, and in 1932, at the height of the Depression, Western Australians voted by referendum to secede. Among the advocates of that secessionist groundswell was one Charles Court. Gina, always in agreement with her father's ideas, helped him when she could.

Delivering his message in his usual blunt rhetoric, Hancock theorised on why secession would work – and why it was necessary.

'People in Western Australia are coming round to the view that the best way of saving Australia from backdoor nationalism is to get effective representation in the Senate by electing candidates on the secession issue, instead of the usual party hacks,' he told *The West Australian* newspaper. 'If the Senate should fail in its duty to protect WA then West Australians should secede . . .' A newspaper cartoon in 1974, under the headline 'Langoulant and the name of the state', showed a chubby Hancock standing proudly next to a pile of iron ore. 'Hancockia, Land of No Mineral Deficiencies', the caption read. Next to it was the insert, 'If at first you don't Secede, try, try again'.

Hancock would not give up, a trait inherited by his daughter. Recalling a trip he took with Gina on a nuclear submarine observation vessel, Hancock suggested to the Americans that they consider the north-west of Australia as an alternative mineral source. 'I said that they should lend us just three of these submarines in exchange for us supplying all the strategic minerals they needed. As I told them, you can have all the armies in the world but they're no good to you unless you have the minerals to make the equipment they need to fight. Everything comes from the earth. You either grow it or you mine it, and you can't even till the soil until you've made the plough. It all gets back to these holes in the ground that people so despise.'

Hancock's pro-nuclear package was wrapped in the same verbal explosives as everything else he supported. 'I don't know anyone of even average intelligence who is anti-nuclear,' he raged. 'That's a lot of claptrap put about by the press and by these people who wouldn't even be able to feed themselves if the government didn't hand it to them. Anything constructive seems to be unpopular these days. You get a whole lot of people howling like hell if a cocky knocks over a tree to grow a bit of corn to feed some people. It's quite ridiculous. I'd like to see Australia nuclear-dependent so that it could be entirely self-sufficient and have the cheapest and safest power in the world.'

To publicise his ideas about mining the Pilbara using a nuclear blast, Lang called on the people he loathed: the press.

'The easiest way to get this ore out, seeing that there's nobody around, is with a nuclear blast. This frightens most people because they think it's an atom bomb, but it isn't, it's a hydrogen bomb.' Gina was the frontwoman to sell the concept. 'A hole will be bored down here, and into this will be lowered a hydrogen bomb, which is about six feet high, and after that will be lowered the atomic bomb,' she said. 'This bomb will be set off and that will set off the hydrogen bomb.'

Citing the possibility that Third World countries could eventually acquire the bomb and use it to mine their own resources, Hancock was obstinate that Australia should have the guts to get in first. 'It would break mountains and mountains of ore for us, at a fraction of the cost,' he said.

Already alarmed by Hancock's cantankerous attitudes and disregard for political nuances, Sir Charles Court regarded Lang's nuclear leanings as the ravings of an extreme-right redneck hell-bent on creating his own wealth the quickest way possible. A nuclear bomb would go off in the Pilbara over Court's dead body.

Hancock pointed to history to back his pro-nuclear push. 'The discoverer of the anaesthetic properties of chloroform, Dr James Simpson, was ostracised by the medical profession, particularly by those members of it who were adept at hacking off men's limbs with meat saws and allowing women to be tortured in childbirth . . .' he wrote in yet another of his pamphlets. 'The innovation of the motor car saw our legislators at work compelling a man to walk in front of it waving a red flag. The initial railway was objected to on the premise that it would prevent hens laying eggs. Nobel, with his invention of dynamite, was heralded as anti-Christ, whose one aim was to destroy the world . . .'

Hancock's nuclear sentiments set him apart as a maverick who bordered on madness, but his attitudes did not soften. If his adversaries didn't like it, they knew what they could do.

He also had clear views about the mining and export of uranium. His dictum was: do it now, while Australia has the chance. In the mid-1970s he expounded his viewpoints on the ABC's talkback radio, where some callers agreed with him. But Barry Machin, then chairman of the Campaign Against Nuclear Energy, did not, and the two men went into battle over the airwaves. Machin quickly learned that the rogue bull would not be swayed.

'I want to ask Mr Hancock why he has always refused to debate the uranium issue in public, because I don't consider this program a real forum for discussion,' he said.

True to form, Hancock shot back that there was no debate. 'The debate was won 29 years ago when the United States Government appointed Dr Edward Teller to look into all the safety aspects of uranium . . . The debate is over, the debate is over!'

'Look, this man Teller you are always quoting, he has a bad reputation,' proffered Machin. 'Listen, he is the person who said that strontium-90 was good for children's bones, during the fallout scare. I don't think you can get away with answering the serious questions about nuclear power by shouting and raving. I challenge you to a public debate in which we can seriously debate some of the misleading nonsense you keep putting over in this one-way style . . .'

Hancock was in no mood to listen. 'You don't have any arguments and you jolly well know it! They are communist propaganda. You are trying to subvert this country.'

'Is that a serious allegation, Mr Hancock? Over the public air, that I am a communist?'

'I'm not saying that at all. For goodness sake, listen, and I'll tell you what the score is. The score is that the rest of the world, with the exception of Australia, has gone nuclear.'

'That doesn't mean we have to follow in their foolhardy footsteps. Did you see that program about radioactive waste on the ABC the other night . . . ?'

'You know jolly well that was propaganda. There were only two true things in it – that nobody has ever died as a result of nuclear power generation for peaceful purposes, and . . .'

Clearly outraged, Machin's response was drowned out by his spluttering.

The interview concluded with Hancock talking over the top of him. 'Listen, listen, listen! Listen, listen, listen! Listen, listen . . . for God's sake, learn something!'

19

HANCOCK WAS NEVER HAPPIER than when he was holding court and pontificating on his favourite subject – mining. Legions of people, from journalists and government officials to trade unionists, sat through countless hours with him as he fed them a steady diet of his views on what Australia needed to return it to its former glory. While the movement for Aboriginal land rights raged around him, tribal elders were holding meetings with mining executives, warning them that company takeovers of their country threatened the very survival of the Indigenous peoples. But Hancock did not budge from his position of self-interest. If he reiterated his opinion loudly enough, he figured one day the bastards would listen.

Incensed at his disregard for their culture and rights, Aboriginal leaders were equally resentful that Hancock, for all his money, did not even attempt to negotiate a middle line. Instead, he dredged up his oft-quoted fear that if Australia didn't mine its own wealth, someone else would.

Pointing to the Northern Territory example, Hancock was scathing. 'The government there have granted Aboriginals mineral rights without them having to discover them – and in the process they have given away the rights to two-thirds of the Northern Territory. This is the most ridiculous thing I could ever think of. The Aborigines have no obligation to find the ore. This leaves them in a privileged position. Aborigines should have exactly the same rights as any other citizen in Australia – they should not have exclusive rights. You can't live off a sacred site.'

The rogue bull resented criticisms that he targeted Aborigines, and voiced this loudly, but if critics were offended by his comments, it was to get a lot worse.

Hancock had grown up with Aborigines; they were his child-hood playmates, and later his workers. To the end of his life, he maintained a healthy respect for these Aboriginal people whom he perceived as maintaining traditional culture and dignity, but his views on those who had shifted into towns and started drinking alcohol were always delivered with the mailed fist. Black or white, if a man was unemployed, he should seek work; if he was drunk, he should get sober; if he wanted to whinge, complain to someone who cared. He would not be silenced.

Wobby Parker, who grew up with Lang at Mulga Downs, was blunt. 'He should have done something right for us people, stuck up for us, look after us better. He give us nothing. We don't worry about him; we don't do nothing when he passed away. He was a rich man, and after he died they fight over his money, but we got nothing.'

Wobby found some comfort in the fact that his son, unlike him, could read and write, and now taught others in the community to do so. There was some comfort, too, in that his people now have the opportunity to do sacred site inspections at Mulga Downs.

Hancock's outspoken views made more temperate white

Australians shudder, and outraged Aboriginal groups. But the older he got, the more belligerent he became.

He also consistently argued that Australia should be exempt from income tax north of the 26th parallel, with a 40 per cent reinvestment clause on capital only. In his lexicon, everyone would win.

In short, he wanted to 'Axe the Tax'.

He was extremely contemptuous of white people who put their hand out to the government for welfare. His abrupt and cynical treatment of those who sought his financial assistance was legendary, although he was a generous benefactor to causes he approved, and to which he gave anonymous donations. He failed to hide his impatience with those who were less well-off than himself, and did not shy from head-to-head confrontations with the unemployed.

He once commented, 'I don't think hand-outs do any good. I think that's where Australia has fallen down. Our national anthem seems to be a tune called "The Government Oughta" – the government oughta feed me, the government oughta clothe me, the government oughta assist me, the government oughta lay down guidelines, the government oughta do my thinking for me.'

20

HANCOCK HAD SUPPORT FOR his secession ideals outside Western Australia as well. Joh Bjelke-Petersen, whom Hancock now regarded as a political genius, was unequivocally batting on his team. Like Hancock, Sir Joh despised Canberra and everything it stood for, and he would not back his cart to anyone, be they prime ministers or overseas trade partners.

In 1976, Hancock escorted Bjelke-Petersen on a voyage of discovery around the Pilbara, espousing as he flew the benefits to be gained from the iron ore treasures which lay beneath them. It was, to those who attended the press conference later held in Perth, nothing short of a mutual admiration society, bordering on veneration.

Their vision splendid for secession of both Western Australia and Queensland was breathtaking. A steel mill would be established in Queensland and in the Pilbara, to milk the coal that Bjelke-Petersen's state boasted and the iron ore of Western Australia. A transcontinental railway would shuttle between the two sites, swapping ore with coal on the return journey.

Sir Charles Court had himself mooted the idea, but the two men did not ask for his input.

What Hancock and Bjelke-Petersen proposed to seek was financial backing from the Middle East to build the railway line. They regarded it as a perfect quid pro quo: the trade-off for those prepared to put up the money would be rights to mine the minerals that were to be found 200 kilometres on either side of the track. Hancock blithely ignored the controversy which sprang from the idea, and criticised the outspoken sentiments of those concerned with environmental protection – the 'eco-nuts' as he had christened them – as the hysterical ravings of left-wing greenies. He had the same amount of patience and time – none – for the call for Aboriginal land rights.

It could work; it would work if Hancock and Bjelke-Petersen had their way. Unrestricted foreign investment was the way of the future. If Jesus could turn water into wine, Hancock could turn minerals into money. All that was required was the combined resources of coal and iron ore, backed by Arab money and a trade-off of minerals.

One of those minerals was uranium.

In 1973, Hancock conducted a secret visit to the Kuwaiti Prime Minister; following that meeting, he made contact with the Royal House of Kuwait and the Shah of Iran. He felt at home in the hot desert sands with men who spoke in telephone-book figures, and he shared their concerns that if they were to invest overseas, there should be no interference at government level. Other issues were also at the forefront of Hancock's thinking. It was becoming increasingly clear to him that the Japanese would continue to stall on signing any contracts for iron ore at this time because of the looming world manufacturing recession, which was to become a stark reality with the oil crisis of 1973. When it hit, Hancock criticised the Arab world in a pamphlet he wrote in July 1974, entitled *Resources Diplomacy or Diplomacy Madness?* That he had visited various sheikhs, the Shah and the Kuwaiti Prime Minister less than a year before in his attempts to shore up financial backing did not induce him to remain silent.

The oil crisis was being felt around the globe. The land of the rising yen, as Japan would become known, felt particularly vulnerable; without oil, they could not make steel. This, in turn, affected Hancock's chances of consolidating any Japanese contracts. He had hoped to muscle in with Marandoo, a site 70 kilometres from Wittenoom, behind Mount Bruce, which boasted high-grade Marra Mamba with an iron content of 62.6 per cent.

Ultimately, none of this came to fruition. The big Australian companies did not need another competitor, and they had the Western Australian Government and the Japanese on their side.

The repercussions of the energy crisis were directly hitting Hancock, and he made his dissatisfaction clear, starting with an attack on the Whitlam Government. 'The list of government misjudgements of our resources is practically without end, yet the government still doesn't seem to understand the impossibility of trying to base an economic policy on such hopelessly misleading data . . .'

He seesawed again, deeming the time was right to take Whitlam into his confidence with regard to his overseas sorties, just prior to the arrival of the Shah of Iran on a goodwill visit to Australia in September 1974. The stage for the meeting between the capitalist Hancock and Labor Prime Minister was Sydney's Kirribilli House, a notably different venue from that of the previous year, when the Whitlams had visited the Pilbara during a Hancock-organised junket. The elaborate setting of the Prime Minister's Sydney home did not impress the so-called 'King of the Pilbara'; he would kow-tow to no one and, until the end of his life, stood by his oft-repeated belief that neither premiers nor prime ministers had any power – 'no bloody power at all'.

Hancock later recalled his conversation with the towering Whitlam, and he did not wrap it in pretty paper. He was adamant that he would not brook government interference at any level in his negotiations; what he was doing was within the law and Big Brother could keep his paws off the project. The prime objectives, he maintained, were to break the Japanese stranglehold as the main market for Australian iron ore, to open up new channels for oil and to bolster Australian defence. The Shah must be kept out of Western Australia when he visited, far away from Court's meddling. Hancock was convinced that Court would make it his priority to turn the tide against any initiative he and Wright proposed. Whitlam graciously did as he was asked; the Shah was fêted, instead, by Bjelke-Petersen.

If the Prime Minister was amazed that Hancock would dare threaten to ride roughshod over the government, he did not comment. Renowned for his exceedingly dry wit, he let Hancock talk.

Despite his insistence that no government minister interfere, Hancock was forced to capitulate when the Shah directly requested a ministerial escort on his Australian trip. Whitlam chose Kep Enderby, his Minister for Manufacturing Industry, who, in turn, invited another minister to the briefing with Hancock. This was the final straw: ordering the minister out, Hancock reiterated in no uncertain terms his position that it was vital the negotiations were kept under wraps. The government, battling voter criticism arising from the current economic hardships, sensed an opportunity to turn a negative into a positive, and newspapers around the country carried stories to that effect. While Hancock received a guernsey in the stories, the main thrust was that the government was looking at the possibility of an exchange of ore for oil between the two countries.

Notwithstanding the red carpet treatment he received, the Shah decided against doing business in Australia. He would, he indicated, be interested in discussing with Hancock the possibility of entering into an agreement with him – if it was offshore. The spectre of nationalisation or, equally unpalatable, socialisation, had frightened the Shah as, indeed, it did Hancock.

21

IN HIS SMALL OFFICE at Wittenoom, Hancock was constantly reminded of his antipathy towards greenies who, he believed, did irreparable damage to business with their petty concerns about the environment. A sign on his desk read: 'Eco-nuts. Let them freeze in the dark'.

But his 'bugger the greenies' attitude held no truck with the Court Government's Environmental Protection Authority (EPA), a watchdog set up to ensure that industry and nature maintained a harmonious balance, and that the landscape was not excessively scarred by mining. In 1977, Hancock forestalled the EPA's objections that the scree at Wittenoom would prove a pollutant to the nearby gorges. Over thousands of years, the scree had been washed down the mountains and lay over it like gravel, which was easily picked up by machinery. A decade before, Ken McCamey had already established that the scree found near Wittenoom had a high iron ore content, but to Hancock's frustration it beckoned him like a mistress he could not touch. The Japanese had not wanted to risk capital on it, and the negotiations – that Hanwright would raise $70 million by 1968 and ultimately produce a million tons of steel by 1995 – had collapsed.

Hancock needed another project, and he was battling a depressed world market. This time, his goal was to remove five million tons of scree from Wittenoom a year to sell to overseas markets to make steel.

In June 1977 Hancock embarked on yet another round-the-world mission to excite interest and capital, with his right-hand man Kevin Dalby, an honours engineering graduate, and Gina, the apprentice mining mogul, in tow. The schedule was exhausting: Kuwait, Switzerland, Madrid and London, where he met the immensely influential powerbroker and money-man Munir Haddad and, later, the then Tory Opposition Leader, Margaret Thatcher. From there, the trio flew to Brussels, Sweden, Rome and Singapore before flying home to Australia. Hancock, now 68 years old, seemed indefatigable. On his return to Wittenoom, with the EPA about to pounce, Hancock figured it was time to take direct action.

In 1990, Lang Hancock gave an interview to Stuart Reid, which is held in Perth's Battye Library. He told Reid that from when Gina was about 12, whenever he travelled overseas, he applied to the school to take her with him, believing that she was going to learn a hell of a lot more by travelling the world with him and meeting world and company leaders. 'You know,' he said, with gruff understatement, 'like the types of Mrs Thatcher. We had morning tea with Mrs Thatcher a couple of times; and Lee Kuan Yew; and meeting the heads of the Kaiser organisation; this kid . . . started at the age of 12 . . . Texas Gulf, Fogarty, all those, she learned to meet them and be on "Even Steven" with them, and this carried on until she went to . . . university.'

Gina's increasing world travels changed the young woman. 'As a young girl she had her father's undivided attention and the whole of the Pilbara at her feet,' a Perth source tells me. 'She did not have to share anything. This seems to have shaped her as a businesswoman and in her personal life.'

After a business meeting with the Iron Lady, Margaret Thatcher, Lang suggested to his daughter that she should emulate the senior woman in both grooming and carriage. Gina took Lang's advice. 'For a while,' says Duffield, 'she was a beautiful young woman.'

Photos of Gina during that period testify to that. Slim, with a broad, open face and flowing hair, she wore little make-up and needed none.

In late 1977, Hancock called a meeting of the Wittenoom townspeople in an attempt to get them to back up his proposal to the Court Government with regard to the scree project. The meeting was a typical bush affair: under the stars, the audience was treated to a free movie – which concentrated on Hancock's achievements – before moving to the main part of the evening, a dissertation on why the project was necessary. He had picked his audience well: like him, they knew that Wittenoom was doomed if it had to survive on tourism alone. Its future lay in mining.

'With Marandoo we were on the verge of signing a thousand-million dollar contract – the largest commercial contract ever signed in the world,' he told them. 'But then along came the steel recession, and we had to look elsewhere. The position is that my daughter and I have been roaming the world . . . associating with everybody who might be interested in this part of the world, to get them into steel and to get things developed. But we have a new concept, to use the scree, and to make Wittenoom the fulcrum not only for that project but for the future of the entire WA iron ore industry.'

Hancock's visions came to naught, his dreams to dust. By 1978, medical opinion about the effects of asbestos dust on workers who were exposed to it was becoming increasingly damning, precipitating the government's decision, in 1979, to pull out of the town. Dr David Kilpatrick, a leading Victorian industrial chemist, used his clout to criticise Hancock for not contributing to the $2 million trust fund for asbestosis victims set up by CSR. His disregard for workers' health, he claimed, was typical of how chiefs treated their Indians. 'He should show more concern for his workers,' Kilpatrick claimed. 'Clearly, the materials they produce are worth more than their lives.'

With pressure mounting on him to address the remaining townspeople, Hancock resorted instead to drafting a letter expressing his opinion on the situation. It was not well received, particularly by the medical profession.

While he admitted that 28 people who had lived and worked at Wittenoom had died from asbestos-related cancer, his statement appeared, in part, to shift responsibility for those deaths to the victims themselves.

'It is essential to repeat that in a lot of cases death by cancer is actually self-inflicted or at least self-aggravated and thus hastened,' he wrote.

Hancock's sheeting of blame for the asbestos-related cancers to alcohol and tobacco users outraged those whose family members had died or were suffering from asbestosis. John Doyle, who was to become a widower from asbestosis, summed up the victims' disgust. 'Wittenoom was Australia's industrial Belsen . . .'

Oblivious to the weight of public opinion against him, Hancock used *The Sunday Independent* to voice his opinion on the closure of government buildings at Wittenoom in 1979. The asbestos tailings used throughout its buildings rendered the town a health hazard and the government, mindful of the repercussions, made the decision to close it down, lock, stock and barrel. Hancock was swimming against the tide, but still he refused to bow to pressure. Under the headline 'City Asbestos

Hazard Worse', the full-page editorial left readers in no doubt about his views.

Hancock's vocal opinions about asbestos damage did not concur with medical evidence. Before the closure of Wittenoom, 20,000 men, women and children lived and worked at the town. By 1990, the dark pall of death that hung over the miners who had worked at Wittenoom was also casting a shadow over CSR. In that year, the company was forced to pay out massive compensation to 322 miners and another 300 cases were backlogged. Professor Bruce Robinson, a researcher in asbestos disease at the University of Western Australia, was brutal in his appraisal of the situation.

'Disease arising from exposure to asbestos at Wittenoom is going to kill people over many, many years,' he warned. Robinson did not stop there, citing examples of the worst industrial disasters in the twentieth century: Bhopal, in central India, where 1700 innocent people died in their beds in 1984 after tonnes of lethal methyl isocyanate leaked from a factory, and from which the death toll is still being counted; and the Chernobyl tragedy, the eruption of a Soviet nuclear reactor which experts believe is a disaster that will still be responsible for deaths generations from now.

Hancock and Wright got billions of tonnes of high-grade iron ore resources in return for purchasing the mine assets from CSR. In addition, they planned to use the asbestos mine equipment and power station to mine iron ore in the vicinity of Wittenoom. Thugs vented their anger at the disintegrating dream of Wittenoom becoming an economically viable minerals centre, shoving the heels of their boots into the thin walls of the asbestos houses, smashing windows and leaving a trail of filthy graffiti in their wake. Hancock and Wright were left to pick up the bill; maintenance alone for the town cost in excess of $140,000 a year.

22

IN 1979, HANCOCK ORGANISED what he named the 'Wake Up Australia' tour, a Qantas jumbo jet which flew journalists and supporters around the Pilbara to look at his mining ventures. To his supporters, it was a brilliant marketing strategy, an opportunity for like-minded Australians to get together and 'Wake Up Australia'. To its opponents, it was nothing more than a propaganda exercise, a futile preaching to the converted which coincided with the publication of the first issue of the Hancock-backed *Free Market* magazine, featuring a suited Hancock, holding an empty wine glass, on its cover. The launch was timed to coincide with Hancock's seventieth birthday in June 1979, and the legend on the giant birthday cake paid tribute to the 'Patron Saint of our Development'. So, too, did the magazine's editorial, which was handed out to passengers on the Qantas 'Wake Up Australia' flight. Those who chose to part with $500 for what Gina described as a 'once-in-a-lifetime trip' were already converts to the cause; the journalists who came along for the ride were likely just as eager to get a junket as they were to report on the trip.

Many of the reports which filtered back to their newspapers and electronic media organisations did not give Gina and Lang the PR they had hoped for. 'For $500 you can fly from Sydney across to Learmouth, in northern WA, stay overnight in a tent, and then fly back to Sydney,' one journalist wrote. 'If that doesn't exactly grab you as the outing of the year, an added attraction will be a steady diet of what Mr Hancock thinks is right with and wrong with this country, with Mr Bjelke-Petersen, to date uncanonised, to second the motion.'

Another journalist, from the BBC, could scarcely contain his cynicism. 'It must have been tough finding a birthday present for the richest man in Australia,' he said. 'So the Patron Saint's birthday has become something of a pilgrimage, a tour of holes in the ground for people whose mission in life is to dig holes in the ground, and all in honour of the great digger himself.'

Gina was peeved. Some reporters, she sniffed, had failed to take the concept seriously, and had even suggested that the aircraft could only fly in a right-wing direction.

Passengers were fêted by flying over Bjelke-Petersen's coal-fields, on to proposed uranium sites in the Northern Territory, into the Pilbara and over the north-west gas shelf. But something was missing.

Hancock.

Making apologies on behalf of her father, who was ill, Gina told the assembled audience that she and Bjelke-Petersen would be co-hosting the flight. The principal speakers, Hancock and Dr Edward Teller, the original drawcards for which the passengers had paid their money, were not going to be on board. Prior to take-off, Gina had offered to return passengers' cheques if they decided not to travel. On her first serious solo public event, the girl who would take over the Hancock reins held herself with dignity and poise. Michael Wright undertook the trip on behalf of his father, who was overseas and could not attend. He was surprised by Hancock's absence.

'Perhaps he was ill, and perhaps he decided he had something better to do. He could be very discourteous at times, if the mood took him. The purpose of the flight was a publicity act to draw attention to the parlous state of Australia and how the government of the day were making wrong decisions. Dad made a recorded, well-thought-out speech on the flight which was effectively interrupted on several occasions by Gina. She has no sense of timing. Gina's interruption of people, particularly those whose views do not exactly match her own, is a common refrain.'

Dr Edward Teller, who consistently flew in the face of public outrage with his outspoken pro-uranium and pro-nuclear views, was recovering from a heart attack in the United States and also unable to travel. The passengers could peruse his ideas, however, when they tired of listening to the other speakers or looking out the window at the coal, uranium or iron ore fields below. Commenting on the Harrisburg nuclear reactor crisis which, as one journalist noted, 'brought us all to the edge of our nightmares', Teller stated: 'There has been considerable damage to the reactor, but minimal exposure to a number of people . . .' The articles in *Free Market* not only concentrated on the views of the controversial Dr Teller but also warned readers of a new plague sweeping Australia. 'Beware! Have you been possessed by a wilderness freak yet?' it asked. 'The symptoms are as follows: Think of a place you will probably never visit. Visualise lantana, mangroves, blackberry and thistle, mosquitoes, snakes and spiders, and nil civilisation. Then vow that the said area never be disturbed. Don't look down: there might be a fortune in the ground. Glory Hallelujah . . . Beauty is in the eye of the beholder, and wilderness is a state of mind, usually fully comprehended after a lobotomy.'

The 'Wake Up Australia' flight was not the first time, nor would it be the last, that Hancock used an aircraft to fly people around the Pilbara, offering them a bird's-eye view of his grand visions. Cynics labelled the exercises 'Hancock Benefit Tours'. But he thought it was grand, and expounded to Reid how Gina had proven to be a superb ambassadress for the tour.

A reporter did an interview with Gina as the flight flew over the Pilbara. Shy but poised and dignified, she held the journalist's gaze and answered each question in a calm voice. Of her 'on the job' experience, she said that her father would be using her more and more over the years. 'It's very important to get a whole lot of experience now,' she said, 'otherwise there's no way I could take over.' She continued, commenting that when she was little, 'I didn't really have a chance to see that much of Dad, I was in boarding school . . . they were the impressionable years, but he's never told me I must think this, must do that. But the last four years I've seen a great deal of Dad . . .' Echoing Lang's opposition to centralised power in Canberra, she opined that Australia would be a damn sight better off if there was less government interference. 'I and my father are very much in favour of the idea of secession, to make WA an independent economic state,' she said in her soft voice.

Charming and pretty, Gina admitted to suffering stage nerves and said she could not give a speech without notes. Even when the reporter asked her questions that she clearly would have preferred not to answer, she held her own against comparisons with her father's abrasiveness. 'What do you think over the last few days?' she quietly shot back. 'I'm not as forthright as Dad, and I do try to be polite but I must admit sometimes I'm not.' Her future, she said, was already full of plans. 'We have quite a few projects on the drawing board . . . Marandoo, bauxite, steaming coal in Queensland, manganese, limestone deposits, a few stations as well – I've got quite a few things I'll be working on in the next few years.'

Asked 'How much is Gina Hayward going to be worth?' she made it clear that it was a question that slightly irritated.

'To be quite honest we don't think of money every day. I'll let you worry about it more if you want to . . .'

The journalist persisted. 'What does all that wealth and power mean?'

'Security of my family is something that is always uppermost in my mind . . . enough for them to have a good education, no financial worries later on.'

One of Lang's favourite pastimes after taking guests on a tour of his favourite Pilbara haunts, during which they would be covered in flies and after which, red dust, was showing documentaries extolling the virtues of his beloved Pilbara. The commentary to *Digger in a Million*, *Dig a Million Make a Million* and *Man of Iron* was delivered in his sonorous, drone-like voice, with Ken McCamey often by his side. But if Lang couldn't do it, Gina was always eager to step in. 'I'd agreed to address the World Symposium on iron ore in Frankfurt,' Lang told Reid. 'Right, well I got sick, so she organised to have a film made, going into all the details of Ronsard, the port and the advantages of it and the downhill railway from Marandoo and the whole box and dice. This film was about an hour's duration and she persuaded the people at Frankfurt in charge of the symposium, that as I couldn't get there, would they look at the film. They agreed to do so, so this film was very, very useful. It's full of all the technical information about the port and railroad, and mining – how it would be conducted and so on.' He added: 'Of course, she's a lot more polite than I am so the relationships were quite good in that respect.'

But Lang also demanded that the young woman who echoed his ideas and whom he continued to refer to as 'young fella' in public, remain feminine and prim. He could be harsh in his criticism of his daughter, who was not known for her stylish taste in clothes, commenting adversely on what she wore and nagging her if she gained weight.

He expected his daughter, as he later wrote, to be a 'neat, trim, capable and attractive young lady'.

Gina had a tough mantle to carry. Lang expected she have the physical charms of a woman but hold her own like a man.

23

HANCOCK MADE NO APOLOGIES for the fact that some of his business deals were negotiated in secret, and recognised that it irritated government personnel – particularly Charles Court. Asked once who he was going to see in Canberra, he replied: 'I can't tell you that, because the moment I mention it they'll run for cover. They'll run frightened. I'm lead in the saddle to anybody – nobody wants to know me. So I sneak up on them.'

On many occasions, he resorted to below-the-belt character assassinations to get his message across, a tactic that made the more temperate Wright shudder and which infuriated those who bore the brunt of the slur. That he sometimes took other people's remarks and used them out of context did not bother him at all.

It was a theme that ran through the Hancock and Court relationship. A thwarted Hancock, pouting and posturing, dripped venom on the minister who refused to allow him his own way. Court, in turn, rubbed in the one fact that Hancock could not escape – he wanted his own mine, and it was a dream he never realised.

He would imbue that dream in his daughter.

Western Australian journalists who watched the two men at close quarters had their own ideas about their relationship. They noted that both were egotistical, driven to succeed, and both held their own uncompromising views about how the Pilbara should be developed. As one wrote: 'An outspoken bushwhacking iconoclast like Hancock could never get on with small-town politicians like the pompous Sir Charles Court – and there was room for only one king of the Pilbara in Western Australia.'

Hancock was not feeling well. In 1980 he had played a hard social round of tennis with his mates from Perth's Kings Park tennis club, a game he found relaxing because, as he noted, 'when you're concentrating on that little ball, you can't be thinking about other things'. But there was a pain in his chest that he was finding increasingly impossible to ignore, a tight, uncomfortable feeling he had not experienced before. All colour had drained from his face, which now had a waxen sheen, and he clutched his chest before collapsing on the edge of the court. While his friends frantically called for an ambulance, Hancock's heart stopped beating. Within minutes paramedics attended, working quickly to revive him.

'I died several times in the space of three minutes, they tell me,' he later recalled of his heart attack. 'They sawed me in half like a bullock and here I am.' Many people doubted that he would survive the open-heart surgery that followed, but Hancock wasn't ready to throw the towel in yet. As soon as he was able he returned to work, but observers noted that despite his protestations it didn't change anything, his brush with death was the turning point for his new perspective on life. Although 70 years old and with enough money to ensure he could live in luxury in his twilight years, he forged ahead with complex business deals at a pace that left insiders wondering whether he was trying to outrun death. The 1980s were to prove a remarkable decade for the rogue bull. His business affairs were to come under the microscope at the WA Inc. hearings, he would be lambasted by a critical press for his deals with communist countries and his personal life would undergo a complete about-face with the death of his beloved Hope and his third marriage, to a woman half his age. In this decade, more than ever before, Hancock, who had always shunned the high life and the limelight, would be held up to scrutiny time and again.

His increasing obsession with getting his house in order was noticed by Ken McCamey, who said that following Lang's heart attack, he was never the same man. 'He used to get all flustered; he'd do things that didn't seem quite right. That's when he started having big spend-ups, too, but there's always a hole in the bucket where things run out. He found that hole later in the Romanian deal.'

It was this heart attack which cemented Hancock's long-held atheist views that there was nothing, and no one, waiting on the other side. Whatever needed to be done, had to be done now.

'I don't worry about death – I died once, and that's all there is to it. It's past. I don't think in the past. You can't change the past so just forget about it. Just look forward and see what you can do.' But Hancock would never be a well man again: his heart attack became a demarcation line between his hitherto good health and the illnesses that would dog him in old age.

Dr Neil Scrimgeour was Lang's GP from 1976 until three years before his death, and had got to know him when he stood for the Senate as a secession candidate. He remembers him as a tough man who confronted life and death situations with his peculiarly pragmatic style. 'Lang had developed a problem with calluses on his foot, and instead of seeking medical advice for it, he tried to hack them off with a pen knife. The result was that he ended up with vascular problems, and doctors warned him that they may have to take his leg off. He was lying in St John of God Hospital in Perth talking to me, and he suddenly said: "Look, if they're going to take my bloody leg off, let them get on with it so I can get back to work." It was a simple statement, announced with no dramatics, and after he'd said it, he went on talking about something else, asking me how my son was getting on.' Dr Scrimgeour was also summoned to see Lang the night he had the emergency heart operation. 'He was refusing to have a body shave, for whatever reason, and it took a while to convince him that he had to have one for the operation. He could be very stubborn when he wanted to be, and he was the sort of man that if he was prescribed one tablet a day for a week, he would take seven at once.'

Never enamoured of flash food, Hancock's diet became leaner following the heart attack. Guests at his table were astonished to find him eating half a lettuce with no dressing, and when he was travelling, he ate store-bought fruitcake wrapped in cellophane, tins of fruit and camp pies.

But his brush with death did not slow him down; typically, he continued to write pamphlets and give speeches that pushed his own barrow. If they offended people, he couldn't give a damn; he had a message to get across, and increasingly little time in which to deliver it. But he grossly underestimated the backlash he received from World War II returned servicemen following a speech he gave in Brisbane in 1981, in which he maintained that a re-armed Japan would only help with Australia's security.

Hancock did not stop at speech-making and pamphleteering. At the age of 71, when most of his contemporaries were retiring, and despite the fact that his health was still precarious following his open-heart surgery, he made the decision to invest in the Australian films *Mad Max II* and *Now and Forever*. Hancock had little interest in movies, and even less in attending gala opening nights. The motive to back the films to the tune of $2.5 million was not just commercial; it was another expression of his backing of free enterprise. He was typically blunt in his explanation that he did not believe in a government-subsidised film industry; when a government put its imprimatur on films, he roared, it equalled no more than a propaganda machine. He pointed to *The China Syndrome* to make his point; that movie, he claimed, was only made to preach the dangers of nuclear power. But there was another reason behind his backing of the two Australian films: his investment came at a time when tax legislation was being changed to lure private investors. Lang's influential accountant and lawyer, Carnegie Fieldhouse, was astute in recognising the tax concessions to be had.

'Carnie', as he was known to his friends, handled Hancock's business affairs for 40 years. An extremely shrewd tax lawyer, his offices in Sydney's salubrious Double Bay reeked of money and sophisticated taste. An extensive collection of bound law reports – some hundreds of years old – lined the walls of his outer offices, reception area and corridors. Along one wall was a false panel containing leadlights of scenes from Dickens. The scene above his meeting table was *The Artful Dodger*.

24

THE LATE JOURNALIST AND author Robert Duffield spent the best part of a year talking and travelling with Hancock in the late 1970s to research his book, *Rogue Bull*. Before his death Duffield recalled the time with a mixture of fondness for Lang and sadness at the events that have occurred since his death.

'I went into the book actively disliking the man and what I knew of him,' he said. 'I wanted to get to know Gina as well, who was then in her early twenties and married to Greg. John, her oldest child, was only very young. I soon realised that Gina was simply a cipher, that she said only what Lang would say. I quickly understood that I needed to go to the man himself. I was opposed to what I understood his philosophies to be, but when I got closer, I realised that there was much more to Hancock than I had imagined. He did not epitomise a power figure – he shuffled around with the aid of a stick – but his dream emanated from him. He lived and breathed minerals, minerals, minerals. I became enamoured of him as a person; he had a warmth that was hard to imagine from a distance, and when I understood his visions, I could see the romance in them.'

Spending time with the Hancocks gave Duffield a personal perspective on the family. 'Lang was an old bear; he loved women and made no bones about the fact that he was a male chauvinist. Hope was a lovely woman – a sophisticated country girl, and no fool. They had a strong marriage, although it appeared that Gina was closer to Lang than to her mother. Gina used "Langspeak" – she didn't appear to have her own personality very much then, she simply paraphrased her father . . .'

By her twenties it was increasingly obvious that Gina was being quietly groomed to take over the Hancock empire. The girlish, feathery voice, which often drops to barely more than a whisper, conceals her will of steel. Duffield noticed it when she was younger: '. . . in order to fit herself for her coming roles as matriarch and priestess of the Hancock dynasty, she has perforce erected around herself a series of armour-plated defence barriers, lest anybody see a little girl inside who could be taken down by the brutal admirals of industry . . .' Gina learned her lessons well, and to Duffield she painted a verbal picture of her definition of beauty. Even then, it was clear that her values and ideals were the complete antithesis of the woman who was later to become her stepmother. Beauty, she said, was not 'neat squares of green land, or paintings, or jewellery, or artefacts, or Paris boutiques. Beauty is the weird, un-capturable colours of the Pilbara. Beauty is ideas – the ideas of what we can do with the vast wilderness by mining it.'

Duffield believed Hancock's strength lay in his uncanny ability to go straight to the top. 'What he did – flying around, identifying and testing the iron ore – was something people like Court could not do,' he said. It was a lesson Gina learned only too well. As Duffield explained, 'Men like Val Duncan weren't interested in dealing with politicians – 'second-hand rogue bulls', Lang called them. They wanted to deal with the immediate players. Lang always espoused his view that he didn't have to worry about public opinion, because that was a job for the politicians. He also believed, in the early days, that he could win Court over with arguments, but that didn't work. So he went about beating him another way, such as pouring thousands of dollars into the National Party to put the edge on Court. The Hancock story is indelibly linked with Sir Charles Court – their joint vision of iron ore and boosting WA society generally, but they were so different in how they attempted to carry out that vision. Court wanted to widen it for the community, for the common people; Hancock saw it from the perspective of a miner. Lang wanted always to stay in the game, to be a player, but his biggest dream – to own and operate his own mine – eluded him. But that doesn't change the reality that Lang was a genuine visionary.'

25

NOW TOO BUSY TO fly himself, Hancock relied on trusted pilots to ferry him around Australia and overseas. In the early days Les Harrison and Tony Abbott (not the Opposition leader) were in the cockpit; Harrison was later replaced by Bob Pruden. The men were the backbone of his business ventures, and he relied on them totally to get him where he needed to be, and get him there safely. Harrison, a former RAF instructor on Vulcan jet fighters, made a habit of showing his copilots how he used to train rookies in low-level flying. Waiting until the plane was traversing water, he dropped down to just above sea level and then handed over the controls of the aircraft. The stunt worked every time: staring imminent death in the face, the young pilots immediately grabbed the controls to avoid plummeting into a watery grave.

By 1974, Hancock had invested in a Learjet which carried five passengers and cruised at 450 knots. But money, Abbott said, did not change him. 'He was a man of fixed ways. He and Hope used to stay at the Australia Hotel in Melbourne, which offered good, old-fashioned service, which Lang appreciated. Wealth didn't change his habits: he always ate fried eggs on toast for breakfast, nothing fancy. And there was no first-class food; that wasn't his style. The in-flight rations were bully beef, lamb's tongue, bread and butter and tomato sauce. He'd eat a cheese sandwich out of a paper bag, and he was happiest doing that.' But although Hancock had simple culinary tastes, Abbott recalled being staggered at his knowledge. 'He was a great conversationalist, a very well-read man who had an unbelievable grasp of literature, politics and industry. He could talk for hours on those subjects, and he used to like detective stories, too. But he wasn't interested in art, the fancy things. He spent his entire time dreaming about the next venture.'

Lang did business with international figures when the rest of Australia was sleeping. Retiring to bed early, it was his habit to snatch a few hours' sleep before hitting the telephones in the hours before dawn. It was a work practice that stayed with him until he became too ill to continue. Hope often joined Lang on his trips, and was a moderating influence on her husband.

'She was like Lang in that she was not a great social person, and she wasn't impressed with the five-star hotels and fancy events.' Spending so much time with Hancock, Abbott had the opportunity to see how he coped with failure as well as success. 'He never gave up, and he never gave in,' he said. 'If something failed, his attitude was to re-think and re-tackle, to try and try again until he succeeded. He was never depressed about failure. He didn't need a lot of friends, although he had many acquaintances, and he was the ultimate workaholic, an early riser who often worked until the middle of the night.'

Lang had little time to play on his overseas trips, and unless he was sick, he never missed a day's work in his life. The pilots were on constant stand-by to fly to the next city and the next meeting. 'I'm not a very social type,' he once commented. 'They put on lunches for me, and things of this nature, while

I'd sooner just get in and talk my business and get out.' But in Paris, Lang did manage to find time to visit the Eiffel Tower, and he told friends later of what he thought about as he stared up at the famous French landmark. 'Looking up at this thing reminded me of the little boy who went to the zoo with his mother,' he said. 'He looked up at the giraffe and said, "Gee, ain't he a huge bastard!" and his mother said, "Don't you dare use that sort of language! How often have I told you not to use the word ain't!"'

'He had a really simple, very dry sense of humour,' an associate recalled. 'And he had absolutely no sense of decorum. A Canberra bureaucrat once asked him: "How many men do you have working at Wittenoom, Mr Hancock?" He replied, "I'd say about half the buggers!"'

To the disgust and astonishment of the maître d' in the best international eateries, Lang often returned food to the kitchen if he deemed it was not cooked. He liked fillet of sole well done, and beef – traditionally served pink – dry and brown.

'We were eating at one of the finest restaurants in Paris one night and Lang had ordered roast beef,' a friend remembered. 'The beef came out as it should, juicy and tender, and he took one look at it and turned his nose up. "That meat isn't cooked!" he told the waiter. "I'm hungry, so cut a few slices off and stick 'em under the grill!" The waiter was horrified, and we could see them muttering in the corner in their own language about this ignorant Australian. But Lang didn't care, he couldn't care less. He called the waiter back and said, "While I'm waiting for the beef, grab me a bowl of chips and a bowl of ice-cream, will you? And bring 'em both at the same time!"'

People who flew with Lang in the early days vividly recall the smell of fly spray in the cabin before take-off; the bush crawled with the unwelcome guests which hitched a ride on board on the bodies of the passengers. Lang dealt with them in the same way he dealt with everything else that stood in his way – he just knocked them down. Michael Wright flew with Hancock on many occasions, and never felt unsafe: 'I felt no fear being a passenger with him. He got a licence from the DCA to repair his engines because there was nobody up there who could fix engines, and what the hell would he do if things went wrong? Being a rough and ready character, he once winched an engine in the branch of a tree. He wasn't interested in cleanliness or precision; this was simply a piece of machinery that he needed to use and on which his life depended. He had about 13 accidents, but none of them were due to pilot error. They were usually the result of mechanical failure. Hancock was fearless, and he would fly between a gap and a piece of cloud. On one occasion he had major engine failure, and so he simply landed on a road. He lost the wings of the aircraft, but it didn't bother him. He just fixed it again and took off.'

Around the Pilbara, stories about Hancock, the 'Flying Prospector' as he was dubbed by the press, are legion. John Hohnen, former Rio Tinto Mining Australia chief and the man who recognised and developed the Mary Kathleen uranium mine, admitted he was in awe of Hancock's flying abilities and bush skills. Hohnen spent countless hours with Lang as he shepherded his small Auster through the Pilbara skies, and with him drank coffee mixed with the condensed milk that he always kept on board. On one occasion when Lang landed the plane on a claypan after a particularly heavy deluge, Hohnen was intrigued as to how he knew the ground was firm enough to negotiate a safe landing.

'Easy,' replied Hancock, waving his hand over the terrain. 'Didn't you see the fresh kangaroo pads going across it?' Lang was well aware that many of his passengers were better acquainted with an office desk than with the wilds of the outback, and he kept a full supply of water on board for any eventuality. Leaving Hohnen in the scrub before taking off to retrieve some papers he had forgotten, Hancock alighted from the aircraft and handed him a gallon of water. 'You had better keep this,' he said, 'otherwise, if I crash taking off or coming back, you'll be dead in four hours.'

In the 1960s, Hancock chauffeured an international reporter around the outback in his aircraft, pointing out to him the minerals on offer in the region. He invited the man to move a rock to see what was in the cave behind it, but the reporter was dubious.

'Isn't it possible that there is a snake in there?' he asked in a querulous voice.

'Oh, very possible,' Hancock shrugged. 'But don't worry about that. That's the least of your problems in this country.'

The reporter didn't agree, and quickly moved along.

Hancock's tours around the Pilbara were all geared towards one goal: everything he did and everything he said was to publicise the potential of iron ore. Passengers recall his stock line, which he repeated on every trip, to every audience.

'Iron to the left of you, iron to the right of you, iron straight ahead of you. Everywhere we look, there is iron, iron, iron.'

That Hancock was a good pilot has never been disputed, but his unorthodox methods often put the fear of God into those travelling with him. He always carried an axe on board the aircraft which he used to chop down the tops of trees before take-off, cheerfully explaining to the alarmed passengers that it made it easier and safer for him to clear the obstacles on take-off.

26

HOPE WAS LOSING HER long battle with breast cancer, and on 2 April 1983 her frail, depleted body gave up the fight. Intensely private about her illness, she did not like to discuss it but those who knew her recognised that her death was a blessed release from the constant pain that dogged her through much of her life.

'She was a charming lady, very moderate, and she suffered greatly in the end with breast cancer,' the pilot Tony Abbott recalled. 'It was a relief when she died, to end her pain.'

Hancock was desolate following her death; his gait slowed, and his general health deteriorated. Never given to socialising, he spent long periods of time alone, sequestered from the world, grieving in solitude. Following Hope's death, Scrimgeour, his doctor, noted a change in his patient. 'He had an air of despondency, and my wife and I were the only visitors he seemed to have at one stage. He was an insular sort of man.'

'Lang's relationship with Hope was unique,' Michael Wright ruminated. 'Hope was the apple of his eye; they adored each other. She generally fell into line with everything he demanded, and he was quite demanding; many domestic decisions that Lang made were of the non-negotiable kind. But her influence, when she cared to exercise it, was very profound. Nonetheless, he could be very cruel by simply being thoughtless. Access to her during her various illnesses was almost impossible; he kept her under tight wraps. He simply made a decision that visitors were persona non grata and as such she was very isolated during her final years.'

Wright recalls that Hope was a generous, if earthy, lady.

'She was one of the most delightful people you would ever meet, and she was a complete foil to Hancock's more abrupt manner. I remember complimenting her on the food she served at Gina's twenty-first birthday party. "There's no point serving crook tucker at a party like this, you know!" she laughed. She had a totally different personality to her daughter. Gina had organised her father's seventieth birthday celebration, which was a black-tie affair. She had sent invitations to everyone but my brother and I, and so we didn't realise the dress code for the night. When I apologised to Hope for not turning up in the right gear, she smiled and said, "Don't worry about it; it's good to see you here." By contrast, Gina reminded me that we could have hired dinner suits. Gina lacks the warmth that her mother had.'

Another family friend recalled that while Hope knew that there were expectations on her to live up to the image of wealth, she was uninterested in its trappings. People were attracted to her warmth, and to her sense of humour. She wore a massive ring on her finger which never failed to attract attention, and she was always gracious when she was complimented on the beautiful diamond. The ring was glass, bought at the local department store for a song. She had a box of them stashed away in the drawer, and when one started looking a little jaded, she would throw it out and wear another.

Hope was buried at Perth's Karrakatta Cemetery, and if Lang was an insular man prior to her death, after it he became even more so. The house seemed cavernous now, and he rattled around it as if searching for something he had lost. After 37 years of marriage, loneliness was an unwelcome companion at his dining table.

Men of Hancock's generation did not cry, and certainly not in public, but it became increasingly obvious to those who knew him well that he was exceedingly vulnerable. Only business deals kept him busy, and he was no housekeeper, as Gina had admitted when she was 12. Hope had run a tight ship on the home front, always there as background support until she became too ill even to play that role. Now, more than ever, Hancock needed someone to look after him.

27

THE FORMER ROSE LACSON'S versions of her early life are as dramatic as the woman herself; if, over the years, the history has sometimes changed, she makes no apologies for that. She was no gutter child, born into peasantry and reduced to a life of starvation and begging. But the truth about her past is slippery, difficult to grasp. Rose is a storyteller, hard to pin down; an accomplished media player, a mistress of disguise, she changes in an instant from flirtatious coquette to a hardened woman of the world. Boasting an innate gift for self-promotion, her conversation is peppered with colourful anecdotes and daring adventures and littered with homespun homilies and the ghosts of ex-husbands and friends.

Rose does not welcome cross-examination about her past. She was, she says with a toss of her dark hair, reared in a cultured and dignified family who were prominent in Manilan society and staunchly anti-Marcos in their beliefs. She also claims that she is fluent in three languages.

'For better or worse, you start with that which all the

past has made you. You cannot dissociate yourself from the stock from which you sprung and from the rock from which you are hewn.' So begins her autobiography, *A Rose by Any Other Name*, with a quote from William Barclay. A month after Hancock's death, a *Sunday Times* journalist travelled to the Philippines to find out just what that stock was from which she was sprung, and their investigations proved contrary to Rose's claims. Her family, he found, was not highly placed in society but were, on the contrary, middle class and struggling to make ends meet. Rose did not appreciate the intrusion.

Always rebellious with a restless spirit that would not be tamed, she enjoyed a close relationship with her father but shared her mother's fiery temperament, a by-product of her part-Castilian background. Rose's parents did not approve of her tumultuous first marriage to Julian Teodoro, which lasted only a few weeks but which produced her only child, a daughter she named Johanna.

In her autobiography Rose wrote: 'So there I was, alone against the world it seemed, an outcast from family and not knowing the first thing about earning a living for myself and my baby. The seventies were merciless years for a separated woman. She was easy prey for men who were only looking for fast flings . . .' From that point, Rose says her life was a tightrope, on which she found a precarious balance based on her good luck, good looks and good management. She married a second time, to a Malaysian who, it was alleged, had become involved in a grubby credit card swindle. That marriage was also brief. In the decade following her separation from her first husband, she claimed she worked as a part-time schoolteacher, interior decorator, accounts executive, marketing manager, insurance broker and panty-hose model. She wrote of being smuggled into Clark Airforce Base, for American military personnel, in the boots of cars to engage in the black market, and frequenting a bar in Manila's infamous red-light district which was owned by her uncle. Rose does not back away from addressing the rumours that she was a prostitute in Manila.

'The idea is ridiculous,' she snorted during our interview in September 1999. 'Ridiculous. I come from a well-connected family, and don't you think that if I had done that, somebody would have blackmailed me for money after I married Langley? I don't care what people think – let them think what they like.'

There are few pauses or full stops in Rose's retelling of her life, the narrative infused with bawdy descriptions, risqué adventures and declarations of childlike innocence.

In April 1983 Rose landed in Perth, a place she described as lacking the excitement and entertainment offered in the world capitals in which she had lived. She claimed she was en route to New Zealand where she intended to look into a new product for the family's food and beverage business. The venture fell through, and she decided to stay with her friend Connie in Perth.

'One morning Connie was reading the newspaper and pointed out an advertisement offering the position of a house-keeper,' Rose wrote. 'I laughed at her – "Connie, you must be crazy. With the kind of life I have been used to, with servants around me at every turn in the Philippines and with a personal maid even when I was romping all over Europe, you can't be serious. I can cook but I'm not very good at ironing. The idea is ridiculous."'

Ridiculous or not, Rose found herself, in early April, at the Hancock mansion for an interview.

28

IN JANUARY 1983, IN Las Vegas, Gina married New York corporate lawyer Frank Rinehart, to whom she was introduced through Joh Bjelke-Petersen. Gina was 28. Rinehart was 65.

'When Gina married the first time, her father thought she was too young, and that her groom was as well,' a family friend recalls. 'But she was determined to do her own thing. The next time, she married someone old enough to be her father. Lang was desperately unhappy about that, too.'

John was six years old when Gina remarried, and later described to me that Rinehart was a demanding, sophisticated and highly intelligent man. 'He was number one at Harvard Law School and believed boys should be treated tough,' he said.

According to associates, Lang detested his suave new son-in-law and he refused to attend the wedding. Gina's once exceptionally close relationship with her father was starting to show signs of strain, which would become more noticeable as the decade went on.

He would undoubtedly have been unimpressed by Rinehart's 1977 conviction for tax fraud, for which he received a one-year suspended jail sentence and was barred, briefly from practising law.

With the birth of their daughter, Hope and, 18 months later, Ginia, Gina and Frank divided their time between living in Australia and the United States. A source who knew both him and Gina described Rinehart as a 'goodly soul' who was very supportive of Gina and the children. 'Lang didn't like him and from what I saw, Gina had the controlling hand in that marriage,' said a source who knew both Frank and Gina. Ginia and Hope were, like their mother, educated at St Hilda's Anglican School for Girls.

Greg Milton agreed that Gina and Frank would bring up John and Bianca. 'I just convinced myself that, in the interests of the children, it was the best thing to do,' he told me. 'I knew very little of Rinehart but I had a lot of faith that Gina would never do anything that was contrary to our children's best interests.'

After his divorce from Gina, Greg Milton's self-esteem plummeted. He drove taxis for seven years, dark years in which he struggled to make ends meet and sought relief from his inner turmoil and insomnia through anti-depressants. 'There were times when I thought suicide would be the easiest way out,' he admitted to me in 2001. 'Not only had I lost everything, I had to readjust to a normal lifestyle. It was a very black time in my life. I was so lonely without my children and couldn't shake my unhappiness. I hoped that in their own time, when they were old enough and mature enough, John and Bianca would try to find me. We had such a close bond when they were little, and through all the years I clung to the hope that one day we would meet again.'

Four years after his divorce from Gina, Greg remarried – a union that lasted seven years and produced a son. A third marriage ended in divorce after four years. 'I was haunted by what had happened in my first marriage to Gina,' he says. 'I couldn't shake it.'

Greg worried that John and Bianca could be at risk because of their name, but he said they had matured into responsible adults. 'Gina has provided great protection for them over the years, for which I am thankful. I followed their progress as best I could, mainly through the media, and whenever I had the chance, I kept press photos taken of them. I believe they are aware of what is expected of them and how to handle the pressure that comes with their name. I am their father – they have an independent right to form a relationship with me if they choose.'

For a moment, Greg became solemn. 'I often wish things were different, that I'd been there during their childhood, but attributing blame is not a constructive process. There are wounds that need to be healed, trust that needs to be rebuilt, issues that need to be resolved. I don't bear Gina any grudges and I hope she achieves her goal of completing her father's work with the minimum amount of stress.' He grinned. 'I've lived the lifestyle of the rich, and while it can be exciting and wonderful, it also brings with it emotional traumas and stress. Money doesn't bring happiness or love, and from experience I know it brings restriction. I'm rediscovering the person I was when I was young and enthusiastic. More than anything, I want all my children to be happy.'

29

ONLY TWO PEOPLE KNOW the truth about how Rose and Hancock met – the protagonists themselves. Rose has offered two versions: the first, that she was standing in a hotel lobby in Manila when Hancock ambled over to her and asked, 'Where's the bloody lift?' and the second, that she met him when she started work as his housekeeper after the planned business venture in New Zealand fell through. What is not in dispute is that just 19 days after Hope's death, Rose started work at the Hancock family home in Dalkeith.

Given the spectacular falling-out between Gina and Rose which began simmering soon after Rose started as Lang's housekeeper, many people express surprise that Gina hired her in the first place. 'It is quite ironic that Gina selected a housekeeper for her father who had no housekeeping credentials whatsoever and whose hands showed no evidence of doing manual work,' one opined. 'Surely one of the key abilities in leading corporate roles is to be able to select appropriate staff?'

What Rose omitted to share with Gina, who undertook the job interview, were some details of her background which later formed such a colourful addition to Rose's conversations: her alleged unceremonious kidnapping by her first, Filipino husband; her second Malaysian husband's alleged involvement in a credit card rort; and the corker of them all, true or otherwise, that she had allegedly worked at her uncle's bar, in the heart of Manila's red-light district. Had she regaled Gina with these stories, it is doubtful she would have got the job.

It is an entertaining, if bewildering, experience to have an audience with the four-times-married chameleon that is Rose Lacson-Hancock-Porteous. Flashy, flamboyant, girlie and garrulous, she could not go unnoticed when she sallied into Perth and was hired as Lang's housekeeper. From that moment, the face of the Hancock family – proud, wealthy and with connections – changed forever. Gone was the jealously guarded private family image, replaced by a public feud of such magnitude that the three protagonists – Lang, Gina and Rose – became dubious celebrities, their names indelibly linked in the public psyche as characters in a real-life version of *Dynasty*. If this was not the legacy that Lang wanted, he was powerless to stop it.

In her dramatic retelling of events, Rose says she was bemused to find herself lying to her prospective employer that she had been a housekeeper in the past. 'Well, I am 34 years old,' she had said, 'unattached and with no intention of getting married.' Told that she would be working for a man, Rose recalls that she was aghast. Reassured by Gina that her employer 'is not the sort of person who would be interested in looking at any woman, he is too busy with his job and running his business', she claims she was placated.

She got the job.

'My first morning was a fiasco!' she recalled. 'I was given a menu listing the meals – mostly roasts – and the washing machine was dilapidated. The vacuum cleaner weighed a ton and was as old as my grandmother . . . At around noon on that same day I heard a key in the lock and in walked Mr Hancock. I had never seen him before. I remember noticing how wise his face looked. I noticed his broad shoulders, the thick eyeglasses and the silver-grey hair on the temple. He looked distinguished. I went over to him and said, "Good afternoon, sir, my name is Rose. I am from the Philippines and I am here to serve you."'

Gina indignantly denies suggestions that she hired Rose; the truth, she says, is that her father had the final say on whether or not she would gain permanent employment after she had served a probationary period. The advertisement in the paper did not mention that the housekeeping position was for Lang Hancock, one of Australia's wealthiest men. Gina, Frank and the children were to live in the house behind Lang's, but from the outset there was a fiery clash of temperaments between the two women. Rose believed that cleaning was beneath her, and that it was a job she took only because she had to. Gina didn't care: Rose was hired help, and she would keep a servant's place.

The clash of the titans had begun.

Tish Lees, an old family friend who grew up in the Pilbara and who knew Lang, Hope and Gina very well, recalls that Lang was as 'lonely as a bandicoot' after Hope's death. 'It was so sad to see the man he became,' she told me. 'He was bereft after Hope died. Our family did what we could to support him. We invited him to join us for dinner at our Perth home and he came along with Gina. I gave him a banjo mandolin to play and we sang old songs, like the impromptu jam sessions we used to have in the bush. Gina commented that it had been a long time since she had seen her father that happy. She invited us to repeat the night at her home about six weeks later.' But the dinner did not eventuate. 'In between going to Gina's for dinner, we had again invited Lang to join us for a meal and he asked if he could bring along a friend. We said yes, naturally. We thought the friend would be a business associate but it turned out to be Rose. We welcomed her but because of that, Gina called and cancelled her dinner with us and cast us off from her life. We were saddened, as we had known her since she was a baby, but it was her choice to behave like that and ours to embrace the woman who made Lang smile again. I told Gina this, and have never heard from her since.'

Within six months, Gina had terminated Rose's employment and demanded she leave the house. Rose moved into an apartment but said she took something with her that no one could take away: Lang's love. Her claims that Gina also evicted her father are vehemently denied by the Rineharts, but what was not in question was Lang's stubborn determination to continue to see Rose. If eyebrows were raised at the huge age difference between Lang and Rose, the couple ignored them. Behind their hands, society sniggered that it was better to be an old man's darling than a young man's slave. Gossips noted, too, the huge disparity in age between Gina and her far-older new husband.

Despite Rose's protestations that Perth was a mere stepping-stone and that she had no intention of staying in Australia, Lang applied for permanent residency for her in September 1984. He also gave Rose a substantial loan to help her establish herself in business. For Gina, this was proof that not only was Rose not going to go quietly, she had no intention of going at all. Furious, she and Frank applied to have the residency cancelled, a move which so outraged her father that he was moved to put his feelings down in writing. In a letter that would later be read to the Supreme Court he wrote:

Dear Gina,

Because of your unwarranted interferences in Canberra . . . I now have to re-double my efforts to obtain permanent residency for Rose, otherwise the money which I have lent her to get established in business, so as to be independent of me, will be lost. As for the children being ashamed of me, I think they are more likely to feel more embarrassed by being picked up from school by a young mother who has let herself go to the point where she is grossly overweight, so instead of listening to gossip and in fact adding to gossip whilst interfering in my affairs, you would be better off to put your own house in order. If you won't consider my well-being, at least allow me to remember you as the neat, trim, capable and attractive young lady of the Wake Up Australia tour, rather than the slothful, vindictive and devious baby elephant that you have become. I am glad your mother cannot see you now. You have accused me of misusing company funds. To this end please do not use any of the company credit cards.

The deteriorating relationship between father and daughter was watched by many close to the family with increasing alarm. Gina moved with Frank and the children to the United States, which Lang appeared to accept. 'She has her own life to lead,' he said and shrugged. 'She knows her husband comes first. In this case, she's gone to America. So I've got to make other plans.' The 'other plans' were guaranteed to upset his daughter.

Rose and Lang were married in 1985 at the palatial North Shore Sydney mansion of Hancock's multimillionaire friend and long-time legal and tax adviser, Carnegie Fieldhouse. If Lang was hurt by the whispers that he was a baby-snatcher and that Rose had married him only for his money, he studiously ignored them.

'I didn't find out that my father had married Rose until after they were married,' Gina later commented. 'I was told after the event . . . I did go to America with the children – we to'd and

fro'd between Australia. I was always concerned . . . for him.'
Quietly, she added: 'I think the less I say about Rose the better.
I don't have any relationship with her at all.' Rose's daughter
Johanna, at boarding school overseas at the time of the wedding,
was also not told until after the event.

Reputed as a genius in his field, 'Carnie' Fieldhouse had
developed sophisticated tax accounting systems to minimise
his clients' tax liabilities. The poolside wedding, attended by a
handful of people, was low-key. Seventy-five-year-old Hancock,
dressed in a smart Givenchy suit, cut an odd figure next to his
34-year-old bride, but a guest who attended the ceremony
remembers it as a dignified and joyous occasion. 'Lang was
happy, deliriously happy, and Rose gave a lovely speech. She
may be a contradiction in many ways, but when she needs to
rise to the occasion, she certainly does so.'

But the wedding was not without its surreal touches: the
cake was decorated with a model train loading real iron ore
onto a dump truck. To Rose's delight, the tabloids had a field
day reporting the wedding, with many giving it front-page
headlines: 'Hancock Weds Philippines Beauty, 36'.

The newlyweds moved into a one-storey house in the
up-market Perth suburb of Dalkeith, a stately, comfortable
house sans the trappings that would characterise their next
home, Prix d'Amour. The later house quickly came to be identified with its new mistress, and was dubbed 'The Rose Mahal'.

Gina failed to conceal her disgust when she spoke about her
father's relationship with Rose on the ABC program *Australian
Story*. 'I was always concerned about my father,' she said with
classic understatement. 'I don't know what else I can say my
reaction was, but I was concerned for Dad. I wanted someone
in his life who would love him and be a very good, trustworthy
friend and companion for him.' She was clearly not amused that
her father had married the hired help. 'I certainly didn't think
he'd have any long-term association with her.'

As a wedding gift, Lang organised for the building of Prix d'Amour in the ritzy Perth suburb of Mosman Park. A prime piece of real estate, the house, with its ostentatious *Gone with the Wind* frontage whose name means 'Prize' or 'Price of Love', quickly came to symbolise a new direction in Hancock's life. Never before given to flashy displays of his wealth, why he did so now was a mystery to many. Hancock's associates from his earlier days found it difficult to understand the apparent devil-may-care attitude he adopted to spending money after he married Rose. They recall that for all his vast wealth, Hancock, as his daughter would later do, had earned a deserved reputation as a person who was reluctant to spend unnecessarily and who never dabbled in frivolities.

A stupendously extravagant two-and-a-half week shopping trip around world capitals followed the wedding, during which time Rose bought furnishings for their new home. Their chartered aircraft groaned under the weight of the goods, but she strenuously defended the spend-up. 'Langley George was a very wealthy man, and he needed a home that would be fit to entertain world leaders,' she said. 'It would not be fitting for him to live in a hovel.'

On one trip to the Middle East with Lang, Rose was furious to find that she had to ride in a Cadillac behind with the women while a sheik and her husband travelled in front in a cream Bentley. Sulking at what she regarded as an affront to her importance, she planned the ultimate revenge. On her return to Australia, she ordered a brand-new cream Bentley, to be delivered to the house as soon as possible. If the sheik paid them a visit in Perth, she told her husband, she would ride up front in the luxury vehicle with any females in his entourage, while Lang and his guest rode behind in an old Holden.

30

THE RIFT BETWEEN FATHER and daughter deepened following the wedding. Removing Gina as director of Hancock Prospecting in October 1985, Lang made it clear that he would not brook interference in the running of his company. The bitterness expressed in a letter from Gina to her father in 1987 would perfectly mirror the ugly fracas with her own children years later. 'You have become the subject of dirty old man jokes from one side of Australia to the next,' she wrote Lang. 'You've been wiped out financially by a manipulating Filipino. You've taken money out of our company in excess of your share and . . . [hidden] the personal till taking in the company books, which is nothing short of a conspiracy against the shareholders. You stoop to lies, blackmail and distortion against your own family . . . Will you let Price Waterhouse examine the books covering these last three years? You know I have sufficient grounds to get them to examine the books with a court order, but I would prefer you agree voluntarily.'

In 1990, Frank Rinehart, who had adopted John and Bianca with their father's permission, suddenly died. 'I thought it was in the best interests of my son and daughter for them to be formally adopted by Rinehart,' Greg Milton told me. 'It would have been too confusing for them otherwise, caught between my world of very little money, and Gina's, with her great wealth.' Gina returned to Australia with the four children, who all carried the Rinehart name, and resettled in Perth.

In a rare lowering of her personal guard, Gina described her late husband, to whom she was married seven years, as 'the finest person I have ever known', and added: 'I have never been through anything as difficult as losing my mother or losing my husband.'

In an interview with Stuart Reid, Hancock fondly reminisced about Gina becoming part and parcel of his business. But his conversation takes a colder tone when he recalls Gina's marriage to Rinehart. 'That [the first marriage, to Greg Milton] didn't work and she married an American, much older than herself, and he was the chief negotiator for Atlantic Richfield, ARCO. Then she had more children with him and, of course, her life was then dominated by him, and he just died the other day and she's pretty distraught at the moment. So there's not much that I'm prepared to tell you about that.'

Though immensely private about every aspect of her personal life, Gina's love for Frank Rinehart has never been in question, nor has how much Lang detested him. 'Lang had a serious fear that Rinehart and Gina were going to try and wrest control of his company,' Willie Porteous told me in 1999. 'I was a friend of Lang's and worked with him in various roles for about eight years and he often mentioned this to me. He lamented that it had come to this with his own daughter. The breakdown of his relationship with Gina was not just about Rose entering his life. It was about Frank Rinehart as well. Lang did not trust him, not at all.'

Gina grieved behind closed doors. 'It must have been hard

for her, regardless of how wealthy she was, to suddenly lose her husband,' a Perth source comments. 'It would have been made harder still by her understanding that she would have to negotiate the tricky vagaries of being the heiress to a fortune, and open to the disingeniousness of new friends with an eye to her wealth and the circling like sharks of opportunistic, would-be suitors. Her father had warned her about this, and suddenly she was alone, again, this time with four children.' Gina, Lang continued in his interview with Reid, 'faded out of the business' while he, meantime, married Rose, who had her own interests. 'One day, of course, my daughter will have to come back into it,' he said. 'I don't know how far that is, but one day that will happen, I suppose, because she's the one that knows the most about it apart from myself.'

'So you keep in touch with your daughter?' Reid asked.

Hancock replies: 'Oh yes, I keep in touch with her, but she's got four children, young, and no husband, so she hasn't got any time to devote to this business at the moment.'

But while Gina suffered over the death of her husband, there were even more turbulent days ahead.

31

HANCOCK WAS NO STRANGER to controversy, but his decision to undertake a barter deal with the despised hardline Stalinist regime of Romanian Nicolae Ceausescu was almost universally condemned. But he had a vision: to open up exclusive new markets in Eastern Europe and to break the stranglehold the Japanese had on the import of iron ore. To Hancock, his idea was a stroke of genius: simple in its concept, promisingly lucrative and a front door to the Eastern European market. That he was 78 years old and unwell did not faze him; he was showing no signs of slowing down. In 1987, he signed an agreement with Ceausescu to barter iron ore with Romania, a coup of which he was particularly proud. Hancock's dream was to be financed by the Romanians, without them receiving any equity. 'Father Christmas has come to town,' he chortled when the deal was signed. Wright was more circumspect.

The trade mission comprised 40 people – union officials, businessmen eager to get in on the ground floor, government personnel and the then-Premier, Brian Burke.

The deal was that the Romanians paid for the ore in steel products; which, in turn, were sold by Burwill International Ltd, a Hong Kong trading company partly owned by Hancock, which was to barter the goods on overseas markets. The nuts and bolts of the barter deal were left to Kevin Dalby who, as a director of Hancock Mining Ltd and Burwill, put Hancock's dreams into practice. It was a complex arrangement, exacerbated by Australian unions screaming that they vehemently opposed importing goods into the country that could be produced locally. Hancock ignored them.

'The deal works like this,' he crowed. 'Three years ahead, they supply me with enough equipment to start the mine, build the railway link and expand the port. With that done, I churn out the iron ore to pay them back. This is only possible because the Romanians have built a canal from a Black Sea port to the Danube River. It is bigger than the Suez or Panama Canal and it opens up all those countries in Eastern Europe that currently consume 98 million tonnes of iron ore a year, while the Japanese consume 100 to 110 million tonnes. Not one scrap of Australian iron ore has ever been sold in this market, so we have penetrated a brand-new market which is almost as large as the Japanese. The other part of the deal is that I have to expand their port facilities from being able to unload 50,000-tonne ships to being able to hand 150,000-tonne ships. We have to freight it in big ships or the freight cost will become enormous.'

Floundering under a $5 billion foreign debt it was determined to eliminate, Romania entered into the agreement to pay for the agreed 53 million tonnes of iron ore using the barter system which was common in European countries. Instead of paying for the ore in cash, it would finance it with goods. When negotiations were complete and the goods sold, the cold hard cash would be siphoned back into Hancock's mining interests.

Hancock could not resist the opportunity to take a swipe at governments who, in his opinion, had been slow to back a barter system. 'This sort of barter agreement has been going on for some time now in Brazil, and we silly buggers have sat back and watched . . . Since the Ludwig opportunity was missed, mining has become stationary in this country. Very little has happened since 1964. This is because the government has clamped down with rules and regulations which have made development impossible. I hope that these stupid things are not going to get in my way now, with the Romanian deal.'

Hancock was under no illusions that the barter agreement would be heavily criticised, but he nevertheless flew in the eye of the storm. When it was noted that the Romanian Government was investing a quarter of a million dollars in equipment at a Hancock mine in part-payment for ore, the union backlash was immediate. Australian workers, they seethed, would be denied jobs because local companies had been left out of the tender process. That was too bad; Hancock simply got on with business.

Asked what she thought of the arrangement, a Romanian who had fled the country and was living in Australia replied: 'My countrymen are weeping, while Hancock shakes hands with the devil.' It was a view shared by many. For those opposed to Ceausescu, the millions of Romanians who watched helplessly as their country became a slaughterhouse and the streets ran with rivers of blood, the dictator was evil incarnate, driven by power and with ice in his veins. Romanians, seeking the same democratic reforms that other Eastern Europeans were demanding, did not find them: where their border neighbours' voices were raised in a spontaneous song for freedom, theirs were met with steel boots and bullets. It seemed that the whole country was bleeding but Hancock, true to his code that business is business, did not bleed for them. Faced with the cold realities that Ceausescu's troops were exercising barbaric practices, including summary executions and overturning even the most basic of human rights, he would not back down. Ceausescu's political leanings or arbitrary punishments of those who opposed him simply did not concern Hancock.

Business was business.

'One paper said there were 2000 people killed and another reported 300, but I'd be very surprised if more than ten students had been killed,' he retorted. 'It does not make any difference because you cannot believe what you read; nobody knows what the real position is.' Amnesty International did know what the real position was, but even their outcry failed to temper Hancock's scorn at the suggestion that Australia should suspend trade relations with the country. 'The calls are without foundation and put together by fools,' he raged. 'Suspending trading links will only harm Australia, not Romania, because 90 per cent of foreign trade is with the USSR.'

Pointing out that in recent years he had negotiated iron ore sales to Romania worth in excess of $1.3 billion, he continued: 'I've put the world's largest unloaders in there and they can build the world's largest canal in the Danube. Before we did that not one tonne of Australian iron ore or coal got into Romania. The time is right not only for sales to Romania but Czechoslovakia, East and West Germany and the USSR. Surely to goodness that is worthwhile, rather than worrying about ten students being killed because they protested about something or other which is none of our business.'

An associate who travelled with Hancock during his Romanian deals recalled that a red carpet was laid out to the airport entrance during one of their visits. Looking out from his private jet, Lang made the comment: 'Look, they've rolled out the red carpet treatment. This must be for us.' Five minutes later, Ceausescu's plane touched down, and he and his entourage stepped out. The red carpet was for him.

In the late 1980s, Federal Government officials who kept a close eye on world affairs were horrified to learn that Ceausescu and his wife Elena were visiting Western Australia in connection to Hancock's iron ore projects, a visit that went ahead as scheduled. But by December 1989, the dictator and his wife were captured and detained as they attempted to flee Bucharest. Tensions were at flash point in the country, and three days later, the people exacted their revenge.

The despised couple was executed on Christmas Eve.

Told of the execution, Hancock accused the new Romanian Government of unfairly trying Ceausescu, and his words were greeted with shudders. 'In part I believe that conducting a kangaroo court . . . and shooting a man who got them out of debt is not the way to start a new democratic government.'

In a press statement released in 1991, Lang boasted that he had managed to negotiate 'sufficient deals in the Soviet bloc' and that this should ensure Australia could 'recover from the present impending depression'. He also used his unique brand of humour to talk up the idea. 'You sell a ship and you have disposed of $25 million,' he said. 'You sell a couple of lavatory seats or Savile Row suits, and what have you got?' Then-Premier Brian Burke, who was a co-leader of the Romanian mission, lavished high praise on Hancock. 'His ability to think things through laterally is amazing,' he said. 'I am sure that one day his power of vision will be rewarded.'

Rose, for once, was a touch more moderate. 'I was always very worried about the Romanian deal because of Ceausescu. He was another Marcos, and look what happened in the Philippines. But you have to remember that through that deal, Lang enhanced the international reputation of Hancock Mining in the booming Eastern Bloc countries, like Russia.'

The reality of the Romanian deal fell far short of Hancock's expectations. Without his own mine in production, the supply of ore was channelled through a South African company and BHP. The deals had already begun to unravel prior to the hated dictator's execution but Hancock carried on regardless.

'I went straight to the new bloke,' he told Western Australian newspaper journalist John McGlue just before his death. 'He started to tell me that they'd entered the era of democracy, he was only the President, he had no power. I said to him, "Look, on President Truman's desk there was a notice that said the buck stops here and that's you." So I eventually won that round. We came away with an agreement.'

Ultimately, though, the grand plans crumbled, symbolised by decrepit, rusting equipment and unloading bays that were offered in the barter deal. That exercise alone had cost a massive $20 million. 'Add to that the other $20-odd million it cost as a result of the "take or pay" contract with Lygren, the European shipping magnate,' the mining insider says, 'several trips in his private jet and the large delegations he funded to Europe, and you get some idea of the magnitude of how much money was wasted on this ill-conceived disaster. Peter Wright had wanted no part of it and without his balanced approach to commercial enterprises, it was always destined to fail.'

That Hancock had apparently turned a blind eye to the human rights abuses perpetrated under Ceausescu and his swing 'to the new bloke' after the people took their revenge made him a sitting target for criticism. Neither did the ironies of the situation escape notice: 'The Arch-Capitalist Lang Hancock, Doing Business with Communists', one headline read.

32

THERE WAS AN URGENCY to Hancock's business dealings in the 12 months before he died, a desperation to fulfil his dream of owning and operating a mine in his own right. Just a fortnight before his death, he expounded that Eastern Europe was the way of the future.

'First of all, there's no country in this world which is a major country that has got their own iron ore. The United States of America has got none. Italy's got none. Germany's got none. Japan's got none. South Korea's got none. China's got none.' He extrapolated on his proposed deal with Russia and Turkey. 'The Russians realise that the Pacific Rim is the only growth area in the world . . . I was supposed to sign a document with Yeltsin worth about $930 million in western investment. I got as far as Moscow. Yeltsin wasn't there. The Russians' set-up got set back six months. But I signed with the world's largest iron ore producer and the world's largest steelmaker for this $930 million development in Siberia . . . When the Soviet breaks up, all the Eastern Bloc next door to Turkey speak the same language and have the same religion. I can see a revival of the old Ottoman Empire . . . I have a deal with the President of Turkey. He came out here, Bob Hawke got blathered for receiving him – which is about the one sensible bloody thing Hawke has ever done.'

Hancock's supporters trusted his judgment in looking at Eastern European markets. His long-time friend Harold Clough, who politely declined to comment about his old mate without Gina's approval to do so despite the fact that his name was forwarded by the Rinehart family on Hancock Prospecting letterhead, described the move in 1992 as a 'very broad vision'. But, he ventured, his great admiration for Hancock was tempered with the realisation that he failed to understand how big companies worked. 'That's both a strength and a weakness,' he said. 'It allowed him to make the decision to break into Romania, but I don't think it's a decision BHP would make. They haven't got the balls.'

At a commemorative luncheon for what would have been Hancock's ninetieth birthday, years later, Sir Joh recalled his overseas trips with Lang. 'He talked me into going to Romania with him, where that communist dictator was who was eventually shot by his people. That was the first time I'd been in a communist country and I didn't know what sort of reception I'd get because I was always accused of being able to see a communist under every bed. Ceausescu was surrounded by so many men with guns, and he would only let people in, one at a time to see him, so you didn't have much hope. He was smaller than myself but he was a ruthless man, with a terrible reputation and I could see the way people lived in fear of the government in those days.' Addressing Gina, Sir Joh added: 'Later, your dad was in the hotel at Bucharest the day you rang him telling him he shouldn't spend so much money, with which I agreed really, and as it turned out you were right.'

In 1995, Gina reputedly paid in excess of A$20 million to Atle Lygren, the Norwegian shipping broker who had negotiated to ship the ore into Eastern Europe, to close off the deal. In real terms, the payout represented at least two years in royalties from Hamersley Iron.

33

MICHAEL WRIGHT – AMIABLE, INTELLIGENT and articulate – sat squarely in the middle of the feud between the Rinehart and Porteous families. As an impartial observer, he said he was often amazed, and more often disgusted, at the vitriol and excess fuelled by the bitterness between the two women. His interest, he said, was in keeping a reality check on the achievements of Hancock and his own father. He was forthright and blunt in his assessment of Hancock's character, but admitted a fondness for him and sadness at the legacy which he has left behind. 'I used to work for him when I left school; I went up to the Pilbara and did a lot of the mineral exploration, working on some of the mines, lead and asbestos before we moved into the iron ore business. I worked at most of the mines, including Tom Price. Hancock was intolerant of mankind; not many people impressed him, but when they did he was generally very loyal to them. My relationship with him was difficult; one minute he reckoned I was the most inept little bastard he had ever met, and the next minute I'd be doing things that nobody else could do.

There were only two people who effectively managed Hancock: one was his wife, Hope, who thought the world of him and who was very good at exercising influence when she wanted to, and the other was my father. Hancock did a lot of the discovery and field work and had the mechanical know-how, but at the risk of being conceited, he wouldn't have lasted a yard without somebody like Dad who knew how to manage him. Fortunately Hancock would defer to my father, which made things a lot easier, because generally he never deferred to anyone. Almost all the negotiations associated with Hancock were carried out by the old man.'

Michael reflected on the beginning of the split between the two men. 'Peter started to get a bit paranoid towards the last ten or so years of his life, quite steamed up about the economy and mad about politicians. He became introverted, difficult to deal with and increasingly querulous and conservative. Hancock became impatient with him, he wanted to go out on his own and start something, and that started the split between the two of them. Not only was the old man not happy to go along with what Hancock wanted, he wanted to actually go the other way and contract. They disagreed philosophically on the economy and on the assessment of the mineral industry; Peter was convinced it wasn't the opportune time to start another iron ore mine, and there were several reasons for that. They also disagreed on Hancock's decision to buy his first jet, which cost an arm and a leg to run. It was incredible the amount of time and effort he wasted travelling; I can't think of anybody who spent so much time travelling to see so many people and who achieved so little for it. So it was natural that they would part company, which they set about doing during the 1980s. The split of the partnership was instigated by Hancock; my father saw no reason to change. The old man went on to expand his ventures into publishing and the like. Forgive my vanity, but the two of them had more successes than failures.

The minute Lang went out on his own he had more failures than successes. God knows how much money he wasted.

'Hancock was a tragedy. He was bright, intelligent and forthright; he undoubtedly had one of the highest intellects of any person I have ever known. But he was completely lacking in intellectual self-discipline. He simply didn't have the where-withal to put things together and keep them working. He had the drive, the brains and the vision, but not the finesse.' He pointed to the Romanian deal to illustrate his point. 'They hadn't even started this venture and he tied up a shipping line. There is just no sense in that kind of approach. The other debacle was his ship unloaders. I lent him some money to get him out of trouble once, but what got me was that he had organised two unloaders, instead of just one. I asked him, "Why two?" And he said, "Oh, look, don't worry about it. You've got to put your reputation on the line, you've gotta show these blokes you mean business." I said to him, "Lang, you front up with a ship unloader in a place like Romania and they'll know you're putting your money where your mouth is." That was the type of business maturity he lacked.'

Michael cringed as he recollected the differences his father and Lang had over Hancock's frequent media appearances. 'Lang had this absurd theory that anything in the media was better than nothing. Every now and then my old man would try and yank him into line, to try and restrict him from being so outspoken to the press. We spent a lot of time trying to hide under the nearest rock when he'd come out with outrageous theories like nuking the Pilbara. And we would simply die every time Rose and he went on television together.'

Under the Hancock/Wright deal, the surviving partner became the managing partner. 'After my father died, Hancock ran some of our affairs on behalf of the partnership. He had a run-in with a group of brokers and I later found that he had a disagreement with about three of them. I said to him, "You can't do that. There's only so many of these brokers in Perth; you just can't go around and fall out with all of them."' The irony of his statement is striking. Even in that respect, Lang would lead the way for his daughter to follow. When he became ill, Hancock's secretary had a standing arrangement to interrupt him in the afternoon and suggest it was time he took a rest. 'But he didn't know what it was to rest,' Michael recalled. 'He'd go into his office bedroom and take the telephone with him. His telephone was a permanent fixture.'

Michael did not hesitate to point out that his father should receive recognition for his part in the Hanwright partnership. 'My father's greatest contribution was in the use of his diplomacy and negotiating skills. Hancock had the visions, but without Peter's management, careful handling of personalities, his caution and diplomacy, the partnership would never have survived and none of the major achievements would have been brokered.'

For all his fondness for Hancock, Michael said he could be insensitive, thoughtless and rude. 'We once had a dinner party for him and Rose but he didn't bother to turn up. He didn't call to cancel; he just didn't bother to show. He behaved like that on many occasions. When he didn't agree with something, he could be emphatically rude. My old man was astute enough to know that it was worth his while to stay with him. He quite liked him, and certainly when they were youngsters they got on remarkably well. Much of the division that happened in the last ten years or so of their life was because they developed divergent philosophical views. They had a shared interest in minerals, but Dad didn't operate the same way as Hancock.'

Peter Wright's sudden death from a heart attack in September 1985 shocked Hancock, but not enough for him to return from overseas to attend his funeral. 'Dad was 78 years old, but despite the fact he was getting on he spent a great deal of his time overseas in his later years. He died in Thailand and Lang was upset and surprised to hear of his death. He was on the other side of the world at the time, and he didn't come back for Dad's funeral. He was too busy doing other things. It was typical behaviour for Lang, but I was surprised he didn't make more of an effort. After all, they had known each other for a lifetime.'

34

THE GET-RICH-QUICK SCHEMES OF the moneyed men of the west were put under the microscope at the WA Inc. Royal Commission, where the corruption and excesses of the mid-1980s were delivered a devastating blow. Australians watched with a mixture of curiosity and disgust as the big men fell like ninepins. For the entrepreneurs who had surfed a wave into shore buoyed by lavish fundraising dinners and a seemingly endless supply of money, the crash was total. One by one, they squirmed under the public gaze as they fronted the commission. By the completion of the hearings, heroes had fallen from grace and reputations were shattered; for some, it was akin to a public execution. Former Labor leader Brian Burke's fundraising conduct was found to be 'reprehensible', with the commission noting that his 'entire evidence about the extraordinary retention and expenditure of cash was most unsatisfactory and totally lacking in credibility'. Alan Bond, once the hero of the masses with his triumphant delivery of the America's Cup to Australia at Fremantle in 1983, was now lambasted for his political donations. Laurie Connell fell in its wake, along with David Parker and casino developer Dallas Dempster.

And into the maelstrom strolled Lang Hancock – uninvited, typically contentious and ready for a fight. He looked all of his 81 years in mid-June 1991, with his shuffling gait considerably slowed and frown lines etched into his forehead. But there was fire in his crusade as he interrupted the commissioner and demanded an immediate audience. Glaring around the room from behind his glasses, his battledress of a casual cotton shirt and joggers mocked the seriousness of the hearings. This was to be one of the last times that Hancock would hold the sabre in public, and he intended to rattle it loudly. He would take this opportunity to defend Brian Burke and David Parker, to explain his relationship with Charles Court and to push his belief that Australia should trade with Eastern Bloc countries. The rogue bull was back, and he did not care that what he was going to say was outside the commission's terms of reference. He would be heard – now. With him was Rose, immaculately dressed, playing to the press in her inimitable fashion and handing them copies of the prepared five-page statement, lest they miss it the first time.

From the witness stand, where he held the floor for almost 50 minutes, Hancock vehemently denied that there was any impropriety in the donations – close to a million dollars by the end of the 1980s – that he made to Brian Burke's political coffers. Hancock had also given to former Deputy Premier David Parker's political machine during his personal election campaign, including a $20,000 donation in 1988. He had employed both Burke and Parker in a part-time capacity to fill the gap left by the death, in October 1991, of Kevin Dalby, who had headed up his group of companies, and he made no apologies for it. Both men travelled with him to Russia and Romania where they were useful to Hancock in a political

161

sense, applying their diplomatic skills to open doors with governments and bureaucrats. It was a skill which Hancock, brusque and impatient with red tape, was sadly lacking. At the height of the WA Inc. hearings, Hancock never wavered from his opinion that both Parker and Burke were young, intelligent and smarter than other people.

Hancock made no bones about the fact that his hostile relationship with Charles Court precipitated his wooing of Labor.

'So I've employed them and I got a lot of criticism for doing so,' he told the press. 'What in the bloody hell, I've got no interest with Labor. The conservative party should have backed me 100 per cent but they don't. I've got no interest in Labor, Christ! They were supportive of me, but they got themselves tangled up in this WA Inc. thing. They wanted to promote the state through the state agencies; that's why they formed this WA Inc.'

But Hancock did not only give to the Labor Party. Though reluctant to admit outright that he had contributed to the ultimately disastrous 'Joh for Canberra' campaign, few – including National Party sources in Brisbane – doubted that Hancock had put his money where his mouth was in the early 1980s. His opinions that Canberra was a parasitic city without an industry and strangled by the dead hand of bureaucracy were well known, as was his unwavering belief that Bjelke-Petersen was the only politician in Australia capable of showing true leadership.

'All politicians ask me for money,' he told the commission. 'I think the Joh for Canberra campaign is about the only chance left for Australia. We need a strong leader and Howard and Sinclair should fall in behind Joh.' That Bjelke-Petersen was discredited by his own party and humiliated by his failed push to become prime minister never fazed Hancock. Until the end of his life, he maintained his loyal stance to his mate, and stood by his claim that he was the only leader who was capable of taking the country out of the darkness and into the light. On this, too, public opinion was overwhelmingly against him, but he never changed his mind.

Hancock ignored the raised eyebrows over his generosity to both sides of politics as studiously as he ignored questions about some of the dubious judgments he made in his personal and business affairs. The contradictions were blatant: while Burke's Labor Party machine was kept well oiled in Western Australia by Hancock's lavish handouts, his opposite political number, Bjelke-Petersen, was riding the same financial gravy train on his journey to Canberra. They were heady days, and fuelled by excess. Brian Burke coined a name for those Western Australian entrepreneurs whose extreme wealth encapsulated the times – Holmes à Court, Connell, Peter Beckwith – Bond's right-hand man – and Hancock. They were the 'four-on-the-floor entrepreneurs', men whose combined bank accounts sang to the tune of multi-millions of dollars.

When the dust settled on the 1980s, the bills rolled in as fast as the money had rolled out. The trail of tears often led straight back to the urban cowboys, the high-flyers of the wild west.

Michael Wright pointed to Hancock's diverse choice of political bedfellows as a classic example of how he overrode decorum and paid the price. If he had second thoughts about his business relationships in the devastating fallout of the Royal Commission, it didn't show. 'His selection of people who orbited around was not always good, and he used to give to either political party as the occasion suited. I remember complaining when he gave Brian Burke and David Parker a job; these two blokes were about to go on trial and Hancock was employing them! But you couldn't tell him anything; he was a didactic, aggressive kind of fellow, probably the most brilliantly stupid human being I've ever come across. He was incorruptible in that he would never take a bribe or anything like that, but he was quite happy to resort to expedience and he was very good at not bothering to see things he didn't want to see.'

As the big men rose in the 1980s, so did they fall following the disastrous stock market crash of 19 October 1987, which the press dubbed 'Black Monday'. In the wash-up, dreams were lost and reputations ruined; some were jailed and others embraced by death's icy fingers.

Hancock remained loyal to David Parker and Brian Burke despite their disgrace. Asked if he would consider employing Parker and Burke in a full-time capacity, he was unequivocal in his response. 'Yes, I would,' he growled. 'They're smarter than anybody else. They're young and they're smart and I am quite satisfied they'll clear their names at this bloody Royal Commission. They've been stupid, financially stupid, but they haven't been criminal.'

In January 1991, Hancock named both Burke and Parker as alternative trustees in his will.

Later that year, Gina was reinstated as a director of Hancock Prospecting Pty Ltd.

And heads would roll.

35

BY 1991, HANCOCK'S HEALTH was rapidly deteriorating and he needed to undergo a triple bypass operation. Given his age – 81 – it was an unpalatable decision to make, and his doctor pulled no punches about the risks involved. It was a life-or-death gamble, with only a 50/50 chance he would pull through. Cardiologist Dr Barry Hopkins, Rose, her maid Carmen, Lang's property adviser Willie Porteous, who would marry Rose after Lang's death, and Rose's interior decorator all accompanied Lang to Alabama in early August. After the operation, Hancock enunciated the fears that he had held.

'For 12 years I've been kept alive by one cardiologist and open-heart surgery, a triple bypass,' he said. 'And it started to block up. I said to my doctor, "What happens if one of them blocks?" He said, "You're up shit creek without a paddle."'

The world's leading specialist in bypass operations, an Australian, was working in the United States. A balloon and stent were inserted into his heart valves and the operation was deemed a success. But Hancock was not out of the woods: his doctors' fears that the surgery would adversely affect his kidneys were realised. A dialysis machine was urgently brought in to control his kidney functions, but the doctors missed the vein when they inserted the machine into his leg. For the first time in his life, Hancock admitted that he was in pain.

'It was absolutely excruciating, you couldn't believe how bad the pain was. So they pulled out of that one. Then they went on the other side of me. When they went there, the vein burst, blood all over the place. Here was my doctor, not allowed to operate. Someone tried to stem the blood. Eventually we got over that and they inserted a gadget clean as a whistle and it took them less than an hour and they fed a tube in that was able to keep me alive. My doctor said, "Let's get the hell out of here." So we came back and they've been trying to repair the bloody damn thing ever since, part of the time in the hospital and part of the time out of the hospital.'

The ongoing dialysis treatment sapped Hancock of his energy, and a desperation crept into his handling of public and private affairs. Foremost among his priorities was the establishment of a multimillion-dollar cardiac institute in Australia. His reasons for that were simple. 'Royalties that go on in perpetuity. What else do I do with them? Give them to the dog's home? Throw them away or do some good with them?'

John McGlue noted that throughout the series of three interviews he held with Hancock in the weeks before his death – one at Prix d'Amour and two at the intensive care unit at Perth's St John of God Hospital – he constantly battled pain, breathlessness and fatigue. 'But he does so with great dignity,' he wrote, 'pushing himself through barriers of pain for no obvious reward. Except, perhaps, that Hancock gets to tell his story again. Maybe this time the bastards will listen.'

Eight years after Hancock's death, McGlue recalled that interviewing him was a bizarre experience. 'It was like walking onto the set of a Fellini movie. He reminded me of an old robber baron, and the setting was extraordinary. He sat at this huge desk, which had cracked and broken glass on top, and railed about his world views in the most bombastic tones. He was in a hurry to get it all said, because he knew he was running out of time. And underlying everything was his express wish that the two women in his life come together. But he didn't understand the dynamics of how difficult that would be. He really didn't.'

Hancock was not given to parties; that was Rose's domain, and she seized every opportunity to throw open the doors of Prix d'Amour and entertain. But this party was different. Twenty guests were seated in the main dining room, the table awash with flowers, as they listened to Danny La Rue croon Lang's favourite love songs. For once, the entertainer was not dressed as a woman; this occasion was dignified and respectful. Lang, his legs swollen and obviously suffering great discomfort, could not sit in an armchair; instead, he was propped up in his wheelchair, his feet resting on a cushion and a blanket covering his body. He looked every bit his age, as if the years, suddenly, had caught up with him, and he was losing weight. A melancholy smile played on his lips, but at least the women he loved most – Gina and Rose – were with him. Guests recalled it was a wonderful evening, but also very sad.

'It was ironic that Lang had paid for this flash party himself,' one guest noted. 'He simply wasn't a party person, and it was very obvious that he was lonely. Hancock didn't wear his heart on his sleeve, but there was a sadness, a vulnerability, about him that night. He looked small and thin, and his eyesight was obviously failing him. He had all this money, but he was just as happy with an old car as he was with the latest luxury vehicle. He may have been a complex man, but in many ways he was a very simple person. Wealth didn't change the essence of him, it only changed the trappings.'

For Gina and Rose, the occasion would be remembered for another reason: it was the last time the two women would be in the same room without their lawyers present. Willie Porteous recalled the occasion when we spoke in 1999. 'I hadn't met Gina before that,' he told me. 'Prior to his death, Lang invited me over to lunch but she refused to come into the house to meet me. She was particularly cool the night I met her at this gathering, and I asked her why she couldn't have the decency to be courteous when Lang was so sick. It wasn't about anyone else but him that night, a fact which I reminded her of.'

Hancock counted on one hand the leaders he admired. Former Singapore Prime Minister Lee Kuan Yew; Britain's former Prime Minister, the Iron Lady of 10 Downing Street, Margaret Thatcher; and Joh Bjelke-Petersen. Just before his death, in the interviews held with John McGlue, he made a last-ditch attempt to put his viewpoints on the record and in perspective. McGlue pointed out that Bjelke-Petersen's reputation had become somewhat tarnished since he left office. '[His] reputation is less than glorious now?' he observed, but Hancock would have none of it. 'That's not his reputation, that's Australia's reputation. Australia's reputation is on the line, not Joh's.'

McGlue pressed on. 'But in relation to the administration of government in Queensland while Sir Joh was in charge, a lot has been said and written in relation to that and a lot of it has been critical.' Hancock stood his ground. 'It's all critical but you'll find very little of it is true. That's the power of the media, to denigrate a bloke, to denigrate a man.'

Media proprietor Rupert Murdoch was also high on his list of people who had the courage to stand alone. 'He's about the only fella who's got the guts to say, "Well, look, I'm paying all these bloody wages, I'm incurring several billion dollars worth of debt and I'm not going to let ratbags tell me what the bloody hell goes in my paper." That's his attitude.' Hancock expanded

168

on why he admired Murdoch. 'Here's a man who's got everything on the line, billions of dollars and his family fortune and everything else and he's going to let someone else tell him what to do? Well, I think that's a bit much.'

Hancock had once said: 'I believe in the essential role of government to keep the peace nationally, commercially and internationally. But I also believe that what governments do best is enforcing the commandments: Thou shalt not steal; Thou shalt not make false or misleading statements; Thou shalt not break contracts; Thou shalt not assault peaceful neighbours. They should leave it at that.' He chose as his heroes people who were all tarred with the one brush. Like him, they were oblivious to public opinion, bombastic in their approach to those who stood in their way, and individualistic in their stand on issues they believed in. And like Hancock, they were brutally honest. In their world, there was no room for anyone who stood in their way. They mowed them down.

36

DETAILS OF THE HANCOCK empire's internal business arrangements are complex and awkward, an entangled maze between companies and shareholders. It is this maze which Gina's lawyers were determined to unravel following Hancock's death.

The company's original structure was changed in 1963: from that point, Hancock Prospecting Pty Ltd (HPPL) was split between Lang, Hope and Gina, each with an equal third share. Lang had also established a Life Governor share of the company, which terminated on his death. In 1972 the structure was again changed with the establishment of HFMF, the Hancock Family Memorial Foundation, a concessionary measure to shareholders to avoid the double burden of company and income taxation. Hancock controlled the new company, and his wife, daughter and Hancock Prospecting staff had varying classes of membership in it. Its operation was kept afloat by discretionary dividends paid by HPPL. It was the family's long-held plan that on the death of her parents Gina would control HFMF. Hope's

170

estate was left to her husband, but she left explicit instructions in a memorandum to her will that Gina and her children should inherit any part of the estate that had been hers. To this end, the Hope Margaret Hancock Trust was established.

The company breakdowns were further complicated in 1989 when Lang made the decision to sell his third share of Hancock Prospecting to HFMF for $23.2 million, a figure which subsequent independent valuations found to be grossly overpriced. He also divested himself of his life governorship, selling that to HFMF for $20 million. Gina's lawyers argued that in the decade from 1984, HPPL assets with a value of $175 million were taken.

Gina's belief that HPPL was labouring under mismanagement grew steadily stronger from 1984; by mid-1988, she and her father attempted negotiations to resolve the conflicts. The basis of Gina's concerns were varied, covering her allegations of Rose's profligate spending of HPPL loans channelled through HFMF, her mother's wishes that she and her children inherit her share, her own removal from the company's directorship and lack of access to company records, the transfer of HPPL assets to HFMF for inadequate reasons and her father's controversial decision to do business in Eastern Europe.

Hancock drew up no less than 24 wills in the six years before he died, and their contents became the linchpin of the ensuing legal battles. The basis of the original will was straightforward, and in line with expectations about what Hancock wanted.

> I revoke all Wills and testaments . . . made by me and declare this is my last Will and testament. I appoint Martin Lawrence Bennett, solicitor of Perth, my stepdaughter Johanna Hancock, my daughter Georgina Hope Rinehart, and Gary Richard Schwab, all of Perth, to be the executors and trustees of this Will. In the event that

such trustees cease to hold offices . . . I appoint Brian
Burke . . . provided that the said Brian Burke is a full-
time employee of Hancock Resources Ltd and is in the
opinion of my remaining trustees of good character and
standing . . . I give, divide and bequeath all shares either
registered in my name or to which I may be beneficially
entitled in Zamoever Pty Ltd, to my trustees upon
trust . . . my said grandson and grandaughter shall survive
me and attain the age of 25 years . . .

It is understood that the owner or registered holder of
my shares in Zamoever Pty Ltd shall have the power to
control the Hancock Family Memorial Foundation Ltd
by virtue of the fact that under the articles of association
of the foundation, ZPL as a Class A member has the
right to 15 out of every 20 votes passed by the members
of the foundation . . .

In grateful appreciation of his loyalty, friendship and
service, one million dollars to the estate of the late Kevin
Walter Dalby, and in grateful appreciation of his loyalty,
friendship and service in addition to all benefits already
paid or provided to him during my life, 500,000 dollars
to Ken McCamey . . .

Hancock also sought to establish a trust, to be known as the
Hancock Cardiology Institute, at Perth's St John of God Hospital
for the purchase of surgery and catheterisation equipment.

The will also stated:

In the expectation that my residuary estate shall receive
from year to year in perpetuity . . . royalty payments from
the sale of ore, I direct my trustees to hold my residuary
estate upon the following trusts, it being my intention to
provide substantially for my wife and her family and my
daughter and her family.

The second-last will, signed in August 1991, was crucial. In it, Hancock directed that the profits from reserves which were then unworked and the royalties that flowed from tenements were to be split between Rose and Gina. This will infuriated his daughter, who claimed that it was in direct defiance of the family's agreement that she, and she alone, would take over the reins of the company on her parents' deaths.

Over the following months, Hancock added four codicils to his will. The first, signed on 20 December 1991, instructed that his wife and daughter were to receive a one-off payment of more than one million dollars each. The second, less than two weeks later, ordered that if his will was challenged by Gina or Rose, then they be removed as beneficiaries.

It read, in part:

> ... in circumstances where during my lifetime I have fully provided for the maintenance and well being of my principal beneficiaries, my wife Rose and my daughter Georgina and I fear that upon my death my principal beneficiaries or either of them might by litigation seek to challenge or contest 1) the terms of my will 2) the validity of my will ... I desire by this codicil ... to absolutely discourage any such challenge or contest ... and desire to make no testamentary disposition for my residuary estate to any principal beneficiary who commences or causes to be commenced any such litigation. Now I hereby direct my trustees as follows, that as on the date of any such litigation ... then such principal beneficiaries are there-after no longer entitled to ... my residue estate.

The third amendment, in mid-January 1992, established a generous trust fund for some of Hancock's trusted employees and the fourth – the kicker – instructed that Johanna, the step-daughter Lang had once adored, be removed as an executor of his estate. Johanna had committed the cardinal sin: she had lied to him when she had forged documents and falsely claimed that she was attending university. For Hancock, this was unforgivable.

Sir Valston Hancock had once commented that 'Hancock's uncompromising attitude is so very obvious in the many interviews given to the press and yet in his personal relations he exhibits an amused tolerance of those who have fallen from grace . . .'

He was not amused this time.

The last codicil also failed to acknowledge the agreement reached between Gina and her father in 1988. Gina held that this will mistakenly gave the impression that HFMF controlled the group's agricultural holdings, and four iron ore tenements and that her father's estate would earn royalties from the development of those tenements.

The Big Australian – BHP – was offered McCamey's Monster in 1991 for $37 million, and in the process of due diligence, it found a discrepancy. The company could not find that McCamey's was owned by HFMF. It also unearthed Hancock's complex deal with Romania, discovering that HFMF's agreement with Atle Lygren, the shipping broker, was ripe for financial disaster. A multimillion-dollar claim was subsequently made against Hancock Prospecting by Lygren.

37

HANCOCK WAS GRAVELY ILL. As 1991 rolled into 1992 he had been admitted to hospital no fewer than three times, and his fear that his time was running out was becoming a grim reality.

With Gina installed at the helm of Hancock Prospecting, Western Australian lawyer Alan Camp was charged with the job of drafting a deed that Lang would be asked to sign, virtually on his deathbed. Either on his own undertaking or under instruction, Camp had earlier broken into Lang's desk to get hold of the will. The deed, which would have the effect of removing shares in Zamoever Pty Ltd, a company that was receiving royalties from one of BHP's iron ore mines, was signed by Lang, ultimately allowing Gina to put her father's estate into bankruptcy.

The intensive care unit was lit up like a beacon, medical equipment blinking in the dark and on immediate alert for any change in his condition. As ill as he was, Hancock resented the interruption, resented his body for wearing out faster than he could get his affairs in order. He had things to do, and do them he must. He hit the buzzer to summon the nurse to his bedside. 'Take me down to the boardroom!' he rasped. 'Now!' Wheeled down the corridor, he took up his allotted position at the massive table and awaited the arrival of those whose audience he had sought. With him waited his heart specialist, Dr Barry Hopkins, and his GP, Dr Alan Hutchinson. This meeting, which Hancock had called, promised to be unpleasant, and his doctors knew that he was too ill to take extra strain.

Gina Rinehart's footsteps resounded along the hospital corridor, followed by those of her lawyer, Alan Camp, and Lang's lawyer, Martin Bennett, who would also act for Rose after Lang's death. Bennett's clients included the late Robert Holmes à Court, who had been impressed with the lawyer's abilities. He had referred to Bennett as a 'lock man', a reference to the reputation he had gained in being able to unlock complex legal puzzles.

For Hancock, who had chaired meetings all over the world and whose power and wealth ensured people listened to what he had to say, this threatened to be the hardest meeting of his life. Realising the precarious state of his health, he desperately needed to try to stem the bitter avalanche between his wife and daughter.

'I want the fighting to stop!' he beseeched. 'I have been fair to all of you. I have cut my cake in half and I want you to be satisfied with that!'

The air was frozen with stunned silence as Hancock outlined his plan to put his signature on a document that left no doubt about who would be in control of his massive but as-yet-unworked Pilbara iron ore tenements.

Hancock Prospecting Pty Ltd.

Gina.

The decision was in line with the arrangements held under a trust agreement that his daughter would take control after his death. With it went the 'big money' Lang had always talked about, the jewel in the crown: royalties that flowed like Bollinger from the Hamersley Iron mines. Over a lifetime, they were potentially worth billions.

If Gina was pleased with the outcome of the meeting, there was no doubt that Martin Bennett, who had been involved in drafting and redrafting the will, was furious. He dispatched a letter to Hancock pointing out in no uncertain terms that his decision to allow Hancock Prospecting to inherit the tenements and royalties ensured that Rose was now effectively cut off from the real income flowing from his estate.

The bitterness was escalating.

Hancock had other visitors to the hospital that week: a man wearing the robes of a Roman Catholic archbishop, and a dark-haired woman who accompanied him. They stopped at the desk to inquire what room he was in, and went along to his ward.

In the days before he died, Lang moved into the guest house behind Prix d'Amour, where he languished in the four-poster bed and received around-the-clock nursing care. The room was converted to a hospital ward, complete with the respirator and dialysis machine which he desperately needed. According to Willie Porteous, Rose made the decision to install her husband at the guest house because it was too difficult for the ambulance drivers to get in and out of Prix d'Amour, and the lift at that property was too small to fit his bed.

When Lang signed the deed acknowledging that the assets belonged to Hancock Prospecting and were therefore not his to bequeath, Rose threw a tantrum. Her version of events of what specifically happened at that meeting has changed over the years, but the essence remains the same. She was concerned, she said, that her dying husband was attempting to do business when he was clearly not well enough. He was also, according to her, labouring under the effects of the drugs which he was taking and not in his right mind. Michael Wright, who last saw Lang the Christmas before he died, did not agree that Lang was suffering from mental deterioration. 'He was lucid and bright that Christmas,' he said. 'I am sure he knew he was dying, but he was well aware that his family affairs had to be fixed up. Lang and I discussed numerous things on that occasion, and he was talking about his future plans.' Gina also saw it differently.

In her interview with *Australian Story* in 1998, she described her concern when she arrived at the guest house the next morning to visit her father. 'I walked in to see Dad and he looked terrible . . . His brow was deeply lined, the whole brow was just contorted; he was lying in bed as though he was absolutely exhausted. Although I wasn't there the previous night there had apparently been an awful row . . . Dad said to me words that I am simply never going to forget.'

Lang allegedly told her, 'Rose nearly killed me last night.'

Gina continued: 'Dad was very ill at the time and couldn't cope with the stress of arguments. We decided to ask Dad what did he want us to do, how could we help.' The day after the altercation in the guest house, Hancock, in an ex parte hearing (at which only one side is represented), requested that a restraining order be placed on Rose. He could barely speak: emotionally and psychologically drained, he was also battling pulmonary congestion, kidney failure and intense pain from the creeping gangrene in his legs. The cocktail of drugs which his doctors had ordered were also taking their toll, and he fell in and out of a fitful sleep.

Magistrate Robert Lawrence, after hearing the evidence, signed the order, which was made up at the nearby Cottlesloe Police Station. Rose was not there and did not have an opportunity to test or reply to the evidence. A hearing was adjourned to a later date.

Tearfully, Rose told the press that she failed to understand why Lang had sought to restrain her. 'I do not believe I deserve this,' she said. 'If my husband thinks it is fair then he must have his reasons and I must accept them. But if he was convinced by someone else to do it, then it is unjust. All I can say is that poison can be venomous.'

Martin Bennett was adamant that Lang had expressed deep regret about the restraining order and that he attempted to undo it just five hours before he died. 'There was an argument about that [the document] – certainly not an hysterical argument – and it was certainly a thing that between husband and wife one could well imagine there would be a discussion,' he countered.

Willie Porteous contends that on the night before Lang died, he was called to his bedside where Hancock expressed concerns about both the deed and the restraining order. 'He called me the next morning to reiterate that it had been a terrible mistake, and to beg me to bring Rose to his bedside,' he said. But it was too late. Hancock was a broken man and his body was giving up the fight, his lungs filling with fluids and the bedroom reverberating with the eerie, guttural gurgle of the death rattles. Those present in the guest house who claim to have heard his chilling scream knew it was the end. The restraining order was never served. Hancock took in one last, deep breath, his body shuddering slightly before he slumped against the pillows and closed his eyes.

It was a lonely ending. Rose was not with him when he died, nor his grandchildren. Instead, he was comforted in his final moments by his long-time confidant and chauffeur, Reg Browne, Gina and his doctor, Barry Hopkins. Gina and the children had spent some time with Lang the night before, and she returned to the guest house the next morning. He was still breathing, the laboured, difficult breaths of a man who had suffered a heart attack. He did not utter one word to his daughter before he died. There were no goodbyes.

John, who had slept overnight at the guest house, was upstairs when his grandfather passed away. He said he could not hear anything in the top room, but vehemently denies that Lang screamed in the seconds before he died. 'I would have heard that,' he said. But other people who were in the house claim they clearly heard it, a sound that one described as 'two high-pitched, chilling screams, about 15 seconds long, a scream that haunts me to this day. You don't forget a sound like that'.

Hancock himself had predicted his own end.

'I'll never die happy,' he once commented. 'I'll be like Baron Thomson of Fleet . . . they say that on his deathbed he was still plotting and planning business deals, and somebody said to him: "Give up, you can't take it with you." And he's supposed to have replied, "If I can't take it with me, I'm not going."'

But go he did. In his final months, he was vocal about what he wanted: peace of mind; a near-desperate wish that his daughter and third wife would resolve their differences; hope that the company he founded would move onwards and upwards. For all his vast fortune, his rivers of gold, all but the latter remained an elusive dream.

38

HANCOCK'S BODY LOOKED PATHETICALLY small under the stretcher blanket. The waiting media, hungry for a scoop, panned the grounds of the guest house in search of family members and filmed the ambulance men as they carefully placed his corpse in the back of the vehicle. But within hours, the news story they had come to get had taken an unexpected, bizarre twist. Detectives from the major crime squad and drug and forensic bureaus, complete with sniffer dogs, converged on Prix d'Amour, grimly silent as they strode past the press and into the house. Lang had only just died and the house resembled a crime scene.

The head of the investigation, Detective Inspector Bill Letch, finally answered the media questions, but he kept his explanation brief. A death certificate had not been issued and the investigation was 'routine', he said. Three days after the investigation, Martin Bennett held a press conference at the house, informing journalists that police had received an anonymous tip-off that Rose was allegedly involved in a murder plot against her husband. He extrapolated on the allegation, saying that the person who had made the call had alleged that 'Mr Hancock would be killed by narcotics and there was some innuendo it would be by Mrs Hancock'. Rose of course denied any such plot, and the police soon reached the conclusion that there was no evidence of foul play.

Bennett uses a persuasive mix of street savvy and charm when dealing with the press, and he used it powerfully this day. His reputation as a lawyer who was difficult to outsmart had already been proven.

'Police behaved with the utmost respect and courtesy to Mrs Hancock and they realised how terribly intrusive was their action at her moment of grief,' he said. He continued that, under normal circumstances, the investigation would have been welcomed to 'dispel these malicious gutter rumours that have circulated about some suggestion of Mr Hancock's death' and added, 'They've found nothing.' While Perth society buzzed with the gossip about why a death certificate had not been issued, Bennett explained that police had wanted to complete their investigation without having to initiate a coronial inquiry. Clothed in mourning black and leaning into the arm of a friend, Rose pleaded with the press to leave her alone until after her husband's funeral. 'I would very much like to speak to you but I'm in no condition to speak to you now,' she said, her lips tight and thin. 'If you will excuse me, from this weekend onwards, please don't bother me any more because the pain is unbearable.'

On the day of his funeral, Hancock's trusted chauffeur, Reg Browne, went over to shake Sir Joh's hand. 'Where were you?' he asked. 'I tried to get you a number of times, but your telephone wasn't responding. Lang wanted you to go and see him.' Sir Joh, recalling the conversation, is contemplative. 'That was a sad part of Lang's life. I would have liked to have helped a little bit spiritually, but he wasn't interested in anything like that.'

Eight years after Hancock's death, Sir Joh remembered Lang with fondness, but said little before adding a rider. 'I think that's about all I can tell you, unless you get permission from Gina that I can talk further,' he said.

Just four days after Lang died, Gina entered a notation in the company books. 'Mrs R. L. Hancock was removed as director of the entity on 1.4.92.'

As the obituaries continued, his body was examined at the state mortuary where it was eventually found he died of natural causes. Chief Forensic Pathologist, Dr Cooke, concluded that Hancock's death was the result of arteriosclerotic cardiovascular disease. It would be a further 17 months before Western Australian police concluded that there were no suspicious circumstances surrounding his death.

39

IF HANCOCK HAD HOPED for dignity in death, he did not get it. Rose had wanted Lang to be cremated in a private ceremony, but the animosity between herself and Gina ensured that the organisation of a simple, elegant service would be delayed. Instead, a macabre act was being played out behind the scenes. As he lay in the morgue, his daughter and wife each made arrangements for two funeral companies to collect his body. An ugly impasse followed: both women applied to the city coroner to have Lang released to them, but they were refused until the situation was sorted out. Rose told the press that she was disgusted with the turn of events. 'My husband's body was kept in the freezer like a criminal,' she fumed. With time ticking on, the deadlock was finally broken and an agreement reached: Hancock would be given a joint funeral, which neither Gina nor Rose would orchestrate.

It was a solemn ceremony. Rose had wanted Lang dressed in the designer suit he wore when they married, but that request was not granted. Looking haggard and tired behind dark sunglasses, she was borne to the ceremony in her Rolls-Royce which crawled to a halt close to where the service was to take place. Encased in black, she dipped her head on the shoulders of her two housemaids, who sat on either side of her in the back seat of the vehicle, where she remained during the service. Gina, protected by her two elder children, looked unutterably sad, sorrow etching her face in a stony mask. When the ceremony was over, the cars transporting the two women separated sharply when they hit the main road.

The family's deep divisions were again broadcast to the world the following day when two competing memorial services were held at the same time. Rose, mindful of Lang's standing in the west, had made overtures to a Perth radio station to invite listeners to hear the requiem mass which she held at St Mary's Cathedral. Just over a hundred people attended that service; the vast church, with its empty pews, echoed with a sterile silence. The guests included staff from Prix d'Amour, some business associates and a handful of people who were friends of the couple. An acquaintance who attended Rose's service remembered it as a curious affair.

'If ever the division between the two women was obvious, it was then,' he said. 'It was bizarre: husbands and wives went to alternate services, lest they be seen to offend either Gina or Rose, and a lot of people who had mixed with Lang and Rose at Prix d'Amour over the years went to his daughter's house. It was a sad way for a man to depart this world.'

Rose, unusually silent, asked that her sister Margie speak from the pulpit, and at the end of the service she swept out, refusing to address the waiting media. Ray Martin, then host of Channel 9's *Midday Show*, had promised his audience an interview with Rose after the mass, but she changed her mind.

In contrast, Gina's service was attended by 600 people, and was a warm and emotional sharing of reflections on Lang's life. The mourners who came to pay their last respects included a veritable Who's Who of Western Australian society; Johanna Lacson, in a defiant snub to her own mother's service, also attended.

A mining insider attended Gina's wake. 'It was held on the front lawn of the old house on Victoria Ave, lined on each side boundary by huge Norfolk pines. Lang had said that his cousin, war hero Sir Valston Hancock, and his wife could live there in perpetuity, but it was not written anywhere. When Lang died Sir Valston and his wife left the house. Who knows why?'

Gina, he continued, had control of the company offices and the addresses of Lang's personal and business contacts – mostly the latter. 'Invitations were designed and hundreds were despatched. The invitees had to make a decision between attendance at the requiem mass or the wake – and most chose the wake because if their relationship was a business one it made more sense to accept the company invitation. Conversely, attending the mass might send a message that one's sympathies were aligned with Rose. The war that was to follow was already uppermost in everyone's mind. As one mining sage said: "A little insincerity goes a long way!"

'Gina chose the young chaplain from her old school, St Hilda's, to add some religion to the occasion. But the chaplain did not have much personal knowledge of Lang and during his address on the podium, he mistakenly referred to Gina's mother as "Rose" instead of "Hope". Everyone assembled noticed the error and would have forgotten it soon after as a simple slip of the tongue. Instead, the mistake is burned into our memories because of Gina's immediate reaction. Tugging on John's sleeve, she ordered him to go immediately to the podium and have the chaplain recant. As instructed, John went to the chaplain and, interrupting proceedings, whispered that a mistake had been made and must be corrected immediately.' The chaplain handled the situation with aplomb. 'He said something to the effect that: "I don't think I made a mistake, but just in case I will read that section again!" This he proceeded to do; the issue was fixed. But this is a classic example of how Gina is focused and driven in every respect and will not let anything pass her by.'

The next speaker, he recalled, was Joh Bjelke-Petersen who delivered the eulogy. 'He did a far better job because his address was based on personal experience and he spoke warmly and lucidly from the heart.'

'He was a strong man in every sense, physically and with his vision,' Joh expounded. 'In more ways than one, he was called the Iron Man and Western Australia and the whole nation owe him a great deal of gratitude for what's been achieved. There will never be another Lang Hancock.'

Martin Bennett, who had played a vital role in drafting the will, predicted three days after Hancock died that any dispute over its contents would pivot on ownership of the Hancock Group's unexploited iron ore tenements in the Pilbara. 'You have to understand the majority of Mr Hancock's fortune lies in West Australian ground . . .' he told the press. He continued that the four major deposits – Mystery One and Mystery Two, Hope Downs and East Angelas – were regarded by the mining magnate as worth 'hundreds of millions of dollars'. These vast iron ore resources were originally properties of the 50/50 Hancock and Wright Partnership but went to Hancock under the asset division arrangement that Gina would later dispute with Wright Prospecting. Martin Bennett made it clear that Hancock knew his will would not please any of the beneficiaries, because 'compromise doesn't necessarily end up with everyone being happy'.

The following day, a queue of curious journalists waited outside the gates of Prix d'Amour, summoned to the mansion by Rose to be given a copy of the will. One by one, they were led into the massive foyer where they were given a brief audience by the distraught and dishevelled widow, dressed in black and hiding behind dark sunglasses. The estate executors had failed to agree on releasing the contents of the will, and Rose decided to do it her way.

'Before Langley's death I said that I would accept anything that he gave me in his will and my position has not changed,' she said in a statement before it was handed out. 'Langley's will reflects his greatness, his sense of the Australian community and his determination to deal fairly with his family and his loyal staff and friends.'

As Rose beat her retreat behind a locked door and the journalists returned to their newsrooms to file stories, her daughter, Johanna, appeared in a Perth court. Lang, with whom Johanna had previously enjoyed a close relationship, had agreed to pay her substantial living away from home expenses if she could prove that she was a student at the University of Western Australia. Johanna obtained stationery with the university's letterhead and forged a document which purported to confirm her enrolment at the university. It was a costly deception: furious, Lang initiated a police complaint and Johanna found herself in the Perth Court of Petty Sessions on forgery charges. She pleaded not guilty. Four months after Hancock's death, Johanna was fined $500 for forging the documents.

Lang's ashes were buried next to his parents' at his beloved Mulga Downs, in accordance with his final wishes. But his liver, heart and kidneys were held at the State Coroner's office, in the event of further toxicology tests needing to be carried out.

The stage was set for a clash of the titans.

40

FOR YEARS, GINA MADE furious claims that the police investigation into her father's death was seriously flawed, and relentlessly pushed for an inquest to be held. The Western Australian Coroner rejected her application for an inquest for the second time in 1998, arguing that no evidence had been produced which would realistically support a charge of manslaughter. He commented that Rose and Lang had stopped arguing 24 hours before his death and that verbal arguments between a husband and wife did not constitute an unlawful act. The real cause of death, he noted, was a 'very serious and pre-existing medical condition'. Gina was not deterred, and asked the Attorney-General to give his fiat to approach the Supreme Court to let them decide if an inquest should be held. John, then working as project manager for the lime-bagging plant at the iron and steel giant Iscor in South Africa, became the family's unofficial spokesperson during that time.

'The evidence our family has to support a call for an inquest is overwhelming,' he claimed. 'I'm shocked and appalled that the

Attorney-General hasn't given his fiat to approach the Supreme Court; since my grandfather's death, a new act has been passed which means a fiat no longer needs to be granted. The irony is, if he had died four years later than he did, our family would not need to go through this.'

Three months after Hancock's death, Hilda Kickett rocked the Rinehart family when she went public with her claim that she was his daughter. Her mother, Kathleen Formosa, had been a cook at Mulga Downs station, a shy, pretty 23-year-old who was part-Aboriginal and part-Asian. According to Kickett, Kathleen caught the 34-year-old pastoralist's eye, and Hilda's birth at Port Hedland in 1943 was the result of their union. Like many children of her generation and race, Kickett spent much of her childhood at St Joseph's Orphanage, where she came to know the priest – later the Archbishop of Perth – whom she called Father Hickey. 'It was practice in those days for half-caste children to be removed from stations,' she said. Hilda claims that over the years she saw Lang intermittently, and that he was a friend of the man her mother would later marry, George Whitby. Her decision to go public was born out of indignation that she was turned away from the hospital when she went with Archbishop Hickey to see Hancock.

'My mother and Lang could never have a future, because Mum was coloured,' she said. 'Old Lang never got the chance to acknowledge that I was his daughter, but I'm positive he would have if I'd been allowed the chance to go in and see him. For all the old boy's faults – and he had quite a few – he wouldn't have turned his back on me.'

While Kickett acknowledges that she has accepted small amounts of money from Gina over the years, she denies that she is interested in financial gain. 'That's not what I want; this is not about money,' she said. 'I walk down the street and people tell me I'm the spitting image of Lang. Gina might have been

190

brought up in a glass castle, but the facts of life are that these things happened, and I don't care whether she accepts it as truth or not. I've got no qualms with her.' It was a kindness she claims she was able to repay 'old Lang' on his deathbed, helping to comfort him in his final days. Her claim has never been confirmed by the Rinehart family.

Hilda's mother, Kathleen Whitby, died in 1985, and Hilda recognises that the onus of proof about her parentage rests with her. 'The Rinehart family want to know why I have never submitted to a test to prove who I am, but they know that Aboriginal people don't do that. I know who I am, and that's good enough for me. I don't have to prove anything to anyone else. I just wondered if it was all worth it, all this mud slinging, and I don't want a messy situation like Rose and Gina. I just wanted to do the history thing, to say old Lang had Aboriginal connections, and quite a few of them. He wasn't the Virgin Mary.' Kickett claimed that for years Lang was an occasional, quiet presence in her life, but that it wasn't until she was 35 years old that she learned that he was her father.

Rose claims that she has met Kickett and that 'where there is smoke, there is fire'. On one occasion, she said, she put make-up on her; later, she commented: 'She is the spitting image of Gina. Only prettier.'

While John Rinehart admitted to me in a 2003 interview that he sometimes gave Kickett small amounts of money, he said that Lang had never mentioned the woman to them.

Hilda Kickett had already publicly spoken about her belief that she was Lang Hancock's daughter when another Aboriginal woman, Stella Robinson also went public with her own claim that she, too, was fathered by the Rogue Bull. Stella, who had eight children, made no claim on the family fortune and sought no publicity; the decision to go public with her identity, she said, was made simply for the sake of history. She died in October

1992 – seven months after Hancock passed away – and proof of her claim to be Lang's firstborn daughter died with her.

Lang, Stella claimed, was just 22 when she was conceived; her mother, Gertie, was one of three Aboriginal sisters who worked at Mulga Downs. She was in no doubt that her conception was the result of a hasty, loveless coming together, and recalled that she had a small friend whom the family talked about in whispers. Her name was Dorothy; they said she was half-white, George Hancock's daughter. Under the welfare department policy of removing half-caste children from their parents in the 1930s, Stella, born in 1932, said she was wrenched away from Mulga Downs, and sent to live with strangers at Moore River, a missionary settlement north of Perth when she was five years old.

It would be 20 years before she was reunited with her mother Gertie. Stella was now a mother herself, but she would be 28 years old before Gertie told her who her father was. In a faltering voice, she recalled her mother's words.

'She told me, "You know the bosses – Hancocks – one of them is your daddy." I am definitely Lang's daughter, I was his first child born on Mulga Downs.'

In the Pilbara, talk of Hancock's illegitimate children is so widespread among black and white communities that mention of them does not elicit any surprise. Professor Ian Wronski was for 20 years the director of the Kimberley Aboriginal Medical Services Council, specialising in Aboriginal health. Based in Broome, his area of influence extended to the Kimberley and Pilbara, and it was in this capacity that he first came to play the role of confidant and adviser to Hilda Kickett and her family. When we spoke in 2001 he was matter-of-fact in his appraisal of the claims, if saddened that the women have had to defend themselves in the face of consistent public denials from Gina and her legal team.

'There is always talk among community people about

Hancock, and lots of others who owned or worked on stations,' he said. 'The reality was that Caucasians who lived and worked in those remote areas had sexual relations with Aboriginal women. I was aware before I met Hilda that she was related to Hancock, and I remember hearing three names: Hilda, Stella Robinson and one other. The Aboriginal people accept this as a matter of course. With the thrust of pastoralism in the early 1900s up into the north-west, Aboriginal people were virtually used as slave labour. That country could not have been opened up without their help. These were not immaculate conceptions; it was incredibly common, and explains today's racial mix.'

Professor Wronski advised Hilda that if she were seeking to establish a relationship with Hancock's family, DNA testing to prove her parentage was the best means available.

'Hilda was always uncomfortable with that idea, although she came close to doing it,' he recalls. 'Culturally, Aboriginal people are averse to dealing with body tissues in relation to the dead. There is absolutely no doubt in my mind that had she gone ahead with the DNA test, the truth would have been proven. I also have no doubt that if she was not Aboriginal, she would have had the test long ago.'

A staunch Catholic, Hilda also took advice from Archbishop Hickey who, Professor Wronski attests, accompanied her in her attempt to see Lang in hospital when he was critically ill. Archbishop Hickey tried to help Hilda with access to Lang, but that access was denied on their arrival. The Archbishop advised her that a DNA test was not necessary because there was a good chance that at least one line of Lang's family would recognise the relationship between her and Hancock. 'She has been provided with flowers and small monetary gifts from time to time from the family, but that has always been a private matter. Hilda has never been materialistic, and she is not interested in money. The key issue for her is recognition of her lineage. The situation is complex and unfortunate, and it is a depressing comment on some aspects of Caucasian society, who refuse to recognise the simple realities.'

Alan Camp, the Rineharts' former lawyer, mediated extensively with the press over the years on behalf of the family. Following Lang's death, he vehemently and indignantly denied that Hancock had fathered illegitimate part-Aboriginal children and that Kickett had been turned away from the hospital.

'Everybody who knew Lang and his family was quite adamant it was not the kind of thing Hancock would do,' he said. 'I've spoken to young men who'd worked around Mulga Downs with Lang and I've spoken to confidants who say nothing like this was ever mentioned or rumoured . . . There is no way that I or any lawyer turned her away from Lang.' Adamant that Hancock did not acknowledge Kickett as his daughter, he was at pains to establish Lang's mental wellbeing at the time. 'He was lucid and clear right to the end; at times he was exhausted but always lucid. If there is any truth in it I consider he would have wanted to see her; he was not the kind of man to turn anyone away. Lang is the kind of person who would have acknowledged her.'

41

IN AN INDIGNANT LETTER to the editor of *The West Australian* a month after Hancock died, W.W. Mitchell, former policy adviser and PR consultant to the Brand and Court governments, vented his annoyance that the rogue bull could take the credit for discovering the Hamersley iron ore deposits. Noting that men who had gone before him had already made mention of the huge iron potential in the region, Mitchell wrote: 'It was after the [iron ore] ban was lifted that one of the greatest deposits of the Pilbara, Mt Whaleback, was revealed by discoverer Stan Hilditch who – while Lang was talking – was patiently discovering, prospecting and proving this vast reserve of very high grade iron. The other major deposit of that period was Mt Tom Price, discovered by Hamersley Iron geologists . . . The fact that Lang Hancock was able to wring a royalty out of the Hamersley consortium was a political mistake of the British partner, Rio Tinto. Many others, whose work was less publicised, or not publicised, did much more for much less than Lang.'

Ron Manners, long-time friend of Hancock and the only person whose name was forwarded by the Rinehart family who agreed to talk to me – either on or off the record – recalled that on overseas business trips he was often asked if he knew Hancock. He replied that he did not, but that he had heard of him. 'After a couple of years I decided that perhaps I should get in contact with Lang, and so I called him in 1974. He was quite brusque, busy as ever, and he gruffly replied that he could spare only ten minutes to see me. We stopped talking five hours later.' Their friendship developed over the years and Manners frequently travelled with Hancock to the Pilbara where they shared an exchange of ideas. 'Lang was direct and candid, and he had a natural ability to question the conventional thinking of the day. He encouraged people to get up and have a go, and he was very often perplexed at how the government got in the way.' Manners believes that Hancock's genius was underestimated. As the Chairman of the Australian Prospectors' and Miners' Hall of Fame, opened at Kalgoorlie in late 2001, he named Hancock as the industry's most influential person. He admits that his choice was not appreciated by everyone, but he was adamant that Hancock be given the recognition he deserves.

He thinks Gina should be given it, too. In 2012, he told *The Australian Women's Weekly*, 'They're the bloody creators. They create wealth, jobs, prosperity. The only problem with Gina is that there aren't more of them.'

Fred Madden, an executive at Robe River for 20 years before joining Hancock Prospecting as Chief Executive Officer under Gina – a position which he left after just nine months – is one person who believes the story of Hancock being the key individual involved in the discovery of the Pilbara iron ore province is myth.

'The Pilbara iron ore resource has been known of for more than 100 years,' he said. 'All that was needed to get it going was a lifting of the ban on the export of iron ore and a demand for the material. Demand came with the development of the Japanese steel industry in the 1950s. The group Hancock was associated with certainly tied up a lot of the Pilbara's high-grade iron ore resources via applications to the WA Mines Department for occupation rights over temporary reserves. Many have become very rich via royalty agreements with iron ore producers and the sale of interests in iron ore deposits.' Headhunted by Hancock Prospecting, Madden was on a three-year contract but bailed out without signing a confidentiality agreement. 'I had a lot of pressure to sign one but I knew if I did I'd have been locked into that company for life. I never knew where I was going, everything changed all the time,' he said. 'I just didn't want to be in that work environment or around Gina. I found her to be nasty and difficult. But she owned the place, so she could behave like that. It was her way. No discussion. You have to be a "yes" man to work there and I wasn't. She has manufactured this story that she was successful in building up the assets by herself, but that's bullshit. Lang left her the assets and she built on them.'

In canvassing opinions about Lang, in 1999 I went to see Alan Bond at Western Australia's Karnet minimum-security prison, where he was then serving a seven-year sentence for defrauding Bell Resources of $1.2 billion (since released). The surrounding countryside was lush and green, and the prison walls could not contain Bond's dreams and reminiscences. The man once dubbed a hero after his triumphant delivery of the America's Cup to Australia in 1983 – the first time in its illustrious history that a non-American yacht took the title – seemed incongruous there, surrounded by blue-collar workers doing time for petty crimes, recidivists and their girlfriends, wearing too-tight skirts, and distressed children wailing goodbye to their fathers when it was time to leave. In his rapid-fire voice, Bond recalled the Hancock he knew.

'After Hope died we looked at all sorts of possibilities,' he said. 'In 1987 we negotiated to buy the entire operation for about $100 million, but we had differences of philosophies. Hancock was a direct, no-nonsense sort of character, but his partner, Peter Wright, was very conservative, not a risk-taker. He should have floated iron ore when the markets were good. Hancock always wanted tomorrow's price; he couldn't come to terms with the fact that he may have to part with control.'

The proposal included the outright purchase of all interests, including royalties, $25 million cash at settlement and another $25 million on commissioning of McCamey's Monster mine and associated infrastructure. It also included a royalty of $2 million a year for the life of the mine, and cash purchase of Hancock's Hamersley royalties. Hancock's response was predictably blunt: any bid for the whole of his interests, he said, would have to be in the billion-dollar class – not millions – to be considered seriously. And, he added, the royalties were not for sale at any price.

Bond described Hancock's single-mindedness as the key to his successes and failures.

'He wanted us to join in the Romanian deal, and we sent a bloke to have a look, but the risk factor was too high for us. He didn't have a feel for the politics involved. He was not interested in you if you couldn't talk business. The big picture made him take the risk in Romania – he wanted to secure a bargaining position with companies such as BHP. He was a total individualist, not a joint venturer; he was the boss, and he made the decisions. For that reason, because of his single-mindedness, he was not readily accepted in business circles.' Bond did not mince words in his appraisal of Hancock's decision to attempt to secure business interests in the Middle East. 'I think they were just grasping at straws. For a start, there is a huge culture difference; the Arabs are cautious, and they can afford to be. They have seen every camel driver with a story to tell, and they didn't need what Lang had to offer.'

Of his legacy, Bond commented: 'He didn't have anybody of equal standing in his youth. His epitaph should be weighed against his business ventures that didn't work. Hancock believed anything was good if it inherently benefited Australia; he was a giant in his own way. His epitaph should read, "I climbed the mountain."'

On the enduring legal problems between Rose and Gina, he was scornful. 'They should appoint an arbitrator and solve the problem. As they say – you come into this world with nothing, and you go out with nothing.'

42

IN 1992, FORMER AUSTRALIAN Prime Minister Bob Hawke
made his reporting debut on the television program *60 Minutes*.
Hawke was a legendary figure in Australian politics, a trade
union president who went on to take the top job, a people's PM
who stood for the little Aussie battler. Producers knew that his
presence on the program would draw a large viewing audience.
But Hawke may have been irked to realise that his segment
would take second place in the public memory to the main
event of the show – the much-publicised 'tell-all' from Rose's
daughter, Johanna.

Rose had hogged the limelight to date but now Johanna was
about to shoot to dubious fame by publicly airing the family's
dirty linen, and it promised to be the best show in town. It was
a lurid debacle that became dinner-party fodder throughout the
country, a sensational stoush which started with a dispute over
ownership of the elegant guest house on the grounds of Prix
d'Amour. Johanna, then 20, had left the palatial home under
a cloud; Rose and Lang had banned her then-boyfriend from

the family mansion. Three weeks later, the feud reached its crescendo, with Johanna doing the unthinkable – opening her mother's closet for the world to see. Rose was forewarned of the interview's contents, and she stood on her dignity. 'I know what my daughter is like,' she sniffed. 'It doesn't surprise me that she would say these things about me. I would never sell my mother to *60 Minutes*.'

The reporter, Mike Munro, sensed a hot story and wasted no time in getting down to business. 'This could become one of the dirtiest family feuds in Australian history,' he observed. Reeling off a list of Rose's alleged sins, Johanna agreed with them all. Her mother, she claimed, had never treated her as she should have. 'She didn't give me a good example,' Johanna whined. She was less critical of Lang who, she said, treated her 'better than my own mother treated me. He was a very good stabiliser in my life'. She said she last saw him in the hospital the week before he died. Johanna sought to explain the relationship between Lang and Rose. 'In the beginning she was fond of him. It was new to her. It was a novelty being married to this man who was success-ful and rich, but she got bored after a few years.' Australians were now perched on the edge of their seats, goggle-eyed at this spectacle, fascinated by this ugly portrait of a family at war but uncomfortable, too, at the betrayal. A few hours after Lang had died, she continued, Rose had told her that she was playing the sympathetic role and asked if it was working. 'She rushed up to me and she took me aside and she said: "Are the press buying the sympathetic act? I'm trying to be a sympathetic wife, are they buying it?" Munro asked the million-dollar question: was Rose a gold digger? 'I don't like to say this, but yes,' Johanna replied.

Munro called Rose to suggest a reconciliation, which was coldly declined: she had already been booked for a spot on *A Current Affair*.

'I do not wish to wash dirty linens in public,' Rose told the program, 'but in such a situation I have no choice.' She talked about betrayal, of being fed to the lions. 'You forgive but you don't forget,' she proffered. She was once bitten, twice shy, a much-maligned mother. Rose's facial expressions ranged from tragic to furious when she described how she had been 'stabbed in the heart' by Johanna's allegations and that she was now mourning both her husband and her daughter. Johanna's public outbursts were 'made-up innuendos . . . it's more than betrayal, it's vicious, malicious'. The daughter she knew, she said, had died when she left London as an A-grade student and came back to Australia a different person.

The respective interviews were so astonishing that immediately the spectre of chequebook journalism raised its head. Industry insiders played a guessing game about how much the women would have been paid, and if they were paid at all. Thirty-thousand dollars seemed to be the agreed sum. Journalist Jacqueline Lee Lewes, in a *Sydney Morning Herald* article, encapsulated the general feeling. 'Even high tack,' she wrote, 'has a price.'

The *60 Minutes* story was the stuff of soap opera, but Rose was outraged. She sued Johanna for libel, demanded she leave her home and, to put the lid on it, took out a restraining order against her. Not to be outdone, Johanna counter-sued, accusing Rose of stealing from her $500,000 trust fund. It took the quiet, gentle persuasions of Willie Porteous – the one voice of reason in the entire fiasco – to reconcile mother and daughter in late 1992.

But there was a rider: Johanna had to agree to signing a written agreement not to give another interview attacking Rose. But there was a sweetener for her: in return, Johanna was paid the $500,000 from her trust fund.

In the Federal Court, Johanna recanted about the *60 Minutes* interview, claiming that what she had said about her mother had all been a pack of lies. She had simply made it up. 'When I did the interview, I was lying,' she admitted. 'Everything I said was a lie. I had a falling-out with my mother and I was a very spiteful person and I was saying all sorts of things . . . So many people were saying I was entitled to this and entitled to that. I was very stupid and foolish and I regret it now.'

Gina's lawyer, Peter Hayes QC, was not impressed, accusing Johanna of lying again – this time on oath to the court. There were, he reminded her, heavy penalties for perjury.

The drama continued when a seemingly exhausted Johanna walked out the courthouse into the loving arms of her mother. If television crews loved it, recording the tears and hugs for posterity, Peter Hayes was less than impressed, telling the court that the public display of affection was a 'most unattractive spectacle' and was all just a publicity stunt. Forthcoming court cases between Rose and Gina, and 'unreliable witnesses' like Johanna, he said, were ploys to poison public opinion against his client.

'This is not a game,' he said.

43

FIVE MONTHS AFTER HER 'Langley George' died, Rose married Willie Porteous. The timing of their marriage outraged John, who sniffed, 'This says a lot about how much Rose mourned my grandfather.' Porteous himself made an admission about their quick decision to get married. 'Lang always asked me to look after Rose after he was gone,' he told me during our 1999 interview. 'So I married her.'

An urbane and charming real estate agent to Perth's rich and famous, Porteous, a Canadian, is good-looking, with the self-assured air of a man who knows what he wants and how to get it. His association with Hancock started in the early 1980s. 'Lang was a man who never lost sight of himself. He had one of the biggest business houses in the world. He wasn't overly generous with money, but he helped people out,' he said.

Rose and Willie deny rumours that they were romantically linked before Lang died, and Willie never lost his composure throughout a lengthy interview. 'I worked for Lang, and used to go all over the world for him, checking out the property

204

market . . . I was the family's real estate adviser.' He consistently defended Rose's often outlandish behaviour. 'She is basically a very sensitive person, she has come from a different culture to Australia, and it is difficult to be suddenly catapulted into the limelight. Lang had asked me months before his death to look after Rose because there could be a lot of problems.'

Willie recalled the change in Hancock following his heart operation in Alabama, and noticed the vulnerability that he had never shown before.

'After he came back from Alabama in 1991, he was obsessed with the sale of McCamey's Monster. In late January, just before he died, he said to me, "Gina is telling me that Rose is killing me and Rose is telling me that Gina is killing me . . . Do they realise I've got enough poison in my body to kill a hundred people? If I weren't so busy, I would have been dead a long time ago."'

Willie admits that he is a far more circumspect character than his wife, and that he has told her in no uncertain terms that he will not play her media game.

'Rose can be a very difficult woman to deal with. She is contradictory, brilliant, a chameleon. I've told her I won't become a clown or any other character in a media circus.' Other people see it differently. The late journalist Matt Price noted that if Willie Porteous is not on the Circus Hancock flying trapeze, he is down on the sawdust holding the safety net.

But despite his understanding of his wife's shortcomings, Willie believes she is the victim. 'This nonsense should have been over years ago,' he said. 'Rose is a victim of a woman who is obsessed with hatred for her.'

Despite the bitter animosity that exists between Rose and Gina, few people doubt that Lang was happy with his third wife, at least in the early days of their marriage. 'Rose gave Lang a new lease of life,' Willie stated. 'She reinvigorated him, dyed his hair black, updated his wardrobe, and looked after him. Rose made Lang feel younger.'

If Hancock was driven by 'iron ore, food and sex', as one associate noted, Rose also reinvigorated him in the bedroom, and was not shy about telling the world that they made love 'three times a day'. Their bedroom ceiling was decorated with mirrors, a veritable love nest with an ornate shell-shaped bedhead the feature of the room.

After their wedding, Rose and Willie moved into the guest house, where Lang had died. Immaculately presented with exquisite furniture, it, too, has sweeping views down to the Swan River. 'I didn't want to live at Prix d'Amour,' Willie explained, with a contemptuous wave of his hand towards the mansion. 'It felt like a museum.' The couple moved back into the big house at the start of the new millennium. In 2006 Prix d'Amour was razed to the ground.

'I was rattling around in that big house with all its memories,' Rose told me, 'and I didn't want anyone else to buy it if we sold. So I made the decision to destroy what was built, and to subdivide and sell the land.' It was a shrewd commercial decision.

Willie says that from the moment they married, he took over the role as Rose's protector. It is a role he has been playing ever since.

In September 1992, Rose commenced the deed action, in which she sought to set aside the deed that was executed by Hancock two weeks before he died on the grounds that he did not have the capacity at the time to understand what he was doing, and that he was subject to duress and undue influence.

It is alleged in this action that prior to signing the deed, Hancock personally owned two assets of significant value: the right to royalties from the McCamey's Monster iron ore tenement and shares in Zamoever Pty Ltd, the company which controlled

HFMF and the repository of much of the Hancock wealth. It is claimed that the deed had the effect of diverting these major assets out of Hancock's estate into the hands of Gina and her children, thereby preventing Hancock's testamentary wishes from being carried out. Gina contended that the deed was valid, but that even if it was not, her father had no personal entitlement to McCamey's royalties or the Zamoever shares, and that he therefore died without any assets to bequeath.

Four years after starting the deed action, in 1996 Rose issued a conspiracy action, alleging that Gina and other people conspired to deprive her of her entitlement under Hancock's will, by certain acts, both lawful and unlawful. One of those acts, she alleges, was a late-night forcible entry, just days before the deed was presented to him at his hospital bed, into a locked drawer in Hancock's office that contained his will. Gina's former lawyer Alan Camp, who had broken into the drawer, was a star witness and was quizzed about both the break-in and the deed. Counsel representing Rose asked why Camp had not simply asked Lang's secretary for access to Lang's desk; his response was that Lang said he did not want his secretary to know. Counsel then enquired of Camp why he had not shown the draft deed to Lang's lawyer, Martin Bennett, and he again quoted the dead: 'Lang said he did not want Martin Bennett to see the deed.'

The action also relied on a complex restructure of the Hancock group of companies in 1995, which effectively removed Zamoever as the controlling hand of HFMF, thereby thwarting the terms of Hancock's will. Gina and her companies denied all of the allegations.

Throughout his life, Hancock failed to achieve his goal of having his own operational mine, but on the anniversary of what would have been his eighty-fourth birthday, a planet, newly discovered by Mike Candy, the director of the Perth

Observatory, was named after him. Candy told the press he chose the name Planet Hancock because Lang was an influential and pioneering Western Australian, and that the planet, 'like a large rock in orbit around the sun', could be largely composed of iron. Planet Hancock, about 460 million kilometres from the sun, is in the asteroid belt between Jupiter and Mars.

44

IN 1995, RINEHART AND former Hancock Prospecting director Gary Schwab made an application to the Western Australia Supreme Court alleging that Martin Bennett's law firm, which in the past had acted on behalf of both Lang and Rose, had a conflict of interest in representing Porteous with regard to Hancock's will. Extracts of the missive Bennett had fired off to Lang following the deed change which had been unveiled at the hospital a month before his death were made public by Justice Scott during his judgement.

'Your decision would effectively disinherit Rose from any tangible benefit above and beyond the money you have set aside for one year's housekeeping,' Bennett had written. 'This may even be lost by Rose if your estate is made bankrupt. How you dispose of your residuary estate must of course remain your decision and always be your decision. A decision, however, of this fundamental magnitude (namely to disinherit your wife) may well have significant further repercussions upon you personally. I also perceive that it will raise a direct conflict of interest in my position as solicitor for both Rose and yourself.' Justice Scott agreed that Bennett did, indeed, have a conflict of interest.

Rose applied to have Gina and Gary Schwab removed as executors of the estate on the grounds that they had a conflict of duty with regard to their role in the litigation surrounding Hancock's assets. The application was dismissed in the Western Australia Supreme Court when Justice White decided that while Rinehart and Schwab were in a position of conflict, the acts of conflict had already been completed. His Honour left it open for Rose to make a further application in the future should the need arise, but the appointment of the Trustee in Bankruptcy to administer the estate has largely obviated the necessity to seek removal of the executors.

Behind the scenes, Gina's lawyers and accountants were working towards a $30 million claim against Rose for misuse of company funds with which, they alleged, she had bought assets and properties. Even her housekeeping money and use of credit cards came under scrutiny. Hancock's own dealings also came in for questioning with Gina's claim that he had acted improperly while director of the Hancock Family Memorial Foundation. Alan Camp was blunt in his appraisal of where the money would go: there was no room, he said, for discussion; it would go to Rinehart and her children. Rose counterclaimed, alleging that her husband was 'cuckoo' before he died and questioning why he would deliberately bankrupt his own estate.

For the lawyers, the legal issue was simple. Who owned the royalties? Could they be deemed to be Lang Hancock's personal assets, or did they belong to the company?

Rose Porteous had found a tough adversary in the woman who said in her early twenties, 'Whatever I do, *whatever* I do, the House of Hancock . . . comes first. Nothing will stand in the way of that. Nothing.'

The constructive trust actions brought by Hancock Prospecting Pty Ltd and the Hancock Family Memorial Foundation Ltd sought to recover the assets Hancock gave to Rose Porteous during their marriage. During his lifetime, Hancock had complete control of the companies; since his death, Gina Rinehart has controlled them.

There were six proceedings, the first of which was commenced in April 1992, a month after Hancock's death, and the last in 1994. The properties included two commercial buildings in Sydney's exclusive Double Bay with a combined price tag of $11.7 million, the ostentatious, six-bedroom Prix d'Amour, worth an estimated $35 million, a Florida mansion worth US$1.6 million, proceeds of the sale of land located in Mosman Park and an office building in Nedlands, Perth. Also in dispute was ownership of Rose's beloved Bentley Turbo, which purred to the tune of $372,000. All up, the assets and accrued interest were valued at an estimated $44 million, acquired between 1985 and 1992. HPPL and HFMF alleged that Hancock, in breach of his fiduciary duties to the companies, used company funds to acquire the assets for Rose; they further alleged that Rose had knowledge of those breaches of duty, sufficient to entitle them to orders that she held the properties on constructive trust for them, and should transfer legal title to them. The trial of the actions was set to be heard in March 1999.

In 1997, Gina was the humiliating focus of a story in *Woman's Day* magazine regarding a claim from her former live-in security guard, Bob Thompson, who also helped look after Hope, then 11, and Ginia, 10. Thompson, a former police officer from New Zealand, pulled no punches about his former boss who, he claimed, had become infatuated and obsessed with him, despite the fact he was already engaged to another woman. Filing a sexual harassment complaint against her through a Western Australian legal firm, he told the magazine that Gina wanted to marry him, despite his repeated assertions to her that he wasn't interested. 'She wouldn't take no for an answer.' Gina, he claimed, ordered him to accompany her on outings to dinner, the theatre and on picnics and asserted he was 'silly' for not recognising that she could give him everything he wanted. 'I'm the perfect woman,' he claims she told him.

The perks of the job were attractive: overseas trips to exotic locations, including a five-day journey on the Orient Express where he claimed Gina sipped champagne while he looked after the girls and a $14,000, three-day stay at a luxury resort at Lake Taupo; sojourns at the London Ritz and on Gina's huge yacht; flights on the private jet and visits to the family property, 'Lang's View', 30 kilometres from Perth. Bob said he was also asked to go and look out for Gina's son, John, then 17 and living in Hawaii. 'John had been kicked out of, or asked to leave, two prestigious military schools,' Thomson claimed. 'It had been a huge scandal, but it was hushed up.'

What was not hushed up in the article were salacious, personal details. 'She [Gina] used to ask me what I did on my days off,' he said. 'She wanted to know if I'd ever slept with an Asian, and what my sexual likes and dislikes were.' Saying that he had to leave, otherwise he would 'go mad', he proffered an opinion about the woman who would become rich beyond her dreams. 'She is an obsessive woman in every sense,' he claimed. 'I was something she couldn't have, so she decided she wanted it more. . . . She thought I was the most wonderful person in the world, no matter how much I rejected her.' Gina, he opined, was not an evil person, but a 'selfish' one, who was just 'incredibly lonely and isolated'.

In 1999, Willie Porteous commented on the Thompson claim. 'He left Perth after that article came out. One minute he was there, the next his phone was disconnected and he was gone, probably returned to his native New Zealand. Maybe it was a case of "this town ain't big enough for the both of us."'

45

FOR ONLOOKERS AT THE court it was pure theatre, with characters larger than life. Rose, stepping out of her Bentley Turbo in designer clothes as if attending a royal gala performance, smiled and addressed the crowd before settling into the witness box, exquisite jewellery dangling from her wrist and fingers. Gina was a study in contrast: avoiding any conversation save with her lawyers, she was icy-eyed and serious, clearly uncomfortable with the publicity this case had attracted. At stake were the properties, furniture, jewellery and money Lang had given Rose during his lifetime. Gina was suing for them, on the grounds that Hancock and Porteous had breached their fiduciary duties by plundering Hancock Prospecting Pty Ltd funds and the Hancock Family Memorial Foundation to buy assets, and that Rose was well aware of what was going on. Rose's lawyers countered that it was Hancock's company, and therefore he could do with the money as he pleased.

The top guns were hired for this showdown which started on 3 March 1999. Gina had the services of former Commonwealth

Attorney-General Tom Hughes, QC; Rose the debonair Melbourne QC Julian Burnside. Reading from a prepared statement, Rose outlined her life with the elderly mining magnate after she was hired as his housekeeper in 1983. While not specific about when she took off the servant's apron and donned the birthday suit in her employer's bed, she admitted that an intimate physical relationship developed between her and Lang soon after she started work and that within two years, they had married. She told the court that she was everything to Hancock – wife, lover, friend, housemaid, secretary and interior decorator all rolled into one – but that there was a price to pay for that. 'I was not allowed to go out for lunch . . . I had to be home by 5 pm,' she stated. She was adamant that she had rejected Lang's offer, made 12 months before his death, of a 10 per cent stake in HPPL. She said no to that offer, she claimed, because she did not want to be involved in a company with her stepdaughter after he died. 'Gina and me in one company – can you imagine that?' she asked the bemused Justice Anderson. At the heart of Rose's defence was her contention that she was a director of the company in name only and that her role was to make the old man happy and comfortable. To that end, she said, she had to 'fly around the world, cook for visitors, stay up late, look good all the time, attend meetings with jet lag, smile at dignitaries . . .'

Hughes produced evidence in an attempt to disprove Porteous' claim that her marriage to Hancock was a true love match and that it never occurred to her to marry anyone else. The document, a Notice of Intended Marriage, was signed by Rose on 29 June 1983, and clearly detailed her intention to marry electrician Louis Michielsen – a man whom she had never met – two months later. The document was signed before she had divorced her second husband, Julian 'Jay' Teodoro, in August 1984. If Gina's lawyers had hoped that Rose would crumble under the admission of this evidence, they were bitterly mistaken. She shrugged off the document as an error, claiming that she had been advised to sign it by Gina's former husband, lawyer Frank Rinehart, as a means of securing her stay in Australia. She was fearful of going through with a marriage of convenience, she said, in case she was caught and imprisoned. Still Hughes pressed on, accusing Rose of travelling to Australia to find herself a wealthy man. The public gallery was highly amused with her response that those type of men were not listed in the Yellow Pages directory. 'Australia wasn't a hunting ground for me . . .' she glared at Hughes. 'The only crime I've ever done is to marry a rich man.' If Rose was aware of the sensation she caused when she announced that she and Lang had made love three times a day, she did not acknowledge it. Neither did she turn a hair when a letter she had sent to Hancock in January 1991 was read to the court, stating that because she had looked after him for years, he should ensure her financial security. If Hughes tried to paint her as a woman who had salivated over Hancock's millions, 'with her ears pinned back', it failed. Her husband, she stated with a haughty toss of her head, deserved better than to be remembered for the 'undignified and uncalled for' public court battle between herself and his daughter.

Unfazed by the QC's verbal brilliance, Rose played him at his own game in some exchanges which left the public gallery gasping.

'[Hancock] showed you what you described as screeds from Mrs Rinehart, in respect,' Hughes said.

'Not screeds, screes,' Rose corrected him.

'When he showed you these screeds – I'm using your word.'

'Scree, sorry.'

'Screeds – letters, memoranda. Is that what you mean?'

'No, he used a very iron term for it called "scree".'

The judge was moved to interrupt. 'It doesn't have a "d" in it.'

'Scree?' Hughes asked.

215

'That's a very iron term for it. Lang would convert them into layman's language. He used them as metaphors.'

'What did you understand him to mean where he described these as screes – S-C-R-E-E-S?'

'There is no "s" in it,' Rose again interjected. 'There is no plural to a scree. It remains as a singular form. It's a collective noun.'

'I'm so sorry,' Hughes sarcastically replied. 'You know so much more about iron ore than I do.'

'No,' Rose corrected him again, 'it's that I just majored in English as a second language.'

Gina Rinehart did not escape the lash. Letters she had sent to her father were produced to the court, which presented a sad, if salacious look at how their relationship had deteriorated since the arrival of Rose in his life. Burnside was as unrelenting with Gina as Hughes had been with Rose: the reality, he said, was that Gina could not accept that her father was in love with his third wife and that it was his intention to provide for her. Forced to read the contents of one letter she had written to her father out to the court, Gina's voice was little more than a whisper. 'Are you wanting for me to trade all my personal belongings, the children's and my home that you – really our company – gave me for my twenty-first? Do you want to give one-third of HPPL to . . .' Her voice faltered, and she stared imploringly at the judge. This was a painful moment for Rinehart, and she wanted to avoid it.

'Is it essential that I read out those words, your Honour?' she asked.

'Yes, it is,' Justice Anderson replied.

She finished the sentence. '. . . a Filipina prostitute?'

In another letter, written in 1989, Gina demanded that her father 'pay back what you have spent on non-company parties i.e., Filipinos'. Hancock responded to the letter with a scathing note of his own. 'I would be pleased if you would leave me alone to live the rest of my life in peace,' he wrote. 'Without resorting to burglary, you will get whatever information you are legally entitled to. If in future you wish to see me you will have to make an appointment otherwise I shall seek a restraining order to stop you being in my office, going through my desk, reading my letters and stealing my papers.'

Gina claimed that while she had initially felt sorry for Rose when she had applied for the position as her father's house-keeper, she quickly realised that she was no cleaner and that she was concerned Lang would contract botulism from contami-nated food. As Rose's stories about her background changed, Gina became increasingly suspicious. 'My father, at one point, said to me after a few months of this that he had never in his life heard of anybody . . . tell so many lies as Rose,' she told the court. 'And that I found very disconcerting, because at the same time that he was recognising the lies, she was obviously having more and more influence on him in my mother's home.'

If Gina wanted to avoid the memory of the day she realised her father and Rose were having a sexual relationship, she could not. 'It was told to me by a number of people and I refused to believe it,' she said. Hughes was becoming impatient with her unwillingness to directly address his questions, and rebuked her. 'Look, would you just please answer the question. I will put it again and please, please attend to it. We will get on so much more quickly.'

Hughes probed again, asking when Lang had advised Gina that he was involved in a relationship with Rose. 'The same day that I asked if Rose could leave my mother's home,' Gina replied.

Recalling a conversation between her father and herself, Gina said Lang had told her he was desperately unhappy and that he wanted to leave Rose. Returning from a six-week trip to the United States, Gina found Lang was still with her.

'He said to me that I was naive and that I didn't understand,' she told the court. 'He said that I had no idea of what sort of things that Rose Porteous would say against my father, what sort of things she would say to the media and the fact that, in his view, she would make up things that weren't even true to try to ruin his reputation if he ended his marriage with her. He said that if he moved back to our property there was no way that he could make this property secure. He told me that it would be in my interests and my children's interests if he stayed in the marriage and did not return to the family home. He said that we would be safer, he would be safer, I would be safer and my children would be safer if he did not return to the family home and if he just stayed in that marriage.'

46

JUSTICE ANDERSON'S JUDGMENT ON the case was lengthy, detailed and pulled no punches about the relationship between Gina and Rose. 'Within quite a short time, a few months, an intimate relationship developed between Mr Hancock and Mrs Porteous and by early 1984 they were cohabiting,' he noted. 'This disconcerted Mrs Rinehart and animosity developed between the two women.' Adding that her father's subsequent marriage to Rose was greeted with displeasure by Gina, he continued that she had become 'genuinely and deeply concerned that Mr Hancock appeared, uncharacteristically, to be reaching into the accumulated wealth of the family companies to enrich Mrs Porteous'.

During the court case, Rose had claimed that she was only Hancock's wife, and totally dependent on him. 'He was the cake,' she said, 'I was the icing.'

Oscillating between brazen and demure during her days on the witness stand, Porteous had the air of an actress taking a curtain call when she finally stepped down. She had played her part in front of the audience – the judge and public gallery– and now had to wait for the court's decision. For Gina, the end of the public grilling could not come soon enough.

It was Hancock's system of complex 'loan accounts' that were highlighted during the court case. Family members would draw down specific expenses against the loan account held at Hancock Prospecting Pty Ltd. Those expenses would be marked against their names, but at the end of June each financial year, the debt would disappear, resurfacing in Hancock's own account where it was evaporated by other companies. Observers noted that the loan accounts were more than likely established for taxation purposes. For Rose and Gina, the system was a two-edged sword when it was held under the microscope in court. Rose's lawyer pointed out that the system worked very well for Gina and her father prior to the arrival of Rose on the scene in 1983. After that, his daughter became increasingly alarmed and infuriated at the substantial amount of money that was directed to Rose. But for Justice Anderson, the issue was not emotive: his verdict, after hearing all the material presented to him from both sides, was based on issues of corporate law. Showing the extreme patience for which he is noted, he stated: 'For myself, I wouldn't think it mattered one jot whether she [Mrs Porteous] insisted or pleaded or demanded or requested . . . the important thing is whether the money was obtained in breach of fiduciary duty by Mr Hancock from corporate resources, whether she knew that was the source from where the money came, and whether . . . the circumstances were such as to implicate her in the breach of fiduciary duty.'

On what would have been Hancock's ninetieth birthday, Justice Anderson handed down his decision. For Gina, the result could not have been worse; for Rose, it was a public victory that she savoured. News crews surrounded her lawyer, Nick Styant-Browne, as he called Rose on his mobile telephone inside the courthouse and told her the outcome. She had opted not to go to court on the day of the judgment, preferring instead to wait at Prix d'Amour for the decision. Justice Anderson ruled that the properties and cash Lang had showered on Rose during their marriage were gifts, and that she was therefore entitled to keep them. He scotched any claim from Rinehart that her father had illegally plundered $20 million in Hancock funds to give to Rose, making clear that 'I am not persuaded the contracts were a sham'. He further ruled that Rose could keep the properties in Australia and overseas, and the Bentley. An elated Styant-Browne told the press that Rose had broken down when she was told of the decision.

'Her reaction is one of hysteria, I'm afraid,' he said. 'She is highly emotional. It was difficult to even understand what she was saying other than outpourings of enormous gratitude.' Describing the trial as an 'incredibly traumatic roller-coaster' for his client, he added, 'It was a four-week trial and she was cross-examined for 13 hours, three-and-a-half days in the witness box involving the most gruelling, relentless cross-examination. It was a very numbing and emotional experience for her. Her character was attacked . . . but in the end it was all irrelevant. This was a case about financial transactions, not the person-alities of particular witnesses. The judge has acknowledged the rights of Mr Hancock's wife.'

Rose later gave a statement to the press, downplaying the opportunity to gloat over her win.

'Today is a double celebration,' she said. 'Today, Lang's ninetieth birthday, I have won justice. Lang's birthday is always a special day and now it is the day I have been vindicated. Today is a private day. I go to church on Lang's birthday, then tonight a private dinner with my husband.'

A po-faced Gina immediately stated that her lawyers were considering an appeal over the decision. 'I maintain that what Mrs Porteous did was wrong and morally wrong and that she relentlessly pursued my father for company money and assets right up to the date of his death,' she said in a statement released through her lawyers.

A day after the judgment Rose, with Willie by her side, held a press conference in the ostentatious ballroom at Prix d'Amour. Looking unusually demure in a dark jacket, she used the opportunity to plead with Gina to stop the bickering. 'It is undignified . . . it is not the way Lang Hancock wanted it to be,' she stated, her hands spread in dramatically orchestrated movements. 'Gina, I am asking you: please, let's be sensible . . . after all, without Langley, the two of us would be nothing today.'

Rose's plea for peace fell on deaf ears. Maintaining her usual stony silence, Gina wasted little time in instructing her legal team to prepare an appeal.

It was not over yet.

47

IN DECEMBER 1997, HPPL lodged a petition seeking orders that Hancock's estate be administered pursuant to the provisions of the *Bankruptcy Act 1966*. In the lead-up to the decision, Michael Kroger claimed that Hancock's estate was insolvent and that he had died without assets. 'He had been an extremely wealthy man but in the last few years of his life, especially during the period of his marriage to Mrs Porteous, millions of dollars flowed out of his assets towards [her] and that left money owing by Mr Hancock personally to his own company – more than $1 million – which the company has sought to get from the estate for some years,' he said. Rose's lawyers counter-claimed that the estate had in excess of $6 million at the time of Hancock's death.

Without adjudicating on these allegations, the court agreed that the estate should be administered by a trustee and in March 1999, Max Donnelly was appointed. Donnelly had a massive task: to conduct an investigation into Hancock's affairs, including all of the dispositions he made in Rose's favour in the two to three years preceding his death. The purpose of the investigation was to ascertain what Hancock's asset position was at the time of his death, to identify dispositions made by him prior to his death and to decide whether to join with Rose as plaintiff in the deed action. The trustee had commenced action to claw back a number of the assets, the subject of the constructive trust actions pursuant to the void transfer provisions of the *Bankruptcy Act*. Gina had indemnified the trustee in respect of the costs of that action. The trustee made no claim in relation to Rose's Sydney properties, or the Bentley, and his claim in relation to Prix d'Amour was to approximately 15 per cent of its value. The remaining assets could only be recovered if he could prove that Hancock was unable to pay his debts on the day of his death.

In March 2000, despite the Full Court dismissing her appeals, Gina made an application for special leave to the High Court in relation to the constructive trust action, an application dismissed in September 2000. Gina was ordered to pay costs.

Three months after the bankruptcy proceedings were lodged, HPPL issued proceedings against Rose and Willie Porteous claiming the return of US$500,000, which was allegedly paid to Rose in March 1992. The basis of the claim was that in a facsimile, Rose requested the money be transferred out of a term deposit held in her name and placed into an account in the Philippines to be operated by herself and Porteous. The statement of claim was struck out on the basis that HPPL could not in any way substantiate its allegation that it was the source of the funds in question. Nor were any of the other allegations in the proceedings found to have been proven. HPPL paid the cost of the proceedings.

Gina Rinehart claimed an out-of-court victory against her stepmother in 1998 when diamond jewellery worth almost $200,000 was returned to the company. The case pivoted on seven items of jewellery, sold to the company by Rose in 1986,

and which were valued by an overseas jeweller at more than
$460,000. A subsequent independent valuation by Hancock
Prospecting valued the jewellery at less than half that amount.
Former HPPL vice-chairman Michael Kroger described the win
as a 'total capitulation', and made it clear that the company
would not stop there.

'The extraordinary sort of lifestyle of the rich and famous
[Mrs Porteous] has been engaging in for 15 years is coming to
an end. Gina Rinehart is delighted with the result, as are others
of Mr Hancock's blood family, and we hope this is the first of
many victories against Porteous . . .'

In 1999, to celebrate the twentieth anniversary of the 'Wake Up
Australia!' flight, the Rinehart family held a commemorative
lunch to which friends and dignitaries were invited.

Daughter Bianca also addressed the crowd at the luncheon
and was effusive in praise of her grandfather. 'He took his
visions for the north-west and sculpted them into what we
know now is an area of substantial economic wealth,' she
stated. 'Most Australians nowadays are familiar with his name,
many are familiar with his contribution to this state, and
everybody I spoke to about this matter, young and old, believes
he should have a permanent place in the visible history of our
country . . . What better way in the world could there be to give
this man and his ancestors the praise they deserve by dedicating
some of the land they love to their living memory.'

Gina, true to her father's creed that nuclear power was the
way of the future, organised for a speech to be read out by
nuclear scientist Dr Edward Teller.

But it was Stan Perron, who had known Lang since the late
1950s, who was most illuminating about his character. Hancock
had run a tantalite mine out of Port Hedland at the time the
United States was paying top dollar for defence; after discussions
with him, Perron paid a deposit of 10,000 pounds to enter the

225

float. To his dismay, the bottom dropped out of the US market virtually overnight. 'Lang owed me about 50,000 pounds at that stage,' Perron commented. They then went into manganese together, and that mine, too, ended up flopping. 'So I lost another 30,000 pounds!' By the time Hancock was involved in iron ore, Perron was reluctant to get his fingers burned again, but Hancock was persuasive. He exhorted his mate to invest 1000 pounds to peg iron ore leases and they ended up splitting the difference; Perron invested 500 pounds on the proviso that he made 15 per cent interest on discoveries over the next ten years. The investment Perron chose to make led to him having a 15 per cent share in Hancock and Wright's royalty from the Hamersley Iron project – which included Mount Tom Price. 'That returned a couple of million dollars a year,' he laughed. 'Lang never asked for help again.' Had Perron known what was to follow – the massive rise of profits to be had from the Pilbara – he undoubtedly would have invested that 1000 pounds.

For years, Gina waged a campaign to rename WA's highest peak, Mount Meharry in the Pilbara, the Hancock Range, to honour her father's role in opening up the area for development. That application was declined, yet, not to be defeated, in 2002, she tried again, this time lobbying then-Premier Geoff Gallop with the same idea. He too declined.

'She was successful in getting part of the Pilbara's Hamersley Ranges to be called the Hancock Range,' the mining source recalls. 'Later, when she entered into the Hope Downs Joint Venture with Rio Tinto in 2005, one of her conditions was that the railway extension required to access the deposit would be named the "Lang Hancock Railway". To rub salt into the wounds, that railway is being extended across Wright Prospecting's only iron ore asset – Rhodes Ridge – which has been the subject of a long-running ownership dispute between the two partners. Gina seems determined to write her father's 50/50 partner, Peter

Wright, out of the history books. Her father, it seems, achieved everything by himself! But if that's the case, how come as soon as Peter Wright passed away, Lang's big schemes became financial disasters? The earlier idea of a separate railway to the coast was canned as soon as Gina entered in the JV, and it became clear that Rio Tinto's railway would be used.'

Gina has also renamed 'East Angelas' as Hope 4, Hope 5 and Hope 6, replacing the Wright name, Angela, with her mother's.

48

THE EVENTS OF 1999 were taking their toll on Rose Porteous. Anointed in June as the victor in the seven-year battle with Gina over the constructive trust actions, she had little time to celebrate the win. By August, she received word that her mother had died in the Philippines, precipitating a rushed trip overseas to attend her funeral. On her return to Australia, she immediately checked into a Perth hospital. Rose had developed a pethidine addiction when treating the pain of a bad back, and was frequently unwell. (She no longer uses the drug.)

After Rose's release from hospital, I was ushered through the electronic gates that protect the property from prying tourist eyes and unwelcome guests.

'Please come to the front door,' a voice announced. The door was a massive fortress, solid and impenetrable; through it drifted the incessant yapping of Rose's beloved poodles, daily bathed in French perfume at her insistence. Muffled voices were raised. There was a problem; they couldn't find the key to open the door. It took ten minutes.

Rose Porteous was painfully thin and drawn in the face, her legs encased in tight pants topped off by a riotously coloured striped jumper which only accentuated her weight loss. Around her wrist was the plastic identity bracelet from her hospital visit. Her face was bereft of make-up, apart from a kohl line underneath her eyes and a hint of lipstick. At first glance, it was difficult to reconcile this person with the glamorous, designer-clad woman who has graced countless magazines. She chain-smoked through the interview (a habit she has since given up), her accent heavily laced with her native Filipina tongue and her dark eyes alternated between calm pools and hell-cat flashes. She was warm, cold, defeated, defiant; a smiling mouth and eyes like granite. She moved from one incarnation to the next with lightning speed. One moment drama queen and flirtatious femme fatale, revelling in her celebrity; the next victim, more sinned against than sinning. She will not be silenced, despite Willie's entreaties. 'When Rose gets mad with me she sometimes goes on radio and declares we are going to divorce,' he sighed. 'It gets tiresome, but I'm used to it. It's like water off a duck's back.'

She did not shy away from the subject of her stepdaughter, launching headlong into her version of events.

'Believe you me, I did not go out with any man in this town. Except Lang, mmm.' Murmured 'mmm's' are scattered throughout her conversation. 'That was the first man I met. My girlfriend tried to match me with all sorts of men, I spoke to them, I was entertained by them, but never did I go for a fling with any of them. Gina sacked me when she found out her father was in love with me. Lang had a voracious, animal appetite for women. He needed a woman, he always needed a woman.'

She was also disarmingly direct about the beginning of her relationship with Hancock. 'He looked at me, and I knew right away, I said to him, excuse me, sir – I always address people as sir – the first time he met me I knew he was attracted. I tried to keep away, honestly.'

Now it's my turn to go, 'Mmm.'

After their marriage, Rose claimed, she literally kept Hancock on his feet. 'He would take me to a disco and every-thing – can you imagine Langley Hancock dancing at Regine's in New York? That was funny – he would dance with me, he loved dancing. His favourite song was "You Made Me Love You (I Didn't Want to Do It)".'

Lang himself admitted that before Rose entered his life he was a recluse.

'Now, I delight in taking her out at night,' he said.

'I have not really grieved over Langley,' she said, 'there was no time to grieve . . . it's not good for my heart.' Lang had been dead for seven years and Rose remarried for almost as long, but that, apparently, was of no consequence. With a dramatic flutter of her hand, the interview was terminated. 'I have not yet had time to mourn Langley George's death. It is upsetting for me to talk about him.'

In 1998, journalist David Leser was given separate audiences with Gina and Rose. 'The hardest part about interviewing Rose Porteous and Gina Rinehart,' he wrote, 'is trying not to appear too goggle-eyed at the contrast between these two mortal enemies, each holding court in her own bizarre citadel . . .' He found Gina to be the complete antithesis to Rose. 'They want to know whether I am an admirer of the late Lang Hancock, and whether I can be trusted to write [the] article in Gina's favour. I can only smile and hedge . . . Three days later, I am back in the boardroom of Hancock Prospecting with my tape-recorder running. The room is charged with a chilly uncertainty . . .' Leser spoke with one of Gina's advisers who, he penned, 'pleaded with me to get the facts right when presenting Gina's story. "Otherwise, it's my cock on the block."' Another employee summed up their feelings tersely: 'I'd rather be killed by Rose than sacked by Gina.'

Rose's celebrations against Gina were short-lived. 'The general public got the impression that Rose had won – but that was not so,' the mining source commented. 'The media did not seem to figure out that there were consequences. First, the law firm Slater and Gordon put their hand out for nearly A$15 million from Rose saying, in effect, "you have won, so we are entitled to our fee!" And the trustee in liquidation of Lang's estate asked that approximately A$15 million be returned by Rose to Lang's estate. This is because gifts given in the last two years before bankruptcy can be "clawed back" by the trustee in liquidation under federal law. The whole saga was very messy but the end result is that Gina caused Rose to have to part with about A$28 million in a relatively short timeframe. So Gina won, although Rose still had sufficient assets to keep her going.'

49

GINA RINEHART DOESN'T JUST move in the big end of town. She *is* the big end of town. Her wealth and name ensures that, like her father before her, she has the ear of premiers and politicians. But her influence could not bring the one thing she most desperately wanted – an inquest into Lang's death. Since his demise, she used her position to lobby people in power to investigate his death for evidence that Hancock met his end through foul means. Her contention was that Rose, far from being a dutiful, loving wife, hastened the end of her father's life through harassment and intimidation.

The details of the new evidence which she presented to the Attorney-General, Peter Foss, were closely guarded by Rinehart insiders in order to protect the identity of the witnesses, but the basis of the presentation was one of Australia's worst-kept secrets. Among the allegations were details that Rose fried Lang's food despite her husband's heart condition and against his dietary specifications, that she tampered with the air-conditioning in the bedroom where he died and that she placed his oxygen

232

in the deep freeze. Rinehart's lawyers, in readiness for the moment when Gina would be given the green light for an inquest, spent countless hours talking to people who had been employed by Porteous during the lead-up to Lang's death and preparing their affidavits. The net widened to include medical staff – doctors and nurses – and domestic employees. Gina's supporters insisted that it was an investigation that had to be held, to set the record straight. That Hancock was 82, and already seriously ill, was not the issue: it was necessary to find out whether his death was premature. Again, the spectre of possible criminal conduct raised its head. Rinehart's lawyer, Wayne Martin, QC, prepared the submission with painstaking care. Addressing the restraining order, he said: 'This would seem to provide a cogent foundation for the proposition that the activities of some or other persons at or about that time may have been independently unlawful, at least during the period after the issue of the restraining order.' He also addressed the possibility that coroners McCann and Hope may have made legal and factual errors by dismissing the need for a coronial inquiry. But the eminent silk did not stop there. Describing the necessity for an inquest as an 'overwhelming public interest issue', he questioned the police investigation following Hancock's death and noted that three professional medical opinions supported the call on the basis that the death may have been premature.

Those against Gina's push – and there were many – claimed that the call for an inquest had become an obsession with her, fuelled by a bitter hatred for her stepmother and a steely determination to bring Rose undone. Michael Wright, who admits to having no respect for either woman, was clearly contemptuous of the situation. 'Rose is what she is, and few people have got any time for her in this town. But Gina is an executive, at the helm of Hancock Prospecting, and she took over that company with great aspirations for setting the world on fire, becoming the empire builder. But this vendetta against Rose has consumed

Debi Marshall

her life. Why she is wasting so much time, effort and money on this thing is beyond me – Hancock's dead, end of story, and she should just get on with her life. One has to ask what Lang would have wanted, and I doubt he would like this scenario.'

Whether Hancock would have liked it or not, the push finally paid off. The first coroner, David McCann, made it clear in 1993 that he had no basis on which to justify the calling of an inquest – that Hancock had died of natural causes. Much to Gina's chagrin, in 1994 McCann determined not 'to make the inquiry file itself available for inspection by any of the persons who have an interest in the circumstances surrounding the death of the deceased'. Through her lawyers, Gina retaliated that McCann had refused to allow her access to view the file or to examine the results of the investigations which he undertook. When the files were finally made available to her, she then renewed her call to Alastair Hope, who made the same decision in March 1998. Since 1996, the law which necessitated an approach by the Attorney-General to the Supreme Court for an inquest to be opened has been made null and void, but Hancock had died before that law became operational. Gina had never accepted the decisions, and doggedly worked with her lawyers to prepare and present the new evidence. Hope was again petitioned and in November 1999 Attorney-General Peter Foss cleared the way for Rinehart to take her presentation to a Supreme Court judge, who would make the decision.

Rinehart never wavered from her intent to sway the powerbrokers to back her call for an open inquiry into her father's death. She badgered then-Western Australian Premier Richard Court with numerous letters to that end; on occasion, she also approached him at functions to discuss the issue. Knowing her determination, many expressed surprise when the announcement was made; not that there was a turnaround of opinion, but that it had taken so long.

In comparison, few were surprised when, two months

earlier, Rose admitted to a Federal Court bankruptcy hearing in Sydney that she had threatened to kill her husband when she realised he had changed his will. If she knew that her verbal admissions could be used against her, it failed to temper her outburst. For those listening to her admissions, the picture she painted was bleak: standing at the old man's bedside, screeching at him as he lay dying. 'I said to Langley George, you've bankrupted the estate,' she admitted. 'I said to him, if this cloak and dagger thing is going on, I'm going to get a divorce right now.' Admitting that she had raised her voice, she continued: 'I said, I'm going to murder you. I'm going to do this and that, and you're going to die a bankrupt.'

Finally, at the end of 1999, Gina got her wish. Rose's alleged behaviour in the weeks leading up to Hancock's death became pivotal in the Rineharts' battle to have an inquest opened into his death. Rose countered that the allegations were ludicrous and an inquest would finally put an end to the nonsense.

'I'm thrilled about this, because Gina was in charge of Langley for that entire period,' she said. 'It's going to bounce back on her. Hopefully, it will finally be the end of all this.' One person who was not thrilled was former Attorney-General, Jim McGinty. 'Gina would not let up until she got what she wanted. She lobbied politically despite Peter Foss not seeing a great deal of merit in her protestations. The coroner, realising the way things were headed, decided to conduct the inquest. He granted it on the basis of fresh evidence.'

The seriousness of the news that an inquest was to be held was somewhat tempered by press reports that Rose had been admitted to hospital following a drug overdose. It was a suggestion both she and Willie denied; the truth, they said, was that the hospital visit was brought on by food poisoning after Rose had baked a custard using a leftover tin of coconut milk. A headline in *The Weekend Australian* said it all: 'Half-Baked Overdose Reports Take the Custard, Says Rose'.

50

ON 13 DECEMBER, 1999, Coroner Alastair Hope reconsidered his earlier decision and determined that an inquest should be held on the basis of receiving a 'large body of additional materials including what was said to be "new evidence"'. But long before it started, there were wranglings. Accusations that the then-Western Australian Governor, Michael Jeffery, had made a 'forceful' intervention to the Attorney-General on Gina's behalf were met with vehement denials. Then-Opposition Legal Affairs spokesman, Jim McGinty, called for scrutiny and investigation of the allegation and then-Premier Richard Court said that his government had 'come under pressure' from Rinehart, who had donated more than $42,000 to the Liberal Party during the 1997–98 financial year. 'We have made it very clear,' he said, 'that the government makes its decision on independent legal advice coming to it.'

For ringside observers, the inquest, which opened in June 2000, promised to be the best show in town, the courthouse a stage to hear allegations that far from being a loving wife, Rose

Porteous had engaged in foul play to hasten her octogenarian husband's demise. Over six weeks, the court heard tales so lurid and tawdry that they beggared belief: headlines of hitmen and black magic, and of sex and drugs; of Gina paying witnesses to 'dish the dirt' on Rose and her counterclaim that the money was given merely so they would tell the truth. A procession of people, from maids to police, lined up to give evidence before Coroner Alastair Hope.

Jim McGinty watched the proceedings with absolute disdain and, 11 years later, is still appalled by it. 'Gina and Rose turned the whole thing into a circus, with Gina paying six-figure sums to witnesses,' he told me in February 2012. 'It was a total disgrace and so against our Australian notion of justice. Gina ultimately failed in what she set out to achieve but in getting to that end result she tied up court resources. She didn't care a damn about other people who had to wait for their own coronial service into the deaths of their loved ones. That was of no consequence to her. In my view it was an example of Gina throwing her weight around because of her money. Money should not buy access to justice.'

The matters examined by the coroner promised to be salacious: bribery; perjury; contempt; stealing; corruption of a witness; conspiracy to bring a false accusation; fabricating evidence; allegations of professional misconduct by legal and medical practitioners. 'It is clear that Mrs Rinehart was not satisfied with either the extent of the police investigation into the death of her father or the results or conclusions which had been reached,' Hope noted. Detective Senior Constable Carter concluded that Rinehart's claim that her father had died as a result of stress inflicted on him by Rose was 'unsupported' and 'appeared to be generated by dislike between the two women'.

The coroner heard that from late 1996 until the start of the inquest, Gina had initiated and directed a privately funded investigation into the circumstances of Lang's death, retaining a number of private investigators and solicitors as well as company employees to carry out investigations on her behalf, investigations which cost a 'vast amount of money . . . millions of dollars'. Payments to witnesses, some described as coming from 'Father Christmas', rivalled the shady deals seen on B-grade crime shows. One witness was paid $40,000 in a car at a Perth car park; Rose's personal secretary, Louise Black, gave statutory declarations about her former employer during the same time she took $200,000 in payments. The court heard that Black refused to 'open her mouth' until she received the money. 'It is obvious that for a woman of limited means these payments would have been seen as being vast and Ms Black would have felt under great pressure to provide information and to continue to cooperate so as to ensure that payments continued,' Hope commented. 'It is not difficult to appreciate the potential for corruption.'

The evidence of other witnesses, all of whom received payments, was astonishing. Rose's employees Heidi Biddle, Carmen Elpa, Maxima Simidrescu and Nelida Stuart accused Rose of screaming at Lang about his will, complaining bitterly that he was too slow to die and using black magic to seduce Willie Porteous.

Hope described some of the irregularities in evidence as being of the 'most gross kind', but some of Biddle's evidence left onlookers rocking with mirth. Claiming to have the powers of 'voodoo', she said that she believed that a '. . . big black man in a tree . . .' had killed Hancock and that as a result she had killed ten white chickens to get rid of his spirit. Stuart gave evidence that Lang tried to ring Rose every day, asking her to come home 'to watch him die' but that she would not return. 'A particularly worrying feature of the evidence of Ms Stuart is that she appears to have signed statutory declarations claiming to have knowledge of incidents which were clearly outside her knowledge and must have been inserted into the statutory declarations on the basis of information provided by another person or persons,' Hope found. 'I did not accept Ms Stuart as a witness of truth.' He did not accept any of them as having credibility.

Hope noted that on learning that she had been effectively disinherited, it was 'hardly surprising' that Rose took up the matter with Lang on a number of occasions. 'Intention to kill is an element of the crime of wilful murder and it is my view that there is not sufficient evidence to establish a prima facie case in relation to that element.'

Hope agreed that Gina's concerns about her father clawing money from the family company for Rose were well founded and that over a period of time Rose had 'urged, cajoled or bullied her husband into spending vast sums of money on her behalf'. He cited a letter from Gina, written in 1988, urging that her father be removed as governing director: 'He has grown notably peculiar in the past few years with aberrant behaviour, seeking media attention and personal aggrandisement. He spends time with people and projects he never would have had before . . . [he] has developed a disregard for truth and is influenced by and under the influence of people who are forcing him into decisions profitable only to themselves. He, with the help of the Company solicitor, has taken more than his share of the equity of the Company. He has sold our family company.'

Lang's chauffeur, Reg Browne's poignant evidence stunned the court. 'To be quite blunt, I was the only friend he had,' he said, clearly upset. 'You can forget his family. He had only one friend and it was myself; he relied on me for everything. And you want me to discuss everything this man did and discussed with me? I object to it. You can put that on record. I really, really object to this.' He continued that Rose had once spoken to him about the possibility of an attempt on Lang's life by poisoning and that she had asked him to be present in the room whenever she was there with her husband.

The lurid details went on and on. Part of the 'new evidence' was that one Ricarello Samiento would claim that Rose had asked him how she could kill her husband; this was cited by Gina's lawyer, Colin Lovitt QC, as conscious intent by Rose to accelerate the process of death. Gina added to the fire, claiming that 'We heard rumours that someone was going to poison my father'. Hope also heard evidence from a Hancock Prospecting director that Gina had paid Hilda Kickett to stay away from the inquest.

Questioned about the investigation which had been conducted at her direction and the extensive payments made to private investigators and witnesses Gina, her voice barely audible, said that she had never heard of the person who appeared to have received $50,000 and she had no idea that $150,000 was supposedly to pay a person named 'Jack' in the Philippines or anywhere else. She was grilled about the steps which appeared to have been taken to conceal the true nature of payments, answering that she had been 'keen to see that the witnesses' identities were protected'.

'Now, could you tell his Worship what you were saying there when you said "Where's a thing about I'm going to murder you, I'm going to do this and that and that?"' Rose was asked. She replied in her inimitable fashion.

'I didn't want to be a part of the cloak and dagger thing that was going on,' she replied, eyes flashing. 'It was very obvious – the poison theory – and it was getting worse. The rumours were spreading around. I was having affairs left and right. It even reached up to my ears that I was having an affair with the manager of Bullsbrook, Rick Fry, you know. I mean, if – it's not being snobbish or anything but your Worship, I've been accused of sleeping with every man in Australia, any man at all. I would have been a very – pretty busy woman but I'm really not that desperate . . .'

The circus continued with lawyers for Rose alleging that

Gina tried to trick her father into signing royalties over to Hancock Prospecting instead of to his estate, an allegation denied by her former lawyer Alan Camp. Hancock had tired of his grasping wife, Camp countered, and wanted only to leave her $1.1 million. Bennett argued, to the contrary, that Hancock had not seemed to realise that having signed the deed in March 1992, his estate would no longer be able to afford the bequests set out in his will.

Lawyer Martin Bennett told the court that Hancock had worried his daughter and wife would fight endless legal battles after he died – a concern that would be proven to be eerily prophetic. Hancock, he said, had hired him in 1991 to stop 'defamatory' correspondence Gina was sending to him about Rose. The letters, Bennett remarked, had been 'so abusive as to indicate more than hostility'. Admitting to not liking Rinehart, he added that she had 'the rudest behaviour of anyone I've ever met'.

Lawyer Alan Camp also gave conflicting evidence at the inquest as to whether he had read certain witness statements and his judgment contains the following typical transcript of a Camp reply in the witness box.

'In light of my answer in that affidavit – I mean, I may have read one witness statement. I don't like to think that I'd say that on oath if – well, I mean, I may have read a witness statement but I most definitely hadn't read through all of the witness statements. Maybe that one was so sensational someone showed it to me, but I don't remember reading it.'

Camp's memory may have been poor, but the witness statement in question was the one which related to a conversation in the Philippines with regard to the alleged hiring of a killer to end Lang's life. It later became apparent that no such discussion had taken place because the supposed killer was not even in the country at the time of the alleged conversation. The coroner would later be highly critical of this information not being brought to his attention, as it was this very information that had largely convinced him that an inquest was justified.

Ultimately, Hope found that he did not accept Alan Camp as credible. 'It is most unfortunate that I do not accept Mr Camp as a reliable witness,' he intoned.

At the end of April 2002, Gina, accompanied by John, braved the braying media and slipped into the rear seat of the small Perth courthouse to hear Coroner Alastair Hope's decision. If she was nervous, it did not show. Keeping an implacable face, she listened as blow by blow Hope outlined her spectacular failure to convince the court that anything other than natural causes was responsible for her father's death ten years before. He expressed concerns about the credibility of Rose's first husband, Julian Teodoro, who was paid a quarter of a million dollars to speak about a plot to hire a hitman in Manila in the week before Hancock died, and said that he did not accept that the death was a homicide. 'In my view the deceased was an 82-year-old man who suffered from very serious heart disease and from renal failure,' he said. 'I accept Dr Cooke's evidence that the medical cause of death was arteriosclerotic cardio-vascular disease, in a man with chronic renal failure. I do not accept that the death was a homicide and I do accept that the mechanism of death involved natural processes.'

While Hope did not recommend any action against Gina, Jim McGinty described the inquest as a savage waste of the state's legal resources and one of the most 'unsavoury and improper episodes ever seen in a Western Australian court'. 'Paying witnesses was so alien to the Australian notion of justice,' he told me. 'There was substantial debate at the time as to whether Gina had committed a criminal offence, if she and others had perverted the course of justice. The issue was the difficulty in establishing that she had paid people to not tell the truth. This was not established. While I had grave concerns about the actions of everyone involved in those payments, from Gina Rinehart through to witnesses, it was the view of the Solicitor-General that it was not enough to bring a successful criminal prosecution.'

It was explained to me by a legal source that it is more difficult to prosecute for what someone has said or done in a Coroner's Court because the rules are not as strict as they are in a Supreme Court. Effectively the Coroner's Court is viewed as a grieving court; its primary purpose is to allow people to air their anger and sorrow and move on.

While Willie Porteous expressed a wish to move on and end any feud, outside the court Gina said very little, beyond stating a desire to examine the judgment before making a decision about what she would do next.

51

IN CONTRAST TO ROSE'S extrovert behaviour and flashy show of wealth, the Rinehart family is closely guarded. 'We're not the type of family that displays our wealth,' Gina has acknowledged. 'We don't drive around in Rolls-Royces.' Hope and Ginia were never photographed as children and around-the-clock security is kept on the family home. The family vehicle is bulletproofed and every word written about them saved by the Australian company Media Monitors.

When we spoke in 2000, both John and Bianca boasted that they were proud to carry the Hancock legacy into the new millennium, despite acknowledging the responsibilities of their name. 'We've always known life is a fish bowl, especially in Perth,' John said. Neither would put a price on their inheritance and claimed that despite their family's wealth, they had to work for their money, and were not spoilt. John wore his wealth with a casual air, the self-assurance of a man in his early twenties who was educated at the best schools and travelled the world; a man who had never experienced poverty and was never likely to. He could, literally, afford to be charming, but the Hancock grit was never far from the surface when Rose's name was mentioned. His jawbone crunched and his blue eyes, a legacy of his grandfather, hardened as he explained how his intensely private family loathe the unrelenting attention they have endured over the years that they have battled in court to prevent further Hancock assets and finances going to Rose. 'We should never have had to spend the money on these court cases,' he spat.

Bianca, then a 23-year-old, slim, raven-haired beauty who was the likeness of her mother at the same age, worked for a while as Gina's PA in the family's Perth headquarters of Hancock Prospecting. She has the same polished vowel sounds as Gina, a modulated, even voice liberally tinged with American inflections gained from years living in the United States and from the rarefied cloisters of finishing school. Relaxed in shorts and runners on a Sunday afternoon in Perth's Kings Park, Bianca was – and remains – the epitome of youth and glowing good health. At family gatherings, where she was frequently called on to address guests and dignitaries, she was grace and charm personified, a woman well able to hold her own as she proudly reminisced on her grandfather's role in Australian history. In the office, she possessed the same confidence; immaculately groomed, professional and helpful. She admitted to being a private person, not comfortable with being photographed, and that she intends to stay that way. She selected her words carefully when discussing Gina, weighing each one as it fell from her mouth. 'My mother is a strong, dedicated woman,' she said. 'It has been so hard for us to accept what she has lived through over the past decade. Her family has always been the most important thing to her, and it's that which has got her through these shattering years.' But her voice took on an authoritative air and her conversation became granite-laden when she reiterated that Gina wanted copy approval for the manuscript of

Debi Marshall

Lang Hancock. Repeatedly, she returned to the subject; increasingly, the request became a demand. Bianca Rinehart was her mother's mouthpiece and, like her mother, she expected capitulation to her will. When that didn't happen, the smile died on her lips.

246

52

KEN MCCAMEY STAYED ON as an employee of Hancock Prospecting Pty Ltd following Lang's death, but in 1995 he was informed by letter that his services were to be terminated. It is clearly a memory which rankled. 'The basis of my termination appeared to be that there wasn't enough work for me,' he told me when we met at his Gin Gin farm. 'Gary Schwab, the [then] director, and Michael Kroger were the people who told me. I was very hurt. I was the only other living person who had worked for Lang, and had found so much for him. Lang left me $500,000 in his will, but it is doubtful I will get that. The company position is that Hancock's estate is insolvent and accordingly it cannot make any bequests to any named beneficiary. I was so upset; I signed a paper which dealt with wages, long service leave, holiday pay, that sort of thing, and which also had a clause about me having no further claims on Hancock monies. This was only half an hour before they had a staff gathering for me, a few sandwiches and soft drinks, and that's when I was presented with a gold pen. Gina wasn't there.

I could have helped her no end, but I wouldn't give that woman a drink in the middle of the desert if I was in such a position to do so.'

McCamey's supporters – and they are legion – are savage about the way he was treated. Lang's former pilot, Bob Pruden, summed up the general feeling. 'McCamey was a gentleman, and he was an exceptionally loyal employee to Lang. He should have lived in luxury, and that is certainly what Lang wanted.' Another insider who knew McCamey well commented that anyone who presented a challenge to Gina's view of history was dismissed. 'This included McCamey,' he said. 'After his termination he ended up a very disillusioned man. I doubt you could ever find a more loyal employee, or one who had contributed so much to the wealth of the organisation for so little in return.'

The gentle bushman did not live to realise Lang's wishes that he inherit half a million dollars from his will for his years of loyalty and service to the company. In early August 2000, Ken McCamey suffered a small stroke, closely followed by a fatal heart attack. Devastated by his sudden death, more than a hundred people attended his service, including Willie and Rose Porteous, Greg Milton and many who had worked with Ken during his years with Hancock.

Willie delivered the warm eulogy, a moving remembrance of a man who sacrificed much of his personal life working along-side Lang in search of black gold. 'It was Ken who discovered the downhill railroad that really made it possible to roll iron ore westward to the coast at Ronsard,' Willie said. 'He visioned and aerial-prospected the coast and he discovered a muddy water channel running 22 kilometres out to the sea through the outer reefs – providing a shipping channel for big ships to reach a port and load iron ore. It was Ken who found some of the most important iron ore mines in the Pilbara – Paraburdoo, Channar, Marandoo and the last, McCamey's Monster . . . Ken was also credited for finding 554 other deposits believed to have reserves

of between 5 and 10 billion tonnes of iron ore . . . You have
marked your life with a large footprint in the annals of this
great country. Your name must truly live on not only in the
hearts of those who know and love you, but serve as a guiding
spirit for the future of Australia.'

Ken McCamey was laid to rest at Karrakatta Cemetery.
Neither Gina, nor members of her family, attended.

Gina went into dispute with both Ken McCamey and the
adult children of Hancock's partner, Peter Wright. McCamey
got nothing from Gina and she engaged in a protracted, if
mostly private, legal battle with Wright's children, Michael and
Angela.

'What's this all about?' I ask my mining source. 'Lang and
Gina are so alike in many ways, but there seem to be significant differences in the way they do things?' He gave a wry
laugh. 'Remember what Hancock said about Gina? He said,
"She's a lot tougher than me, but she's not ruthless; I think
you'll find she's very fair." I think he got the first bit right.
Lang's intentions towards Ken were never honoured. Gina put
Lang's estate into the hands of Ferrier Hodgson, receivers. It
was bankrupted after Lang signed the deed on his deathbed
and despite around $15 million being recovered by the trustee
in liquidation from Rose, no money flowed to Ken's family.
In later years, Gina had her staff show a slide at international
iron ore conferences listing all the ore bodies discovered by
her father. Today, these particular slides are omitted from
the conference slide sets available on the Hancock website.
McCamey's name also does not appear on the fiftieth anniversary commemoration to Hancock.'

He cites the maxim, *a lot of litigation needs a lot of lawyers*
to conclude his point. 'There is always money for that, but not
for McCamey. Regardless of what reasons Gina proffers for
this, there are a lot of people in Western Australia who will not
forgive her for this. He died a shattered man.'

53

PRIOR TO THE MINE'S closure in December 1966, for seasoned miners, Wittenoom quickly established a reputation as being the toughest area in Australia to work. Desperate to find men who would come to work at Wittenoom, let alone stay there and keep on labouring in the primitive conditions, the company resorted to recruiting vagrants who had spent a night at Her Majesty's pleasure in the Perth lock-up. Their choice was simple: pack their swag and hotfoot it to Wittenoom, on board the MacRobertson Miller plane that flew daily into the site, or go back to jail.

Robert Vojakovic was 21, a fresh-faced Croatian displaced from the war who migrated to Australia in the early 1960s. Word was, he recalled, that there was work at this little place called Wittenoom – tough work, for sure, but a job. Like many of his fellow migrants, he gravitated to the ragtag settlement. He arrived three months before Christmas. The heat was unbearable, the iron barracks, with no privacy, air-conditioning or doors, were nicknamed 'Death Row' and the only social outlets for the men were drinking, gambling and fighting. It was jungle law, he recalled, dog eat dog, survival of the fittest, where men who were nursing hideous memories of war and trying to rebuild their shattered lives were stripped of their dignity. It was the wild west at its worst, barbaric conditions in the mine, barbaric conditions in the living quarters. Fresh off the boat, the majority of the workers had no money to leave Wittenoom, and it became their prison. Many men who opted to take their chances there failed to heed the warning not to use the credit system at the company-owned store; if they were in hock to the company, they would be refused an air ticket to leave until the debt was cleared. The town's remoteness made walking out over 180 kilometres of arid ground an option for only the bravest, most desperate or foolhardy men, and the company's drivers and pilots were under threat of suspension if they took any workers out in their trucks or planes. For the migrants who despised the emptiness and lack of culture, every potholed, dusty road led to hell.

In the identical asbestos-built homes, clumped closely together, the kitchens became the focal point for the few migrant women who, desperately homesick and unable to speak English, conversed in their native tongue and tried to make the best of what they had.

'Poker was a big game, and many men lost a week's wages in a night,' Vojakovic remembered. 'I had never played in my life, but one night, Christmas Eve, I asked to be dealt in for a game. The stakes were high, you didn't mess around with these men.' Through the long night, Vojakovic relied on beginner's luck and nerves of steel to keep risking his stake, and by dawn, he had amassed 500 pounds – more money than he would have earned working at the mine after expenses, more money than he had ever seen in his entire life. He piled the filthy notes into his swag, shouted his disbelieving mates to lunch and made his way to the airstrip to fly out of this hellhole. 'The ground staff bloke knew that he was risking his job by smuggling me out of there, but I offered him 40 pounds,' he recalled. 'I told him, "All this is yours if I get on that plane tomorrow."' He snatched up the money and I got the flight the next day.' Vojakovic would come to understand that the winning run on poker which financed his escape from Wittenoom had probably saved his life. He never forgot the mine, nor the men; twenty years later, when he read in the Western Australian newspapers about the asbestosis victims of Wittenoom fighting for justice, he took over as president of the fledgling Asbestosis Disease Society.

When I visited Wittenoom in 2000, Vera Yugolano and her husband, Umberto – once a gun miner poached by Hancock – had lived there for 35 years. I was warned they were extremely loyal to Gina and would not talk about the family. Out there, so far from Perth, so far from the legal eagles, the couple were the proverbial guards around the ragged Wittenoom palace.

From the water tower perched on the hill above the township, Mulga Downs station stretches as far as the eye can see. It is achingly beautiful country, where the flat lands merge into the Hamersley Ranges that tower above it. The road to the station gate was still partly flooded from a recent deluge of rain and birds gathered to drink from the overflow. The station sign was written on an old letter box – 'Mulga Downs' – but the then-manager of Mulga Downs, Steven Hoosen, had been given instructions that I not be allowed in. He was polite in the way that bushmen are, but unapologetic about the refusal. Mrs Rinehart had said no, he told me. And that was the end of the matter.

Paul Fitzgerald, a former Catholic priest whose ministry covered around 300 kilometres of the Pilbara, left the priesthood in 1972 and returned to Wittenoom in 1990 to help in the fight to save the town. He ran the guest house where

I stayed, a former convent complete with single beds in a dormitory where nuns prayed to God to save the souls of the rough-and-ready mine workers and of the displaced Aboriginals. 'If I thought it was that hazardous, I wouldn't live here, and my lungs are perfect,' he told me. 'It's the country here that is so spectacular. It's very humbling and makes you think spiritually.'

Wittenoom is more than a ghost town: eerily quiet, the slight breeze on the days I was there seemed to carry the names of the dead, names written in asbestos dust. They echoed down from the now silent mine site, past the charcoal-coloured tailings that spew over the hills, the obscene signature left from days gone by. They echoed down the ravine, into the shadows of the cool inviting waterholes and around the mostly derelict township. They echoed through the neglected cemetery, with its concrete slabs and plastic flowers left years ago on the now untended graves. There are 60 plots, many unmarked save for the iron spikes that stand to attention and beckon the observer to tread softly here. The rock-hard earth did not invite burials; explosives had to be used to dig a grave. The latency of asbestosis and mesothelioma ensured that the men and women who worked at Wittenoom and who have died from the disease are buried in other places, usually the homelands they had left with such high hopes.

A former miner at Wittenoom saw the irony of the workers dying back in their homelands, years after they had bartered their health and youth down the hellish mine. 'How convenient for the company that the disease takes so long to become evident, and for people like Hancock who didn't believe people died from asbestosis,' he said. 'Otherwise, one half of the town would have been burying the other half.'

Fourteen hundred and fifty kilometres away from Wittenoom, on the office wall of the Asbestos Disease Society in Perth, a painting by artist Steve Benedict, who once worked at Wittenoom, serves as a grim reminder of the mine's history, the people who died from exposure to asbestos and those who capitalised on it. The iron spikes are a ghastly feature of the painting, lined up in the front driveway of Prix d'Amour, the house that Hancock owned with Rose. Down the side of the mansion, the ghostly, gaunt figures of the dead miners march away from the house, into eternity.

Robert Vojakovic does not accept that entire families – the men who worked at the mine, the women who dusted their work clothes before washing them and the children who played in the lethal tailings that were laid around the town – should die before their time. 'This disease is no respecter of men, women or children, and it does not differentiate between rich and poor. Mesothelioma has an exceptionally long latency period. Wittenoom was a polluted community, filthy to the core.'

The cartage of hessian bags containing the asbestos fibre from Wittenoom to Roebourne and onto Point Samson was carried out by an independent contractor which mainly employed Aboriginal labour. More than 6000 Aborigines were exposed to blue asbestos in the Pilbara region, but it was not until 1984 that Indigenous labour was included in statistics associated with the deadly mineral.

On average, three former residents of Wittenoom who lived or worked in the town after 1966 contract mesothelioma each year, and lodge claims against the state, the Ashburton Shire, CSR, Midalco, Hancock and Wright. Victims are often in advanced middle age and live only a short time after diagnosis. The compensation covers medical costs and special care. In addition, liability is largely covered by public liability insurance.

Lang Hancock's attitudes to the dangers of asbestos are well illustrated by his expressions of faulty logic. In a widely circulated 1990 letter to the government and shires, he wrote, '. . . sunbathing causes more cancer, yet you do not prohibit it. It [the press] is wrong about nuclear power which is the safest power there is – falling trees have killed more people than nuclear power has done, yet you do not advocate cutting down all forests . . .' He also once affirmed that 'there is no asbestos in the town that is of any harm to anybody'. Gina is more restrained in what she says about asbestos disease but she does not accept claims at face value.

Despite the relatively small net amount that the company has to pay, legal sources say that the cost of the lawyers involved in hardline negotiations far exceeds the gap that has to be closed to conclude a settlement. 'None of those involved in these cases can understand why Gina takes such a hard line,' one told me. 'It doesn't make sense: if even one of these cases ended up in court, the legal costs would then be substantial. In addition it would put the whole issue in the spotlight and more claimants would be attracted. At present, because of the age of the victims, co-morbidity and lack of knowledge, claims are often not lodged.' Wrongful death claims are often filed by family members of a pleural mesothelioma victim after the person has died. The disease is usually not diagnosed until it has reached a late stage and death often comes within a year of diagnosis, before the case can be organised and prepared for presentation. These suits seek compensation including monetary, loss of life or financial support. After Hancock and Wright's public liability insurer has covered most of the cost of a claim, Hancock Prospecting is left with a residual exposure of around 1 per cent of the total claim, which can vary depending on the specific circumstances.

'I remember an occasion where a claimant, in a wheelchair with multiple tubes and breathing with the assistance of an oxygen mask and flanked by legal representatives of the six defendants had to adjourn to wait for Gina to take a phone call before a decision could be made,' my source says. 'This is the human, tragic face of the mesothelioma claimants. I was tempted to pull the cash from my own wallet to close the gap that day.'

Today, Wittenoom is a town that has virtually been erased from history. Almost all the buildings have now been demolished and large warning signs appear at the turn-off to the town and multiply as the township becomes closer. There are more wallabies, kangaroos and water dragons than people in the main street.

Robert Vojakovic is still President of the Asbestosis Disease Society in Perth and in 2011 was honoured for his 32 years of devotion to helping asbestosis disease sufferers. 'The ADS pioneered litigation arising out of Wittenoom,' he says proudly. 'Any claims arising out of exposure post-1966 are all resolved. None took longer than about four months. I don't think that Rinehart would even know who the claimants are. It's all handled by her lawyers and insurance.'

'How many people have died from exposure at Wittenoom – miners, visitors, transient workers, residents?' I ask.

'More than 2000. For every two cases of asbestosis, there is one case of mesothelioma. Asbestosis is a slower death than mesothelioma. There are also a host of other diseases that go with it.'

I ask Robert about the people I met when I went to Wittenoom and surrounding Pilbara areas in 1999. 'The former priest, Paul Fitzgerald, who thought Wittenoom was safe? Is he still there?'

'No, he's retired. He has asbestosis. He refused to make a claim.'

'What about Umberto, who worked for Hancock post-mining with his wife, Vera?'

'He died from asbestosis. I personally settled his claim. Vera lives in Perth now.'

'And Wobby Parker, the Aboriginal elder? Where is he?'

'He died. His wife had mesothelioma; she died as well.'

He takes a deep breath. 'You know, the staff at Mulga Downs station didn't want to testify that Wobby's wife had worked at Mulga Downs, just as Wobby had. She'd worked there since she was 12 years old. We needed witnesses to help with her claim around 1998 but she died, unsuccessful. It was ironic, really; the person who refused to give the statement also developed meso and asked if I would settle her claim. I did. She has since died.'

He gathers his thoughts again. 'All the Aboriginals got asbestosis. At least they're looked after in Western Australia. I once took a blackfella to a New South Wales hearing and the bloke there said to me, "Uncle Tom can wait outside. If you don't like it, leave." I told him that if he was in WA, we'd thump the shit out of him.'

Gina, Robert said, attended primary school at Wittenoom. 'She is just as much Wittenoom as any person there. She would surely have been exposed to tailings. I knew a couple of girls who went to school with her. They are both dead from mesothelioma. One was in her late 30s, the other early 40s.'

The small office that I visited in 2000 has now grown to having the largest library on asbestos research in the world, and employs 18 people. 'Gina wanted a statue of Lang Hancock in a prominent part of Perth,' Robert recalls, 'but there was opposition to it. I was one of the people who opposed it. I give Hancock credit for being a pioneer, but if there is a statue of him, it should be at Wittenoom. Make it as big as the statue of Rhodes! Gina and all her crowd could go out there and pay homage to the King of Asbestos, leader of the Hancock dynasty. But they'd have to clean the place up, first. They couldn't go tramping over all those deadly tailings. At the moment Wittenoom is sadly contaminated, but cleaned up we would have a beautiful site to offer to the world.'

He ruminates on how Hancock himself escaped asbestosis. 'He reckoned he ate more asbestos than any other person in the world. He was a ruthless bastard who worked hard for what he got; he didn't care about collateral damage. He was once asked if he would put some money towards medical research for the disease. He said no; that essentially, to make an omelette, you've got to crack a few eggs.'

'If Lang was at risk of asbestos disease, what about Gina?' I ask him.

'She is in the same boat as I am to get mesothelioma,' he answered bluntly. 'Latency time is around 30 years. I haven't met Gina but if I did speak to her, I would tell her to have a check-up.'

54

IN A LETTER TO Lang Hancock in mid-1985, Peter Wright had bemoaned that their long alliance was breaking down. It had, he wrote, 'changed from a unique partnership which everybody admired, envied and many tried to break – to which you and I were proud to be intensely loyal and which was amazingly successful by any standards – to an association which I simply find difficult to believe'. To observers in 2001, a legal battle between their offspring was yet another sad chapter in the severing of all that once was in the partnership between old friends, Hancock and Wright.

In 1983, Hancock divvied up the interests he had accumulated with Wright, writing them down on two pieces of paper which were given to Carnie Fieldhouse to formalise as an amendment to the Partnership Agreement. The decision to carve up their assets was a simple action to avoid what both men feared most: fights among their descendants.

Finalised and signed in mid-February 1984, the agreement listed all the assets and interests, excluding royalty interests, of the partners in two schedules of supposedly equal value. The schedules included iron ore, coal, manganese, base metal and limestone interests of the partnership – all of which were deemed to be equally owned by the partners. Each schedule was supposed to be of equal value and each partner would take control of one schedule. Central to the agreement – and later, to the court case – was clause 4, which stated that 'each partner shall have the option exercisable at any time during the continuation of the partnership to require the transfer of the Hancock Prospecting Pty Ltd (HPPL) interests to HPPL and the transfer of the Wright Prospecting Pty Ltd (WPPL) interests to WPPL'.

Wright's schedule included the Rhodes Ridge Joint Venture, one of Australia's richest undeveloped iron ore groups. Its potential is limitless. Unlike the increasing proportion of Western Australia's iron ores which require further processing to achieve a saleable grade, Rhodes Ridge ores – known as 'direct shipping' because they do not need upgrading in a processing plant – can be mined, crushed, screened and loaded on a carrier bound for East Asia.

In late 1997, a letter under Hancock Prospecting signatory was sent to Wright Prospecting, suggesting that the partnership put in place by Hancock and Wright should be dissolved. In return, they offered for HPPL to buy out 25 per cent of Wright Prospecting's interest in Rhodes Ridge. WPPL would have none of it, upping the ante by responding that it would exercise its option over Hancock Prospecting's 25 per cent of Rhodes Ridge, as stated in clause 4 of the 1984 agreement.

That wasn't an option for Hancock Prospecting. The exercise of the option, it wrote back, was now ineffective; the 1984 carve-up was superseded by a 1989 management deal. In effect, the validity of the agreement itself was denied – despite HPPL having taken possession of all the assets in its schedule under the terms of that same agreement. 'Litigation was inevitable but

Wright Prospecting was reluctant to do that,' a mining source tells me. 'But years dragged by and discussions proved fruitless.'

The gloves were off. 'Eventually, and reluctantly, in 2001 Michael Wright and Angela Bennett took Hancock Prospecting to court. 'In the simplest terms,' the mining insider says, 'HPPL had taken the most valuable assets, yet Gina would not agree to transfer this one asset to WPPL in accordance with the Partnership Agreement. Effectively she had taken her half of the lollies and then wanted half of WPPL's as well. That would have given her 75 per cent of the assets when it had always been a 50/50 partnership. The base metals, oil and limestone assets in WPPL's schedule proved to be worthless. Gina apparently had no regard for the long history of the partnership, for the trusting relationship that had always existed between the founders and for her fiduciary duty to her partner. Former senior employees claim she ordered them to "get after the Wrights and get half of Rhodes Ridge". The Wrights were unprepared for such an approach and believed that Gina would eventually do the right thing. For this reason it took them almost a decade before the matter was listed for a hearing in the WA Supreme Court. It took a further six years before a hearing and then a further two and a half years for a judgment. Now, they must wait years longer for the appeal processes to be exhausted. From her history, no one expects that Gina will ever throw in the towel.'

The appeal, he says, will probably be heard in the second half of 2012.

This case was also not without its quirky touches. In a deter-mined attempt to shield herself from the press, the notoriously media-shy Angela Bennett – Michael Wright's sister – hid her face behind a towel as she walked in and out of the court-house. Michael Wright also avoided the media and went one step further, snapping his own pictures of the photographers and television cameramen who were filming him. This family too has its own issues. In his evidence, Wright admitted that his sister had criticised his business acumen and that their relationship is strained.

In 2009, Angela Bennett sold her 7567-square-metre Mosman Park property for a cool $57.5 million to mining millionaire Chris Ellison. At the time, the price set a record in real estate terms.

Noting that 'It is very evident from the correspondence between them that they were concerned in 1982 and 1983 to settle the partnership arrangements so that the assets and interests of the partnership would benefit them equally with provision for their approximately equal division into two groups of assets of roughly equal value', Justice Michael Murray applied common sense in recognising the spirit of the long-time friends' 1984 agreement and its reflection of Hancock and Wright's close working relationship. 'The two men speaking for HPPL and WPPL had been friends and partners for a very long time,' he intoned. 'They clearly intended to deal fairly, each with the other.' Justice Murray also commented that Carnie Fieldhouse had drawn up both partners' contracts. 'He appears to have proffered advice to both Mr Wright and Mr Hancock, even in circumstances where, in relation to the subject matter in question, their interests may have been potentially in conflict,' he said. The ruling, which took two and a half years, was definitive. The 1984 agreement remained in force and Hancock Prospecting had breached it by failing to transfer the holding as requested.

No one who knows Gina underestimated how she would react to the news. But she didn't give the press an opportunity to salivate over a long media conference. Instead, they were treated to a benign statement from Hancock Prospecting, stating, in effect, that they were 'very disappointed' with the judgment that HPPL should relinquish its legal 25 per cent interest in the Rhodes Ridge Joint Venture to WPPL.

'Very disappointed' was a gross understatement. The ruling not only clawed approximately $1 billion from Rinehart's wealth – then estimated at $3.4 billion – but also deprived her of the potential to earn billions more from the Rhodes Ridge deposit. Worse, she had to admit defeat and hand 25 per cent of the Rhodes Ridge Joint Venture to Hancock's business partner, Wright Prospecting.

In 2002, Gina hosted a function for 700 guests in the garden of the Dalkeith home her parents had owned, extolling the virtues of her father and his achievements, on the fiftieth anniversary of his discovery of iron ore. Reminiscing about the days of getting up at 6 am to start an airborne reconnaissance of the Pilbara with Lang and others, Gina rolled film of Lang and told the audience that his long association with Peter Wright was 'honoured by both without a written agreement for most of their long and productive lives'. It was an admission that raised some eyebrows among those in the audience who had questioned Gina's decision to go into battle with Michael Wright and Angela Bennett. 'It might have been better for her to have steered away from that subject,' one guest remarked. Far from taking his hard-earned money and retiring to the good life 'thousands of miles away from any destructive media and the jealousy they wrongly inspire', Gina concluded that Lang instead 'chose to invest his wealth and his life in this country, to explore and develop his beloved Pilbara and to attempt to educate his fellow Australians regarding the advantages of free enterprise over central planning and the "sound good" but impractical socialistic utopian government policies'. She could have been talking about herself.

Gina started her speech by describing how, 50 years ago, her parents climbed into their tiny Auster aircraft and took off from the bush airstrip. 'But,' she said, 'storm clouds were gathering . . .'

If only they had known how much.

55

GINA RINEHART IS KNOWN as a relentless litigant; a combination of her immense wealth and determination ensures that she can – and does – run litigation seemingly without end. Over coffee in Perth, the mining insider rattled off a list of stoushes she has run through the courts. He counted them on his fingers, in rapid succession. 'Where do we start?' he said. 'There are: 1) The legal challenges with Rose, which included the "constructive trust" case before the Supreme Court; 2) Lang's inquest in the Coroner's Court, and putting Lang's estate into bankruptcy; 3) The legal battle against Carnie Fieldhouse, which would have horrified Lang. Now that Carnie is dead, Gina is going after his legal indemnity insurer; 4) Gina's claim against BHP for around $200 million over McCamey's Monster, in which she argued that BHP had failed to honour a contract with Lang which put Lang into financial difficulty, and so he had to sell McCamey's Monster to BHP at a fire-sale price. She wanted the full value; 5) Attempt to gain access to the BHP railway under the ACCC, a long-running saga;

6) Dispute (along with Wright Prospecting Pty Ltd) with Rio Tinto over royalties that are being withheld from specified areas at Channar and Eastern Range; 7) Defending mesothelioma claims; 8) Dispute with her partner, Kumba Resources, over Hope Downs; 9) Dispute with her partner, Wright Prospecting, over Rhodes Ridge; 10) Dispute with Stan Perron over royalty claims; 11) Disputes with her own children; 12) Dispute with her former bodyguard who claimed sexual harassment by her; 13) Falling-outs with her accountants, managing directors, security personnel, and political advisers; 14) Disputes with people on the ground including engineers and geologists; 15) A parting of the ways with approximately 16 law firms in Perth and around the country and the resultant sacking of very senior legal people, including senior counsels.

'The thing is,' he continues, 'Gina is prepared to run these actions at the same time as pursuing real projects. That takes a lot of dedication. You have to be very driven to run so much serious stuff in parallel. Just changing legal representatives and counsel takes a lot of effort. The new team has to be briefed and brought up to speed. Then there is her political activism; her opposition to the carbon tax and mining tax, her push for a Northern Zone for immigrant workers – it goes on and on. She never seems to run out of energy for any of it.' Or money to fund it. The monumental legal battles with Rose cost tens of millions of dollars. Rose's former lawyer, Nick Styant-Browne, who went head to head with Gina's counsel on more occasions than he would probably care to remember, described Gina as an 'indefatigable' litigant. 'Styant-Browne reckoned that she exhausted the best lawyers in the country. Losing was just not in her vocabulary.' That, he says, is the reason most people don't talk openly about her. 'In a nutshell, they are terrified of being sued and, inevitably, dealings with her end in tears.'

Former Attorney-General Jim McGinty, one of the few people to allow his name to be used on the record, agrees.

'I can understand people wanting to remain anonymous,' he says. 'Most people in Western Australia are fearful of Gina's influence. Money talks. But I don't agree that she wields too much power. Buying into media, for example, is not an indication of power – it's an indication of wanting it. People on both sides of politics are reluctant to engage with her unless they have to. Unlike other major players, such as Twiggy Forest, there is no measure of enthusiasm for dealing with Gina.'

Hancock Prospecting Pty Ltd headquarters is situated in West Perth, in a salubrious modern office block just minutes from the CBD and trendy cafes and bars. A bust of Lang Hancock greets visitors at reception, beyond which is a locked door leading to the offices. A silver model of the aircraft Hancock flew is perched atop a lump of ore, with the legend: 'This scale model is of the Auster J5 Autocrat flown by Langley . . .'. A gilt-framed eulogy to him, handwritten by a calligrapher, leaves the visitor in no doubt as to who founded this company.

The atmosphere inside HPPL is deathly quiet, as sterile as a hospital. Tables, chairs, walls: all white. But Gina's deep love of the Pilbara is evident in her choice of family photographs that grace the walls. Gina, young and impressionable, sitting side by side with her father on an ancient, ochre Pilbara rock; sitting with Bianca on a similar rock; a painting of her beloved Pilbara, a gift to Gina from a senior executive at Rio Tinto.

The sterility of the office environs reflects the seriousness with which Gina's employees are expected to take their job. There is no 'home away from home' welcome here. Gina occupies the same corner office as her father before her.

'No pun intended, but it can be a minefield working there,' one former insider told me. 'Gina has kept some employees long term but she's regarded as demanding and exceptionally tough, even among the toughest business men. It doesn't matter who it is: from secretaries to senior legal counsel; she wears the pants, she drives the hard bargains. She doesn't just want control; she demands it. She drives her staff as hard as she can. Forget downtime; she thinks nothing of emailing employees in the wee small hours of the morning and employs two personal assistants – one for the early shift and one for the late.'

Another former employee, who left the company of her own volition less than a year after starting work and who requested anonymity, also noted that morale at Hancock Prospecting is depressingly low. 'People walked on eggshells. It didn't make for a happy working environment. Security is particularly tight; the Hancock secrets are kept well and truly under lock and key. Every document deemed to be high security is kept in a locked repository, to which very few people have access. Employees have their right index finger scanned, and they have to enter a code when moving from any room entering into a corridor. There is a cold atmosphere in the company, a general feeling of distrust, and I was more than happy to leave for that reason.'

Little, it seems, has changed.

Employees recall that while Gina treats staff well, the atmosphere in the company is oppressive, and only the most robust survive. 'People at executive level have their own skills and talents and expect to be able to utilise them,' one told me. 'But you can't do that with Gina. She makes all the decisions. Even if you are the lowest employee, she has her finger on the pulse.' Her siege mentality with the media also ensures that company secrets are in permanent lockdown. 'God help anyone if they suggest courting the press,' he said. 'It's her way or the highway.'

With few exceptions, the mention of Gina's name in Western Australia's mining, legal and social circles invariably brings a shudder. 'I won't talk about Ms Rinehart' is the common refrain. Pressed as to why, the answers are similar. 'Say the wrong thing or, worse, go into print with it, and she'll come down on you like a ton of bricks,' one mining executive told me. Another laughed outright before putting the phone down. 'You want me to do what? Not a chance! This city is too small.' Yet another was bluntly forthright when I asked for assistance. 'I am a busy boy . . . so I am unable to assist you. Sorry.' Many anonymously bemoaned that Gina will likely best be remembered for her pathologically private nature, which reaches even beyond Australia. Chris Rinehart, the son of Gina's second husband Frank from another relationship, lives in America, but when journalist Jane Kadzow requested an interview with him, he responded: 'Gina prefers the family not interact with the press.' Even if he had wanted to say something positive, he said nothing at all. 'I respect her wishes and decline an interview,' he said.

Gina's father did not have the same approach to keeping his employees in the dark. Hancock told Robert Duffield in the 1970s: 'I expect the same loyalty from the office boy as from my top men. I trust them not to betray our secrets to our enemies. But I want them all to know as much as possible about what's going on – otherwise how can I ask them to be loyal?'

Like her father before her, Gina Rinehart does not waste words, and does not discuss her private life. When she has to speak at a court hearing, she does not dress her language in flowery adjectives; on the very rare occasions when she speaks to the press, or instructs a lawyer to do so on her behalf, there is always a reason for doing so.

Always.

56

JOURNALIST TIM TREADGOLD WRAPPED it up in one short, sweet sentence. If the insatiable Asian demand for iron ore continues, he said, then Gina is 'perfectly placed to ride the dragon to incredible wealth' – much more wealth than she has now. A long-time Gina observer, Treadgold encountered first-hand her media-siege mentality when trying to gain an interview with Gina. He told Jane Kadzow that Gina had sent him a story about her business that he thought read as if she had written it herself. 'It purported to be based on my questions and her answers,' he said. 'But I'd never asked the questions. I didn't know whether to laugh or cry.'

In 2006, Gina made her first appearance in *Business Review Weekly's* (*BRW*) billionaires list. Luck played a hand. The rise of her wealth, from a mere pittance of $900 million to a staggering $1.8 billion, resulted from the convergence of two forces: a 70 per cent increase in iron ore prices and her 50 per cent sale, under a government deadline to meet certain guidelines, of Hope Downs to Rio Tinto. The relative speed of the project after approval now ensures at recent prices that HPPL could net around $1 billion after tax per annum from its 50 per cent share in the Hope Downs Joint Venture. In addition, it is thought that Rio Tinto is paying a royalty to HPPL on the value of 50 per cent of production from Hope Downs. The size of the royalty is highly confidential.

A$1 billion after tax per annum. Alan Kohler, who makes even stultifyingly dull stock market figures sound interesting on his nightly ABC finance report, put it in a nutshell. 'It has been estimated that when Hope Downs reaches full production of 45 million tonnes annually, Mrs Rinehart will receive an income stream of $40 million . . . a week.' Like a tsunami tide, Gina's estimated paper wealth just continues to rise. Last year alone, it leapt from $4.75 billion to $10.31 billion, doubling this year to $20 billion. 'That's the sort of money that could make a serious dent in the problems of the Third World,' a source commented to me. The figures are just so mind-boggling that it's hard to keep them in perspective. In 2011 Forbes crowned her Australia's richest person and, later, the richest woman in the Asia/Pacific region. However, SmartCompany, the Australian internet business news service, predicts that based on her iron ore and coal portfolio her personal net worth could rise to more than US$100 billion if China's growth does not come off the boil. At this rate, Gina may soon be wealthier than the richest woman in the world, Christy Walton, whose family own Wal-Mart Stores.

In January 1998, the Western Australian Government's *Prospect* magazine announced a joint venture between Hancock Prospecting and Iscor Ltd, the South African iron ore miner and steelmaker. In return for a 49 per cent stake in the resource, Iscor had agreed to outlay up to $20 million evaluating the Hope Downs project, a former H&W asset, which Gina had inherited from her father. By 2001, Kumba Resources had spun off from Iscor. But by 2004, there were escalating tensions. While Anglo American moved to a stake of 66.6 per cent of Kumba, Hancock Prospecting and Kumba were still reviewing the terms of the joint venture. Six years had passed since the announcement of a deal. Mark Drummond encapsulated the problems in *The West Australian* that year. 'The reason those development issues are not being addressed at Hope Downs is because Hancock Prospecting and South African miner Kumba Resources have become estranged joint venture partners,' he wrote. 'And if industry speculation is any guide, their relationship has degenerated to the point where Ms Rinehart has filed for divorce.' Drummond ventured the theory that Gina had 'sought to exploit a change of control clause in the joint venture agreement to bring about those arbitration proceedings. That trigger is based on Anglo American assuming effective control of Kumba'. Drummond was on the money. 'It was the change of control issue that Gina used to eventually get rid of Kumba so that she could then conclude a joint venture with another partner,' a source told me. 'Prior to them parting company, Gina had issued invitations to hundreds of business contacts to attend the announcement of the JV with Kumba and to hear about the feasibility study of an iron ore mine at Hope Downs. Negotiations with Kumba had still not been finalised by the time of the announcement, but the announcement went ahead regardless. Several WA ministers and the Premier himself, Richard Court, were there; such was the ability of Gina to gain the attention of the government. One sage remarked that the major companies would have been unable to attract as many ministers to the announcement of a new operation – let alone the announcement of a study! There was no likelihood of a mine being initiated for some years.'

The negotiations for a new partner also became a saga. 'At one stage Mitsubishi thought it had a deal with Gina. The Perth representative advised his head office in Tokyo that the deal had been done. But then Gina slid a piece of paper across the table saying words to the effect: "These are my further conditions!" The representatives were shocked. Then, out of the blue, Gina announced that a JV had been concluded with Rio Tinto, which took the media by surprise. It was not known that Gina was negotiating with Rio Tinto.'

When Anglo American, one of the largest mining companies in the world, swallowed Kumba, Gina took the opportunity to break her contract with the company, utilising the 'change of control' provisions in the agreement. 'There was a legal stoush which Gina won – but at a price. Kumba had to be paid hundreds of millions to exit the project. She had played off different suitors but Rio Tinto won the prize in June 2005.'

After years of delays, the pressure was on to execute the dream of her father. It was now or never. 'Ultimately,' the mining insider said, 'it propelled Gina to conclude a 50/50 joint venture with Rio Tinto.' The timing could not have been more advantageous. The price of iron ore skyrocketed soon afterwards, paving the way for the massive windfall that Gina enjoys today: more than A$1 billion a year after tax. 'The Rio Tinto deal was very generous,' he said. 'I wonder if they have ever regretted it; after all, the profits that Gina is making will mostly go into a new iron ore project that will compete with Rio Tinto!'

Gina, he ponders, seems to like the challenge of pressure-cooker situations. 'She put herself in a difficult place by announcing the deal with Kumba without it being finalised. Years later she was desperate to get rid of Kumba because the government had set a deadline of end June 2005 to get a project organised, following an extension of the previous deadline of end 2004. The settlement with Kumba left Gina very little time to finalise a deal with her current partner – Rio Tinto.'

Since the project start-up, he said, there have been ongoing issues between Gina and Sam Walsh, Rio Tinto's head honcho. 'Gina keeps her fingers on everything,' he tells me. 'She complained incessantly about Rio Tinto's ore pricing system which was based on the average price in the previous quarter. She pointed out that when iron ore prices are rising, the price received by Rio Tinto is always below the price obtained by other sellers. Gina was not prepared to accept the argument that when prices are falling the reverse situation would apply.'

An essential criterion for Gina's next iron ore project, 'Roy Hill', he said, is control. 'But at the rate Gina is accumulating profits from Hope Downs it will not be long before she has the cash needed to control more than 50 per cent of that project. Then she will be receiving the letters of complaint instead of writing them!'

He recounts a short story about the amount of fear that Gina imbues in people. 'One of the several ore bodies that constitute Hope Downs was known as "Luncheon Tree", named after a tree that was of historic significance to Lang and Gina: it was under that tree that Lang had lunched around the time that particular ore body was discovered. Around the time of Kumba's involvement, there was a bushfire in the area and the "Luncheon Tree" was lost to the fire. Gina's manager at the time, Richard Jupp, was distraught, trying to work out how to break the news to her. "How am I going to tell her that the tree has been burned?" he said.'

Gina's holy grail – to own and operate her own mine – is now within striking distance. Secured in a joint venture with South Korea's Posco, the world's third-largest steel-making company, and STX Corporation, a South Korean holding company who provide trading services, negotiations with Australian and overseas banking institutions to back Rinehart's company to the tune of $7.2 billion for Roy Hill are now on the brink of being finalised, as are government approvals. All going to plan, the first shipment of iron ore – and the realisation of her (and her father's) lifelong dream – is only two years away.

Lang Hancock – Rogue Bull and Flying Prospector – had amassed his vast wealth from selling mining tenements to companies who, in turn, established mines; his income came from the 'rivers of gold', the royalties that flowed from those mines. But although Gina's name is still inexorably linked with her father's, she is now poised to hold her own, in her own right, among the big boys of mining. Once regarded as a woman who has built her legacy and fortune on her father's name and inheritance, she has now proven that she is more Rogue Bull than Pilbara Princess. And she just keeps getting bigger. Her iron grip on the tiller has ensured that she hasn't just gambled on her luck but capitalised on it through canny business investments and clever contracts with those who can afford to put their money where their mouth is.

57

GINA KEEPS A LOW profile for her philanthropic support, which includes the Hancock Family Breast Cancer Foundation, founded in memory of her mother, and whose objectives are to fund and promote research and to help provide support for women affected by the disease. Friends say that suggestions from former association members that Gina has failed to give the foundation wholehearted support have hurt her deeply.

Gina also supports the Hope Scholarship Award Program for girls and has worked with the Mannkal Economic Foundation, which mentors young Western Australians. She is a director of the South-East Asian Investigations into Social and Humanitarian Activities (SISHA) which campaigns against human trafficking, and has made contributions to a cancer centre at St John of God Hospital in Perth's ritzy Subiaco, as well as supporting the St Hilda's Anglican School for Girls hall, named in honour of her mother. As his estate was bankrupted, it is unknown whether she has secretly heeded her father's wishes, placed in his will, for a cardiac institute to be built at a Perth hospital.

Critics argue that given Gina's enormous wealth, her philanthropic work is grossly inadequate. 'Gina is unknown in West Australian philanthropic circles,' Jim McGinty told me. 'I work in various philanthropic roles in Western Australia and the general consensus is, "don't bother with Gina". Last year, *The West Australian* newspaper published a list of our most significant women,' he says. 'Gina's name was on it, and featuring prominently underneath, a listing that she made donations to St John of God Hospital. Well, I was Health Minister at the time that that particular cancer wing was opened and I can assure you that her contribution was negligible. I laughed when I saw it.'

McGinty claims Gina's values on these sorts of issues need revising. 'I don't mind people making dollars,' he said, before comparing Gina's philanthropy with Twiggy Forrest's. 'Twiggy makes a lot of money but he also puts his hands in his pocket and returns money to the community; that's the sort of people West Australians admire. We have a warmth, too, for the likes of Alan Bond, and his larrikin spirit. There is a mindset in the west that people are all in favour of others getting out there, doing something extraordinary. But Gina is the exception to this. Her view of the world is seen as very self-centred.'

Self-centred or not, Gina has also won some recognition for her work, including the Australian Export Heroes Award in 2009 and the Telstra West Australian Business Woman of the Year the same year.

Gina's charitable donations and choice of causes are often compared, adversely, with the donations and causes supported by the Bill and Melinda Gates Foundation, which lends its famous name to the wealthiest and most generous private foundation in the world, tackling poverty eradication, public health and education. In 2010, Bill Gates and Warren Buffett devised the idea of the wealthiest people in America pledging at least half their net worth to charity during their lifetimes or at death.

An article in *Crikey* by Australian philanthropist Daniel Petre noted that this concept would never work in Australia; that a $5 million gift from a billionaire is nothing to be applauded. 'We either stop lauding thanks for the crumbs offloaded by our most wealthy, or we start offering similar thanks to Mrs Smith whose $100 donation is a greater proportion of her net wealth.'

58

IN AN EXCLUSIVE INTERVIEW with me for a national magazine, Gina's first husband, Greg Milton, told me he always dreamed that one day the son and daughter he'd not seen since they were small children would make contact with him.

Greg – who had reverted to his real name, Milton – had always maintained a dignified silence over the break-up of his seven-year marriage to Gina. 'Because I was Gina's first husband, I have to a degree lived in the shadow of the Hancock family, with all its wealth and power,' he said. 'But the time has come to re-establish my own identity. We need to get on with our lives and start healing old wounds. I will never lay bare intimate details of my relationship with Gina. That will always remain private, but I won't hide any longer. I'm a mature adult, with my own mind and my own life.'

In 2000, I was commissioned to research and write a profile of John Rinehart, who was then working for Iscor Ltd, a major South African steelmaking and resource company. John had recommended a secure hotel for me to stay in, but the country

278

was rife with violence and I felt unsafe going alone. Then writing the biography of Lang Hancock, I decided to travel with my brother and researcher, Wayne Marshall. I had not met John before but he was genial on the telephone and more than happy to discuss his business situation and relationship with his mother, Gina. That is, within reason. 'I can't tell you everything, of course!' he joked.

We arrived, jetlagged, to a cacophony of colour and sound – women's kaftans in peacock shades of fluorescent green and purple and their headwraps high as church pillars, and the exhortations of taxi drivers to get in their vehicles. 'Get some rest,' John suggested. 'I've organised a welcome for you tonight.'

We hoped it was a more encouraging welcome than the newspaper headline we saw as the private car organised by John drove away from the airport. 'Brother and Sister Raped and Murdered.'

John has none of the ruggedness of his grandfather, Lang, or the gruffness of personality. The second thing is his modulated, warm voice and the third how unaffected he appears to be by his family's immense wealth. John has an open, unassuming manner, and smiles readily.

The first night we arrived, John and his then Australian girlfriend, Jess – a pretty blonde who was quick to smile – hosted a South African barbecue, a braai, in our honour. Present were members of the South African rugby team, lean young men at the top of their game with an appetite for a good time. John was a gracious host, pouring wine, uncorking an old bottle of Port, cooking the meat. It was clear he relished entertaining.

The next morning we went with John to the Iscor mine, where a cheeky family of monkeys scampered up the barren escarpment, pausing momentarily to wait for their young and scratching their scarlet bottoms with sheer indifference to their audience. The hard African sun beat down, unrelenting in its intensity and, in his hard hat and immaculate blue shirt, John looked the epitome of a mining heir in waiting. 'I was very, very close to my grandfather, Lang,' he told us later. 'This is in my blood. It is all I want to do.'

John, who was educated at Perth's exclusive Christ Church Grammar before studying at the prestigious Phillips Academy in the United States, has an easy familiarity with luxury that serious money can buy. He is used to the best: at three months, he had his first trip in the family's private jet; at seven, he joined Lang and Gina as guests of the Sultan at his Bahrain palace. He invited us to join him and Jess at a private wildlife resort an hour from Pretoria. The road leading to the resort was pitted and dry, and the surrounding bush was made up of spinifex. It seemed disappointingly ordinary but as we rounded the corner, there it was: low-slung chalets with thatched roofs, an open-air bar with languid fans, rooms decorated with leopard-skin floor coverings and a long jeep laden with native fruit and exotic culinary luxuries. Between the plates of food, gleaming silver buckets held bottles of champagne and wine. At dusk, zebra and giraffes casually sauntered past, their backdrop an African sun as big as a watermelon. Mesmerised, I turned to speak to Wayne. A lone tear rolled down his cheek. 'Paradise, eh?' John smiled.

The following day, we followed John and Jess to Sun City. They immediately checked into the opulent Palace of the Lost City hotel that overlooked the scenic valley like an African citadel. Its towers, embellished with elephant tusks, could be seen throughout the huge complex and the hotel was surrounded by lush botanical gardens. Wayne and I exchanged worried glances: could we afford to stay here? The answer came in a heartbeat: absolutely, yes. It was not every day we got the chance to do this.

Here, among the opulence of safari-style marquees adorned with plush cushions to offer respite from the sun, luscious fruit served on silver trays and the pungent smell of coconut oil on ample-waisted, bikini-clad tourists, the difference between the haves and have-nots was stark. At dinner that night, I apologised to our African waiter for wasting some of the food on my plate. 'Oh, it will not be wasted,' he assured me, smiling and taking my plate. 'I will take it home to my family.'

John was driving; I was the passenger as we headed back towards Pretoria. We chatted about his life and travels, and his father, Greg Milton's name was mentioned. 'He's a good-looking fella, John – just like you,' I said. He grinned at the compliment, and then realised what I had said.

'Have you met him?' he asked.

'Yes.'

He pulled the car over to the side of the road. 'When?'

'Last month.'

'Did he know you were coming over here, to meet me?'

'Yes, he did.' I hesitated. This was way out of my area and I didn't know what response I would get. 'Look, he's given me his phone number to pass to you. He wants to know if you would call him, or would you give him your phone number? He's desperate to get in touch with both you and Bianca.'

'Is that what he said? Really? He wants to see us?' John was weeping openly now. 'Please – give him my number.'

At Christmas, the call came.

'Hello, Greg? This is your son, John.'

Greg, who has now converted to Islam and lives in Asia with his new wife, could not describe the joy he felt at hearing John's voice. 'I was shaking with nerves,' he later told me. 'It was a total surprise. We met that same night and talked until the early hours of the morning, catching up on the past.'

There was a lot of catching up to do. They had not seen each other since 1981. John organised too for Greg to see his daughter, Bianca.

59

WHILE RESEARCHING AN ARTICLE entitled 'The Iron Lady' for the *Good Weekend* magazine, journalist Jane Kadzow admitted that, like me, she had found it difficult to get people to talk about Gina. And, as also happened to me in 1999, she was refused any help from the Rinehart camp unless Gina could see the copy.

Cynics questioned the timing of the article's release, shortly after Gina's increased stake in Fairfax shares. Was this the last opportunity, they asked, for Fairfax journalists to be able to write it as they saw it? But despite the obstacles, Kadzow found some telling vignettes.

During the Queen's visit to Australia in October 2011, Prince Philip and his wife attended a garden party at Government House, where the Prince 'stopped to chat to a middle-aged woman in a broad-brimmed black hat', Kadzow wrote. The woman was Gina Rinehart, who replied somewhat coquettishly to his inquiry about why she was on the guest list that she was 'merely a loyal subject'. The Prince, not known for his patience, repeated his question as to why she was there, but Gina still would not disclose who she was. A fellow guest who overheard the exchange later commented how modest Gina was to not reveal her identity. 'He looked a bit annoyed, in fact, because he was looking for a straight answer,' she said. The Prince moved on, but not before suggesting to Gina that she was perhaps there because she had 'the largest hat in Western Australia'. They both laughed. Not one to doff his metaphorical hat to anyone, if he realised that he had just exchanged greetings with Gina Rinehart, who financially outstrips his wife, Queen Elizabeth II, the Prince did not let on.

But the hat story did not end there.

Waiting on a response from Gina as to whether she would talk to her, Kadzow fervently hoped that she hadn't seen any online articles about the garden party exchange, in *The Age* and *The Sydney Morning Herald*, headlined 'Prince Philip Pokes Fun at Gina Rinehart'. The article quoted a guest at the party claiming that the Prince had said: 'That hat could poke someone's eye out.' Alas, the article was seen. Hancock Prospecting Information Manager Mark Bickerton wrote to Kadzow: 'Regarding the recent discussion with HRH at Government House in West Australia,' the letter says, 'other media who were present reported it was a very happy and relaxed discussion between HRH and Mrs Rinehart . . . Your publication however chose to make the extraordinary and unbelievable claim that HRH told Mrs Rinehart that her non-pointy hat was pointy and may poke someone's eye out! Obviously HRH would have seen many hats over the years and would not choose to stop to speak to someone for the purpose of criticising their hat, including a hat worn in honour of his wife, the Queen. This is an insult by the *SMH* to not only Mrs Rinehart, but importantly HRH.'

Clearly, *we are not amused.*

'And no,' Kadzow concluded, 'she doesn't want to be interviewed.'

*

Like her father, who preferred an austere personal lifestyle prior to his marriage to Rose, Gina rarely indulges in the high life unless there is a business opportunity attached and is known to be frugal in her personal spending. But she is acknowledged in the industry as a good payer, her staff salaries well above industry standards. 'I guess that is necessary to have people stick around,' a former insider says. 'I don't think she splashes her money around needlessly.' He recounts a story of when John and Bianca were staying at the Dalkeith house years ago. 'John, then an adolescent, left a towel drying over the pool heater, which started a fire,' he says. 'A neighbour called the fire brigade but the fire truck couldn't get through the gate. So the neighbour let them through his property. The fire engine then crashed through the fence to get to Gina's property. The fence remained broken for a while and eventually the neighbour phoned Gina's office to have it fixed. He was told, "Go ahead – fix the fence – and Gina will pay half!" Somebody obviously forgot to remember that the neighbour's fence was broken in order to save her house from fire! Then again,' he reasons, 'maybe the fence was rotten anyway and so her office took a commercial line; they think that they are a target because of Gina's wealth.' He considers a press report which stated that former employees regarded Gina as a 'penny pincher'. 'I don't think that's right,' he says. 'I think it's more a case of Gina rationalising things, such as payouts to Dalby and McCamey. The situation with her children seems like a control thing, rather than penny pinching. Maybe she believes they are not yet capable of handling the money and power? Her refusal to hand over Rhodes Ridge is understandable if put in the context of Gina's belief that her father did everything and that the Wrights have gained more than they deserve from the partnership. But the truth is that Lang needed Peter very badly; once he was not part of his endeavours they went completely off the rails. Also, keeping Rhodes Ridge locked up in litigation gave Gina a free kick with her Hope Downs project. Hope Downs should have been developed after Rhodes Ridge, but it has been operating for years and Rhodes Ridge is still tied up in an ownership dispute.'

According to her friends, Gina is careful in her personal spending, eschewing the spectacular trappings of great wealth. But as much as she is driven by a powerful work ethic, her money does afford her some luxuries: holidays at Versace's resort in Italy; accommodation at the Paris Ritz; a permanent penthouse suite on the cruise liner *The World*. But even at leisure, it seems Gina can be demanding. A former employee of *The World* recalls the staff reaction to news that Gina was coming aboard. 'Nervous. Really nervous. Like a lot of extremely wealthy people, she can be very demanding, and she sets a high bar.'

60

PRIOR TO HIS DEATH, in order to cover a large debt to HPPL, Hancock sold his Life Governor's share in the company he founded to the Hancock Family Memorial Foundation for $20 million. When the Life Governor's share changed hands, it lost its special powers and then ranked pari passu with other shares. 'That is the reason why Gina is claiming that the amount paid for the share was ridiculous and is one of the reasons she was suing Carnie Fieldhouse,' my source says. 'Now she continues to sue Carnie's legal practice insurer, LawCover.'

It was a sale that would come under bitter scrutiny, with the foundation later alleging that Fieldhouse had a negligent conflict of interest by acting on behalf of both Hancock and the foundation. In short, the foundation claimed, they had paid too much. Far too much.

Gina and the foundation want damages.

Inherent in the claim is the loss of value on Lang's Life Governor's share and that the directors of HFMF approved the transaction because it was what Lang wanted. 'Incredibly,' the

286

source says, 'the foundation put out their hand to the New South Wales Law Society to help. The society has a collection plate of sorts, taking contributions from all New South Wales lawyers to help finance discretionary professional indemnity claims. But they didn't win. The discretionary clause meant there wasn't an insurance contract between Carnie and the society.'

Long-time associates of Carnie are savage about the legal wrangle that followed Lang's death. 'Carnie was more than a family lawyer – he was treated as part of the families,' a source tells me. 'I doubt either Hancock or Wright thought he was in some way an Artful Dodger. They had retained his services for decades and thought highly of him. I imagine they would both have been devastated by Gina's legal actions following Lang's death.'

He ponders other reasons the foundation – Gina – instigated legal proceedings against Carnie. 'Perhaps Gina was so upset that he was at her father's wedding to Rose that she could not forgive him. Perhaps she thinks Carnie had a hand in the bitter acrimony between her father and her, which was later sorted out? Carnie saved the partnership a fortune in tax, so it seems ironic that Gina's company would sue him. Much of his work was done by a staff lawyer who was never made a partner, but Carnie himself had a huge job. Hancock was once one of Australia's biggest taxpayers and relied implicitly on his judgments. The litigation against him was not only stressful, it hurt him very much. It's very hard to understand the reasons why Gina turns her back on the people her father so trusted.'

Approached to talk about Hancock in 2000, Carnie was polite but firm. 'I have made it my practice to not discuss Lang in either a personal or a business sense over the past four decades,' he told me. 'I do not intend to change that now.'

In November 2007 Carnie went to his grave, still abiding by his promise.

61

GINA MADE NO BONES about her strident opposition to the Federal Government's proposed Mineral Resource Rent Tax (MRRT), which replaced the Resource Super Profit Tax (RSPT). The MRRT was mooted to tax profits that flowed from the exploitation of non-renewable Australian resources. In theory, the idea was to tax 30 per cent of the 'super profits' from iron ore and coal mining in Australia; in practice, it was negotiated that a company would be liable to pay when its annual profit reached $75 million.

The MRRT had the support of some major players, including trade unions, BHP Billiton and the Rio Tinto Group. But it had some extremely potent opposition: the mining industry, mining organisations, lobby groups and the Liberal and National parties.

One of the most vocal opponents was Gina.

In 2010, she threw off her private mantle and joined Atlas Iron chief David Flanagan and Fortescue Metals Group boss Andrew 'Twiggy' Forrest at an 'Axe the Tax' rally opposing the scheme. Forrest, like Gina, has some powerful allies, including billionaire James Packer and media mogul duo Kerry Stokes and Rupert Murdoch. And, like Gina, Forrest didn't mince words on the proposed Minerals Resource Rent Tax. It was, he stated, 'economic vandalism' and a 'mad dog's breakfast'.

The 2000-strong crowd held up placards exhorting the government to 'Mine your own business' and 'I don't want to lose my job' while Gina, with Twiggy, stood on a makeshift stage on the back of a flat-bed truck, microphone in hand, bellowing to the crowd.

While Flanagan and Forrest introduced speakers, in between ringing a large bell and repeating the mantra, it was Gina who caught most attention. Her usually deathly-quiet voice was raised in a holler, her cheeks flushed from the heat and exertion as she implored the crowd to let its collective voice be heard in Canberra and for Canberra to 'Axe the Tax!' By the end of the rally, she had virtually lost her own voice.

Gina's exhortations did not sit well with everyone. 'Under the Constitution the states own the minerals and so the proposed federal tax on mining is morally unconstitutional,' a source tells me. 'But the Feds have designed it as a tax on profits rather than as a royalty on the mineral extracted; they would probably win if there were to be a High Court challenge. This is yet another example of where the law is an ass; even the title of the new tax says it is a tax on minerals! Everyone knows that the Feds are imposing the equivalent of a royalty on minerals and thereby usurping a right that belongs to the states.' He gives a simplistic comparison. 'Suppose the Feds decided to impose an extra tax on rent from houses. There would be a revolution! Owners of houses would argue that they should not have to pay a higher tax than others because it would be discriminatory. The owners could elect to increase the rent – and that would be OK. But in the case of minerals, they are owned by the state governments and the mining companies are like tenants: they pay the rent set by the owners; a royalty. That royalty is usually a fixed percentage of the value of the mineral extracted. So Gina has a valid argument – but she is not a good look. The billionaires banded together on their makeshift stage – Palmer, Forrest, Gina – arguing that the new tax is unfair. Not a good look at all.'

He attended the rally and recalls thinking how out of touch Gina was with the common man. 'There she was, standing there with a string of bloody huge pearls around her neck and yelling out against a tax that would have flown through to the person on the street,' he said. 'Could someone perhaps have advised her that this was not the most strategic tack to take?'

Jim McGinty, too, was less than impressed. 'Gina has a particular view of the world and she wants to make sure that point of view is heard,' he told me by telephone from his Perth home. 'Her opposition to the mining tax is a classic example. What an unedifying spectacle that was. She has inherited her wealth but she doesn't want to share it with anyone. How many billions does she need, actually, to be happy? There are two ways that the wealth from mining can be distributed through the community: one is through taxes, the other is through wages paid to individuals. Gina doesn't want either. She wants to keep it all for herself. The other big players, Rio and BHP, accept the need to make a contribution.

'People in the mining sector,' he continued, 'are doing incredibly well but there are many more people who are struggling to make ends meet. Gina has said that "We should, on humanitarian grounds, give more of these people the opportunity of guest labour work in Australia, so that they can feed and clothe their families and pay for medical and other pressing needs." What this actually means is that Gina wants to turn the Pilbara into an economic-free zone, which is code for bringing in cheap African and Asian labour to help build ports, railways and mines. Import them, exploit them, then send them home with a pittance. It's not right.' Unions also strongly oppose the idea, as does her mining partner, Rio Tinto.

Whatever its merits, the anti-tax rally proved to have far-reaching consequences and was another nail in Prime Minister Kevin Rudd's pro-mining tax coffin. A staunch and vocal advocate for the tax, just two weeks later he was unceremoniously dumped from the Labor leadership. His successor and former deputy, Julia Gillard, was in a conciliatory mood; shortly after consultation with large mining firms, the new government announced changes in the form of a watered-down tax that appeased mining and business.

While Rudd's June 2010 overthrow was regarded by many as a treacherous, Machiavellian act, numerous political commentators cited the vocal opposition to the mining tax from both the super-rich and blue-collar workers as a strong contributing cause. Rudd didn't stand a chance: as the ABC *Four Corners* program 'The Comeback Kid?' noted, in 2010 foreign-owned mining companies spent a whopping $23 million on their anti-mining tax campaign.

62

FOLLOWING AN UNSUCCESSFUL ATTEMPT to settle matters in a mediation hearing in 2011, 88-year-old Stan Perron, who bankrolled Hancock and Wright in 1959 to the tune of today's equivalent of $13,000 in return for a 15 per cent royalty from all iron ore produced from Hamersley's operation, is now set to battle both HPPL and WPPL through the courts over his claims to both past and future royalties from the 'Brockman' mine, a group of Rio Tinto iron ore deposits about 60 kilometres north-west of Tom Price.

In July 1992, a Rinehart executive advised Stan Perron that Hamersley Iron was mining at Brockman but that his 15 per cent share did not entitle him to a claim on any royalties flowing from it.

Initially, Perron accepted the advice from Rinehart's representative. But on a blistering-hot day, as he inspected the massive expansion of Rio Tinto's Pilbara operations, Perron came to the belief that geographically, his interests fell within the Hanwright royalty group and that he may, resultingly, be entitled to a significantly higher royalty flow from the 1964 deal he had made with Hancock and Wright. At present, Perron gets 15 per cent of Hancock and Wright's 2.5 per cent royalty on some of the areas mined by Rio Tinto Iron Ore.

In his claim, lodged in WA's Supreme Court by Perron's trust company, SP Investments, Perron states that: '. . . the Brockman royalties are part of the royalty payments payable by Hamersley Iron pursuant to the royalty agreement' made decades ago with Hancock and Wright.

Within three years, Rio's new Brockman 4 mine is poised to be a massive operation, buoyed by feeding Asia's voracious appetite for high-grade iron ore. From start-up, it will produce 22 million tonnes a year, a figure that Rio claims will double in a few short years. 'Based on today's iron ore prices, by 2014 this massive mine could generate up to $150 million in annual royalties for the Rinehart and Wright families,' my source explains. 'If Perron's area is deemed to encompass Brockman 4, the figures are staggering; potentially hundreds of millions of dollars over 20 years. Other deposits are in the same category, so at current prices the argument concerns a royalty flow of about $30 million per annum, continuing for at least 20 years.'

He shakes his head. 'More litigation. It just never seems to end. Perron, Hancock and Wright had been good friends during their lifetime. Again, it's a shame it's come to this.'

In the bold move of putting her money where her mouth is, Gina founded the climate denial lobby group Australians for Northern Development and Economic Vision (ANDEV). Its policies echo that of her late father's visions, and demand the creation of 'a special Northern Economic Zone stretching across the north of West Australia, the Northern Territory and northern Queensland, where companies can bring in tempo-rary labour'. Australia, it warns, is facing a real threat as the government makes growth in a competitive market increasingly difficult by imposing new taxes and forcing mining companies to move their business overseas. 'Other countries have governments that look to the future,' it says. 'Ours just looks down the road to the next election.' ANDEV's other demands include no super tax or equivalent, lower personal income tax or tax rebates for those who live and work in the Northern Zone, and lowered or eliminated payroll tax. Its membership includes some big-hitters with controversial views: John McRobert, the former adviser to the extreme right-wing Pauline Hanson; Mannkal Foundation chairperson and long-time friend of Gina, Ron Manners; and Ian Plimer.

Like her father, who would not back away from airing his controversial views in the face of harsh criticism, Gina would not be defeated in her crusade against the government's carbon tax. In a sentiment that eerily echoed Lang's disdain for bureaucracy, she demanded that these taxes be dropped, or risk bureaucracy becoming the only growth industry in Australia. We should demand from our politicians, she railed, that they have a majority by referendum before they introduce any new taxes.

Using her nous and clout, Gina appointed a well-known figure to help bolster her dismissal of theories that global warming is induced by humans. This time, she turned to geologist and Professor of Mining Geology at the University of Adelaide, Ian Rutherford Plimer, one of Australia's most prominent climate-change sceptics, to further her cause, appointing him to sit on the boards of two of her leading companies. Plimer's controversial view – that man-made climate change is a myth – has ensured him global attention, much of it negative. But Gina was generous in her praise of him, describing Plimer as one of the 'leading sources of reasoned and factual information in Australia on global warming and climate change' today. Whilst Plimer has many vocal critics, his supporters believe he is a dedicated academic not influenced by his association with the mining industry or his ownership of mining shares. They argue that his ideas should be challenged using logic or science. Climate change is an emotive issue and one which is inexorably linked in government policy to the contentious carbon tax, which will tax polluters on the per-tonne of carbon they release into the environment. By 2015, this tax will change to a trading scheme where the market will dictate the price. While its supporters claim this is the best way to manage the reduction of carbon output and in turn reduce climate change, Gina and her cohorts disagree.

Plimer, a life member of the Australian Skeptics, describes the proposed carbon-trading scheme as one which could potentially destroy the Australian mining industry as well as create massive unemployment. In this view, he has powerful allies, including Gina and Scottish politician and former newspaper editor Viscount Christopher Monckton, whose peerage is inherited. Gina gave Monckton a free forum by bringing back to life the Lang Hancock Lecture, which she sponsors at Fremantle's Notre Dame University and where he spoke during his early 2010 tour of Australia on climate change. But the eccentric Scot is not a lone ranger; behind him is the Galileo Movement, so-named after Italian Galileo Galilei, the 'father of science' who proved that the sun did not orbit the earth. According to the Galileo website, he stood up publicly and almost lost his life to ensure objective science replaced superstition, ideology, ignorance and state control. The Galileo Movement's godfather is talkback host Alan Jones, and the movement is also backed by the full weight of Gina Rinehart, who underwrote Monckton's tour of Australia. Reluctant to admit who had paid his airfares, the Viscount fudged the issue, claiming to be unencumbered by being a paid mouthpiece and not having any knowledge of the finer details. The ABC's Wendy Carlisle tried to nail him on the subject: '. . . there have been some reports that Gina Rinehart brought you out here.'

'Well I think that's extremely unlikely . . . In the old days they could have done such a thing quite cheerfully and nobody would have batted an eyelid and everybody would have understood that if their workers' jobs were as directly under threat as they now are, that would have been a perfectly acceptable thing to do . . . And so I very much doubt whether she had anything to do with it, and that is a question, in any case, for her and not for me.'

In a 2011 ABC *Drum* opinion piece, journalist Graham Readfearn summed up his take on Monckton's views: 'Among other things, Lord Monckton argues that attempts by governments and the United Nations to reduce emissions of greenhouse gases from deforestation and burning fossil fuels are part of a conspiracy to install a world government. In Lord Monckton's eyes it's all a socialist plot.' *The Australian*'s columnist Phillip Adams could also not let the opportunity pass to have a dig at the climate change deniers. 'Praise the lord for Lord Monckton! For Ian Plimer! For Andrew Bolt! Not only does this evil axis of scientists tell lies [about the greenhouse effect] but they've also doctored the weather to frighten people with huge droughts, cyclones and tsunamis to prove what they now call "global warming".'

63

LIKE HER FATHER, GINA'S move into publishing was geared towards control of media to push her own ideas. But she would do it bigger and better, just as she intends with her own mine. Gina's escalation of shares in Fairfax, from her original 4.9 per cent holding, for which she outlaid $100 million, to almost 13 per cent – which cost around $150 million – got the punters talking. Suddenly, Gina Rinehart's name was on everyone's lips. 'You couldn't go anywhere without hearing it,' a Perth resident told me. 'Everyone was talking about her opposition to mining taxes, the feud with her kids and her buy-up of Fairfax shares at a time when you can't even give a newspaper away. But, you know, the overriding sentiment was a line from that old Beatles song: "Can't Buy Me Love".'

Gina's entrée to becoming a major shareholder in Fairfax did not change the mantra of those who work there who insist that the company's independence of thought will remain strong. With an eye to a bargain, Gina had again lucked out, picking up the shares at an historically low price. The question was, in a digital age, why would Gina want to buy into traditional media? The answer, according to Fairfax business journalist Adele Ferguson, is that 'traditional media is still the most effective way to influence state and federal politics'. Citing other major players such as Kerry Stokes and James Packer who have long recognised the clout of traditional media, she continued that Rinehart's raid was timed just before the release of a report into media convergence. 'There is no doubt there will be sweeping changes to the way media companies and content are regulated, which will further loosen cross-media ownership laws.' If that is the outcome, Gina will have jumped the gun with an advanced position in cross-ownership.

If, in turn, the recommendations became legislation, it would create a climate for takeovers. And therein is the rub. 'Buying a stake in Fairfax and pushing for a board seat does two things,' Ferguson wrote. 'It gives Rinehart influence either overtly or more subtly, and it gives her a seat at the table in any potential takeover with the ability to either encourage it or block it.'

Gina's expansion from mining to media was widely considered a grab for power and to influence public debate, and not one based on financial considerations. As Tim Treadgold told the ABC, Gina could buy Fairfax with loose change.

Commentators and political players flooded radio, television and print media with their viewpoints, many warning that Australia could end up seeing a super-monopoly by the super-rich for media control. Their fears were heightened by footage of Lord Monckton, posted online, preaching to the converted at a Mannkal meeting in July last year. He could not have made himself plainer. Australia needed a proper dose of free-market thinking and they should encourage 'super-rich' backers to invest in a local version of Fox News, he told his captive audience. 'Frankly, whatever you do at a street level . . . is not going to have much of an impact compared with capturing an entire news media.' It is a strategy that mirrors Gina's views.

In a lively interview in early February, Queensland-based mining magnate Clive Palmer told Tony Jones on the ABC's *Lateline* that he found the idea of following in Gina's footsteps for a stake in the media 'very attractive'.

'You could have an east–west play with Fairfax,' he said, jolly and smiling. 'Gina should come from the west and buy 15 per cent and we could buy 30 per cent from the eastern side of Australia and really get the place humming again . . . She's a very, very smart woman so if she's going after Fairfax there must be something in it.'

'. . . what would be in it, one imagines,' Jones countered, 'is the ability to exert influence on policy, on government policy particularly in the mining area. Do you think that should happen?'

Palmer answered no to that question, but agreed that he would seriously consider 'going into some kind of media partnership with Gina Rinehart. 'Absolutely . . . we've certainly got excess money to spend . . .'

As media commentators studied the question of just how much power and, in turn, influence should be afforded to minority shareholders, it was suggested that Gina should be given a dose of her own medicine, and be barred from getting a seat on the board until 2068 – the year which she had secretly extended the vesting date of trust fund to for her children. Would the board want her there, anyway, after all the adverse publicity she has recently attracted? 'The other issue, of course, is that she's got her feet in both camps,' a journalist source said. 'She's on the board at Ten and wants to get onto the Fairfax board as well. She should get out of Ten if she wants to be taken seriously for a board position at Fairfax. She's also into getting her message across online in a big way, and guess who is the star of online media? Fairfax.'

In increasing her Fairfax share, in early 2012, Gina flew under the 15 per cent limit bar of Australian media ownership rules. The government's cross-media review was established to address changes that might be needed as a result of the growth of internet-based media. This raised the suggestion that Gina's move may have been timed to give her a strategic position across different media in case ownership laws are relaxed. In Western Australia, Fairfax controls Perth radio station 6PR and several regional newspapers. Combined with her interest in Channel 10, it potentially adds up to considerable influence and a dangerous concentration of power. If the review were to recommend abolishing cross-media ownership rules, Gina would be in a strong position to increase her control or to block others from attempting the same in Western Australia.

The interim report of the Finklestein Inquiry was mainly concerned with abolishing the Press Council and replacing it with a new government oversight department to make the media more accountable. It certainly stirred up some strong sentiment among journalists. Bob Cronin, group editor-in-chief of West Australian Newspapers, described it as 'the most outrageous assault on our democracy in the history of the media' – a mild description in comparison to some others.

Lang himself had grand visions for media control, which he expounded during the 'Wake Up Australia' era. The power of government, he wrote, could be broken by obtaining control of the media and then educating the public. 'Control of the press could also be obtained by several of the big mining groups banding together with a view to taking over one or more of the present giant newspaper chains which control the TV and radio channels, and converting them to the path of "free enterprise".'

A Western Australian political watcher, who asked to remain anonymous, vented his spleen about the rising power of Australia's super-rich. 'It was once incumbent upon kings, queens and other rulers to take care of their subjects,' he told me. 'The current rulers of this country are people like Ms Rinehart who take the resources and profit from the nation and give us little more in return than a spray from the back of a truck screaming "Axe the Tax", which is not the slightest bit becoming for one who holds the mantle. She should realise that taking a huge profit from our collective resources without being prepared to share a little more with her fellow Australians is unacceptable. Her growing media interests are worrying as it would appear that she'd like to take a leaf out of Rupert Murdoch's newspapers and other media interests and have a go at running the country for us. Fairfax already has a stranglehold on around 30 per cent of our newspaper market, and Rupert's got a lion's share of the rest. Kerry Stokes has his fingers in the pie at *The West Australian* newspaper and at Channel 7 and Packer/Murdoch and Gina are on the board at Channel 10. Gina and her cohorts want to mould the media so it toes their party line. It's scary. Very scary indeed.'

Another commented that if Gina seriously wants to influence media in Australia, then people need to look at the sorts of ideas she supports. 'Some of them are the whacky anti-Canberra concepts her father had, such as wanting WA to secede. That's like a child stamping its feet because it can't get its own way. She also supported his proposal to use nuclear explosives for port development and mining, though she doesn't appear quite as vocal about that now. She takes extreme positions on major issues such as economics, taxation and climate change while at the same time wanting to import cheap Asian labour to the north of Australia to make herself even *more* money. This is bundled up in the platitude that it's a humanitarian gesture. So what sort of influence would she have on media, given the opportunity?'

Gina surrounds herself with the best people in the business, whose backgrounds range from legal, operational or financial experience in various industries, mining or government. To earn a place in the inner sanctum is particularly difficult; to keep it, even harder. In an oft-seen picture of Gina sitting at a glass-topped table in the boardroom of Hancock Prospecting, she looks the epitome of a corporate boss. She is posed identically to a photograph taken of Hancock in the 1970s, at the same table. The only difference is that Hancock holds a lump of iron ore in his hand. 'That picture of Gina tells a thousand words,' the mining insider comments. 'Not just "like father, like daughter", but "make no mistake who's the boss". To work successfully for Gina, you've got to fall into line with her demands.

In 2011 Gina recruited the Honourable Cheryl Edwardes, the first Western Australian female Attorney-General in the Court Government and former Environment Minister, as head of government relations. Edwardes defends her boss against accusations that her hugely expensive forays into the Ten Network and Fairfax Media were instrumental in buying Gina political clout. Instead, she countered, it was 'definitely a business decision', adding that if Gina wanted to influence debate, she could simply use her website to do so. 'The question is, what effect will Gina's media shareholdings have on her ability to platform her ideas?' a source asks. 'It remains to be seen if her political influence and pushing of her right-wing ideology will increase now.' He adds that Gina has a determination to succeed that he has rarely seen in another individual. 'Remember that young girl who warned that nothing would stand in the way of the House of Hancock? Well, she's now a middle-aged woman who pushes all the boundaries to get what she wants.'

Gina's executive director and right-hand man, Tad Watroba – the only other full-time board director next to Gina whom she trusts to speak to the media – has been with the company since 1991, joining shortly before Hancock's death. A Polish refugee, 65-year-old Watroba is fiercely protective of Gina, a loyalty she rewarded two years ago by renaming her Alpha coal project in Queensland Tad's Corner. On his birthday, he

302

was also rewarded with a piece of Gina's poetry, in which she annointed him as 'earning her trust'. This time, the poem was not set in stone but posted on the ANDEV website. Other executives include her Chief Financial Officer Jay Newby who, along with her daughter Ginia, alternatively sits on the board, managing director Paul Mulder, general counsel, Terry Walsh, executive general manager for carbon steel Barry Fitzgerald, and chief development officer, John Klepec. With the avalanche of press reports following the fracas with her children, she has also contracted media adviser, Ian Smith, of Bespoke Approach, to help her negotiate the overwhelming public interest she has drawn.

64

FIFTY-TWO-YEAR-OLD NEWS LIMITED JOURNALIST and commentator Andrew Bolt is best known for three things: his extreme conservatism and right-wing politics, his close professional affinity with people who share his views on the nonsense of man-made climate change and his repeated question, 'But by how much will the carbon tax lower the world's temperature?' In Bolt's world, no cause is sacred. Lefties, Muslims, pokie reform – they all get a relentless serve. And Bolt has some very powerful, super-wealthy allies prepared to back his mantras, including John Singleton, James Packer and Gina Rinehart. Known as a very smart operator, opponents of his right-wing viewpoints consider him as something of a ventriloquist's dummy for those who give him the opportunity to espouse their views in a public forum. And he espouses them with the short, sharp language of a radio or television grab and with an eye to tomorrow's headlines. His style is to corral his interviewees, round 'em up and hit them with a verbal volley in order to elicit responses to his questions. Carbon tax is 'the most brazen fraud'; the mining super-profits tax is a 'meat axe to our mining industry'; his opinion of the benefits of reducing CO_2 emissions that: 'even if we cut emissions today, global temperatures are not likely to drop for about 1000 years'.

Then, like a magical rabbit out of a hat trick, he appeared on his own Sunday morning television show on Network Ten, the *Bolt Report*. The timing of the program – shortly after Gina got a seat on the Ten Network board – raised serious questions about her influence. In conjunction with his gig on Sydney radio station 2GB, where his equally conservative talkback colleagues Alan Jones and Ray Hadley voice their right-wing opinions to a huge audience, this new program delivers Bolt some pulling power. And that, according to Singleton, is a good thing. 'We have been able to overtly and covertly attack governments,' he told journalist Jane Kadzow. 'Because we have people employed by us like Andrew Bolt and Alan Jones and Ray Hadley who agree with [Gina's] thinking about the development of our resources, we act in concert in that way.'

But not everyone agrees that Bolt's television program was gifted to him from Gina on a silver platter. '[There is] no way that would have happened against the better judgment of Ten's programmers,' editor in chief of *Business Spectator* and *Eureka Report*, Alan Kohler, commented. He added, wryly, 'No doubt they were ready to try anything to combat the dominance of your correspondent [himself] in the 10 am time slot on Sunday.'

Forbes magazine cut to the chase. Rinehart, it said, was breaking free from her 'mould of ultra-wealthy heiress' to use her money for influence, most notably in her campaign against Australia's environmental reforms, including taxes on 'extractive industries like mining that have a heavy footprint'.

In February 2012, Kohler cautioned that Gina Rinehart is likely to find investing in Fairfax Media a 'deeply frustrating experience, whether she's trying to influence the newspapers or just make money'. 'She was raised on mining and right-wing politics and was taught by her father that owning media was a source of influence, along with giving politicians money directly and nagging them, and everyone, endlessly about the benefits of small government and the evils of environmentalism,' he wrote. 'Gina is not a nag like her father and she hangs onto her money like a limpet, although she is starting to dabble in media companies. But she will need to buy more than 15 per cent of Fairfax to have any say – even if she does manage to get on the board.' Lang, he wrote, had made a 'lot of noise and gave a lot of cash to favoured politicians' but mostly 'wasted his breath and his money', although he added to the rise of right-wing politics around the world in the 1980s. He continued, 'Gina Rinehart appears to be an unreconstructed Thatcherite/Reaganite as well as a full-blown climate sceptic . . . As for buying 235 million Fairfax shares at 81.8 cents as an investment – it's a Roulette play, in my view . . . there are far better speculative plays in the industry Gina Rinehart knows best.'

65

IN MAY 2011, RINEHART wrote against what she called the 'global warming fear campaign' in an opinion piece entitled 'Australian Business Leaders – Where Are You?' in the mining industry magazine *Australian Resources and Investment*. In a nutshell the article encapsulated her views and left many open-mouthed. But it was a perfect forum. If you don't trust the majority of journalists to quote you correctly and push your views, why not write the story yourself?

Gina hit her pet topic early. 'Some mainstream media like to attack me because I speak out against a carbon tax,' she wrote. 'It's a pity more business executives don't speak out, because really this proposal should have been dropped long ago. Let me say how very proud I am of my fellow Australians, who, in recent polls, are voting in the majority against a carbon tax. We are showing we can think for ourselves, and are not swayed by the global warming fear campaign.'

Citing the example of a highly educated 27-year-old she had recently met overseas, she wrote that this young entrepreneur had opined that Australia, with its great resources, needs a reduction in taxation levels to provide 'better incentives' and that we should also reduce approvals, permits and licence processes. Yet what is Australia doing, she asked? 'Not only maintaining its taxes, but bringing in two more very messy taxes – MRRT and carbon tax – which will seriously undermine Australia's competitiveness and increase our costs across the board.'

Gina then moved to an attack on mainstream media's scare campaign about carbon-induced global warming. 'The theme has now changed to carbon dioxide-induced "climate change"... Even before human civilisation, the world went through ice ages and periods of global warming. There will always be changes that affect our climate, even if we close down all thermal coal-fired power stations, steel mills and other manufacturing operations, putting employees out of work and drastically changing our way of life. I have never met a geologist or leading scientist who believes that adding more carbon dioxide to the atmosphere will have any significant effect on climate change, especially not from a relatively small country like Australia . . .'

Gina's take on the carbon tax or the MRRT on thermal coal was its own fear campaign. She warned the government was not providing all the information it should and that unemployment would be a direct result. 'It is not just the rich mining companies that would be affected, but every man, woman and child in Australia, not to mention blue-collar workers whose jobs in steel mills, power stations and manufacturing facilities would suffer or disappear.'

And what for, she asked? 'It won't stop China and India from continuing to emit carbon dioxide on their own account. These nations understand that you cannot raise a population's standard of living without also increasing energy consumption.'

We need to become a country that the best in the world want to immigrate to, she wrote – a country with enough wealth to properly care for its increasingly elderly population, to enable us to defend ourselves against internal crime, war and terrorism. And she raised the spectre of non-permanent migrant labour. 'In addition it is important we do not prevent or delay guest labour from working in hot and remote areas of the country where Australians are often reluctant to work. Guest labour for pre-construction and construction is essential, particularly in remote areas.'

There are some issues to consider in this article. How much is Gina wanting to pay the guest labour? Is it our standard wage, or less? What of our own unemployed in Australia? The Pilbara is now flooded with people, men and women seeking work and big bucks in just those remote areas that Gina is referring to. And her opinion of climate change? Why *hasn't* she met a leading scientist with opposing views to her own? She seems to have met everyone else.

In an essay in *The Monthly* magazine in February 2012 which mauled the self-interest of the super-rich, Treasurer Wayne Swan vented his outrage at what he called the 'rising power of vested interests'. Referring to the slogan on a T-shirt a young man was wearing a decade ago – *Greed is good. Trample the weak. Hurdle the dead* – he commented that the words encapsulated a growing sense of unease in Australia at that time. 'Today,' he continued, 'when a would-be US president, Mitt Romney, is wealthier than 99.9975% of his fellow Americans, and wealthier than the last eight presidents combined, there's a global conversation raging about the rich, the poor, the gap between them, and the role of vested interests in the significant widening of that gap in advanced economies over the past three decades.' The power of those interests, he continued, is undermining our equality and threatening our democracy. He cited Rinehart's foray into Fairfax Media as an example. She did this to further her commercial interests and to wield greater influence on public opinion at a time, he wrote, when it is critical that the economic resources boom helps strengthen the entire economy.

Liberal frontbencher Christopher Pyne didn't agree. The essay, he sniffed, was an example of 'class warfare and the politics of envy'. Clive Palmer didn't agree, either. Swan, he said, was an 'intellectual pygmy'.

66

IN SEPTEMBER 2011, NEWS that Gina's three oldest children
– John, Bianca and Hope – were taking court action to remove
their mother as trustee of the Hope Margaret Hancock Trust
on the grounds of alleged 'serious misconduct' was met with
a mixture of derision and astonishment. Suddenly, the meticulously constructed veil of privacy that Gina had battled for years
to keep tightly around the family was torn away when personal
emails between herself, Bianca and Hope were splashed across
newspapers around the globe. The emails were submitted into
evidence in a Sydney court, but the children's email addresses
were not obscured. With the veil now lifted, Australia could
finally glimpse some of the reasons Gina is so controlling of her
children's money and why she believes they don't need to take
court action against her to get it. Equally significantly Hope
who, with Ginia, was kept closely guarded from the media by
Gina, was suddenly propelled into the spotlight by her own
doing.

'What a sad irony,' one Perth source commented to me. 'For all Gina's money, she failed to stop their private lives hitting the limelight and the media circus that followed publication of those details. Whatever you think of her, it must surely have hurt.'

At the heart of the dispute is Gina's claim that all four children agreed in a signed 2006 document that there would be no airing of dirty linen but that family disputes after that time would be resolved in private, via mediation or arbitration. Gina tried desperately to keep it all under wraps, winning an interim non-publication order at the start of proceedings in late 2011. Justice Paul Brereton stated the obvious. 'This is not the first occasion of discord in the family, which has immense wealth, no small part of which resides in the trust. In the past, the affairs of the family, including such discord, has attracted considerable publicity in the media.' By October, Justice Brereton gave the judgment that he intended to dismiss an application by Rinehart that there be a stay on court action, directing the family into mediation. It kept grinding through the courts: prior to Christmas, suppression orders on the case were lifted but a stay granted until February 2012 and later extended by the High Court of Australia until early March. Gina's team pushed for the suppressions, while Hope, John, Bianca and media lawyers opposed them. Gina's lawyers tried again, this time for a non-publication order based on fear of personal and family safety. This failed to win over the sympathies of the New South Wales Supreme Court, who dismissed it in early February. Instead of the desired outcome, Gina's failed and costly legal attempt to suppress the nature of the legal action resulted in Australian and international media salivating over every juicy morsel made available from the court documents. It effectively kicked wide open the doors of the House of Hancock so the world could see inside, and became the latest chapter in the ongoing dynastic saga. But this time the contents of the emails from

Gina to her children were so caustic and personal that one felt like a voyeur reading them.

Gina's youngest daughter, Ginia, 25, who was afforded a Swiss boarding school education, worked for a time as a publicist at Faberge in London and is now partnered with Ryan Johnston, son of Beach Boys Bruce Johnston, has sided with her mother. For her efforts, she now boasts official positions within Hancock companies. Following the lifting of the non-publication orders, details exposed in the explosive emails immediately became dinner-party fodder. The personal email Hope sent to Gina in July 2011, in which she outlined her expensive taste in food and nominated the 'few things' that she wanted for her birthday, was met with incredulity. 'Hi Mem,' it started. 'I need a few things for my birthday (cook so you can be sure April [daughter] is fed right, bodyguard so that the kids are safe and housekeeper that is good [with] kids so if I need to go out I can) and I found a great agency here that sources the best, here are the descriptions and costs, I would buy them myself but I'm down to my last $60,000 and your [sic] only paying my husband $1 a year . . .' Hope outlined the job description of a chef/cook who would prepare 'detailed menus and food for most or all family and social events' and would be responsible for anything 'food or kitchen-related, including organization, clean-up, shopping for all food-related supplies and menu planning'. She nominates the annual salary range: $40,000 to $225,000.

The latter figure astounded restaurant insiders. 'The normal chef's range is more like $65–$100,000 a year,' Victorian restaurant consultant Tony Eldred told me. 'The top end usually requires working hours of between 55 and 65 hours a week; extremely family-unfriendly. Only three or four chef jobs exist in Australia that pay more than $250,000 a year. If you advertised that kind of salary you'd be inundated with fast-talking con artists who fancy themselves as the next celebrity chef.' The bottom number is too low and the top number is too high, and paying more doesn't guarantee better quality. You'd probably lure anyone who can open a baked bean can to apply for that sort of job. There would be a queue of twitching misfits lining up for the position if you advertised the top end scale of money.'

In another email, sent the following day, Hope pleaded with her mother to remain in the United States, saying she could not live in Australia or Singapore. 'It's not fair on me to have to live there and horribly unfair for me to have to expose the kids to that,' she wrote. 'It's hard enough being a kid, let alone the peer pressure that comes from being the wealthiest one in the country.

'I love America, the girls love it. I'm happy here. Your media is minimal and positive here. I really do need a safer apartment but ironically I can't afford it! I don't want to have to move back to one of your "desirable" countries again just to save every cent I can so I can finally live here where I'm happy, my children are happy and I can offer them the best school and universities in the world. It's not fair that you are selfishly pressuring me to move to Singapore and Australia just because you hate America.'

Hope berated her mother for her lack of comprehension about publicity of her extreme wealth. 'I don't think you understand what it means now that the whole world thinks you're going to be wealthier than Bill Gates,' she wrote. 'It means we all need bodyguards and very safe homes!! Especially the children who are small and easily targeted for kidnap. No country (not even Singapore) is safe. I don't have the money to protect myself or my children and it scares me. I should have enough money to have a bodyguard, housekeeper and cook. Even my friends who have nothing compared to your wealth have more staff.' Hope detailed the cost of a bodyguard's annual salary: $55,000 to $100,000. And housekeeper: $35,000 to $55,000.

I flash back to the letter written in 1833 from John Hancock

to the Surveyor-General, begging for his entitlement for an inch
of land to put their feet on:

> Sir
>
> wee Beg leave to inform you, that wee have been Residence
> in this Colony nearly three years and not having an Inch
> of Land to put our feet on, not so much as a villa grant
> or a town alotment, wee shall feel much obliged to you
> if you would give us instructions for selecting of such
> Grants or town alotments as wee are entitled to in this
> District . . .

Later, with the tussle continuing in court, a security expert
warned that Hope was at most risk of harm. 'Kidnappers tend
to be amateurs,' he wrote, '[therefore] the odds are greater they
will be caught so they are more eager to silence their victims.'

Soon after Hope's entreaties to her mother for cash, Bianca,
who was a director of Hancock Prospecting and HMHT
Investments until she was replaced by Ginia Rinehart, entered
the fray, with a gentler approach to her mother seeking funds
to upgrade her family's security. 'Chum,' she starts. 'No doubt
you heard about the unnerving situation yesterday involving
a bomb and an 18 year old girl at home in Mosman. Thank
goodness Hope and family have moved overseas as we all otherwise would have been so much more concerned. However, the
fact is although we were not targeted this time, we are, by all
accounts the highest risk family in all of Australia for future
similar attacks.' Referring to her partner, Sasha, and young
son, Nicholas, she added: 'I am not comfortable that [we] have
adequate measures in place to minimize risk to our personal
safety. Although we have recently beefed up our security at
home (added motion sensor cameras), this will do nothing to
protect us should someone enter the house. Especially with

Sasha travelling so frequently with work, if we are to remain based here in Australia I would like to have security personnel present . . . Unfortunately I do not have the financial means to achieve this, and ask that either you consider sponsoring such an arrangement or please make funds available so that I may consider our options in this regard.' She signed it 'Love, Biancs'.

The same year, Bianca and her family moved to Canada.

Seemingly unaware of the irony of having a reputation as being a queen of litigation, in an email to her daughter Bianca in September 2011, Gina censured her to act responsibly and stop the 'lawyer feast'. 'Enough is enough,' she wrote. 'Your ill-considered action is also now causing media attention and jeopardising also the very lives of our family. . . . It was again also absolutely unnecessary given the significant dividend payments that were to start for you in January 2012, payments far, far greater than what you have been receiving from the Trust, and which could have continued to keep you in expensive homes, endless holiday travels, and increasingly very privileged lifestyle for life, without you having to work, but given the work I've done . . .' Poignantly, she signs it 'Mother'. Much of the contents of this email were also copied to Hope.

Paul Barry

67

ANY CORRESPONDENCE BETWEEN JOHN and his mother has not been made public. I recall what he told me during our interview in South Africa. 'It is a good thing for me to get away from her for a while. But because I am overseas does not mean I'm not 100 per cent supportive of her and the company. Hancock Prospecting is going to be my main thrust in life.'

Now, it appears that is not the case. Out of favour, John's salary from Hancock Prospecting ceased in late 2011 (after court action commenced, and Bianca was removed as director, replaced by Ginia). Gina now has three of her adult children, plus her grandchildren, scattered around the globe.

Federal Liberal MP Alby Schultz's wife, Gloria, a close friend of Gina, described the situation as very sad. 'Gina loves her children. Adores her grandchildren. I know she is deeply hurt by it,' she told Jane Kadzow. But adman extraordinaire John Singleton was less selective of his words. Singleton has known both Lang and Gina for decades and is one of the few people comfortable in airing his views about the girl who, he told

Kadzow, 'sees it as her destiny to fulfil Lang's dream'. Of her children, he said, 'The business comes first. Being a parent is secondary. It's just, "Where do they fit into the dynasty? Are they iron or are they coal or are they uranium?" If they don't fit into the company, there's no role for them.'

Other Australian dynastic families have managed to find a way to successfully incorporate their children into the family companies. 'The Murdochs and Packers are great examples of how that can work,' a journalist comments. 'John Symonds, founder of Aussie Home Loans, is worth around $600 million but he's not just handing over the money to his children. He's teaching them the tricks of the trade. It could have been very different if Gina had seriously worked out roles for her children.'

One person who decidedly does not fit into the company is Hilda Kickett, who watched the fracas from her Geraldton home. She would not comment on the feud but told *The Daily Telegraph* that John and his sisters had all been very generous to her and that there was nothing she wouldn't do for them, including Gina.

The timing could not have been worse. In the week that *Forbes* magazine crowned Gina as the wealthiest woman in Asia, and also anticipated she could easily become the richest woman in the world, a 44-page security consultancy report, commissioned by Gina, was delivered to each of the children. The report, compiled by a global risk consultancy and code-named Project Tara, outlined the living arrangements for each and compared their safety with incidences involving high-profile public figures such as American television host David Letterman, heart surgeon Victor Chang who was murdered after he was described by a newspaper as 'filthy rich', and the Beckham family.

In documents released by the court, during the proceedings Gina's lawyer, Paul McCann, also gave examples of disparaging comments that have appeared on social media sites since the court action began. 'Gina Rinehart, by all accounts, is a disgusting, selfish and exploitative tyrant. She deserves the internal family strife she has engendered,' one read.

The security report warned that the family's combination of 'wealth, youth and acrimony' was likely to keep media interest on the boil and therefore raise their public profile, and continued that lifting of the suppression order 'risks exposing the children and grandchildren to serious security risks' such as kidnapping, robbery and murder. They would also become a target for 'crowd sourcing', where mobile phones are used as conduits to instant updates on individuals, downloaded in real time to sites such as Facebook and YouTube. 'In simple terms, it means that the children, and their children could be anywhere on the globe and have their movements monitored and tracked by the public or worse, criminals,' a social media commentator tells me. 'It may seem benign but it's a form of stalking, really, and the stakes are high for wealthy people.'

Just how high the stakes are became apparent when McCann upped the ante by giving Hope, John and Bianca a deadline to end their opposition to the suppression orders, threatening them that if they refused to comply, Gina may call a halt to insurance policies taken out for them and her five grandchildren against ransom or kidnapping demands. This latest power tussle between Gina and her children was seen by commentators as a high-risk chess move on her part. If the children did not agree, she may make good her threat and remove their safety net. If that happened, she would potentially expose them – and her grandchildren – to the huge risks associated with being the offspring of a multibillionaire.

'We can only presume that your clients' previously stated concerns for the personal safety of their families and themselves have now completely and entirely disappeared,' he said. 'Under these circumstances, it seems your clients would place no value in the continuation of "ransom insurance" that is currently provided to them and/or their young children. Indeed you may consider such insurance to be wasteful expenditure.' He continued that the children had 'two options' – to either confirm 'they are no longer concerned about their personal safety or that of their young children . . . so the insurance policies can be cancelled' or to drop their opposition to the suppression orders.

68

THE SAD AND POISONOUS acrimony between Gina and her three children, and the reasons John, Bianca and Hope took the action against their mother, became explosively clear by March 2012, with the suppressions lifted and the release of private emails between the four into the public domain. Australia's wealthiest woman wanted her children to allow her to remain as the trustee of the Hope Margaret Hancock Trust, established by Lang in 1988 – a trust that owns a quarter of the shares in Hancock Prospecting.

The sudden emergence of Bianca, John and Hope onto the media stage via court documents or the occasional press statement from John begged the question as to why they were silent for so long. The answer lay in legal confidentiality agreements which ensured that over most of the past decade they have been banned from going public with any private disputes, divulging issues raised in any court actions or starting legal stoushes, the latter tied up in 'non-disparagement' clauses preventing any denigration of their mother.

Lifting of the suppressions allowed the fractured dysfunction rampant within Australia's richest family to be revealed. Unsurprisingly, it showed the power struggle between Gina and John that has raged since 2003 – the same year John and I did a magazine story in Perth – over control of the trust.

On letterhead marked the 'Chairman's Personal Assistant' in September that year John sent a missive to his mother's legal representative complaining bitterly that he would have to wait until his sister, Ginia – who was not born when Lang had drafted his wishes – turned 25 before he could realise his portion of income from the trust. That was almost a decade away. He also penned an accusatory letter to Gina, blaming her for using her control of the trust as a 'tool of power over her children'. The result was the 'Porteous Settlement Deed', signed by Gina, John and Bianca.

By the following year, John was forecasting what was to follow, outlining in strong language his demand that, based on his not receiving any trust monies, Gina's controlling manner with distributions and her alleged illegitimate movement of assets from the trust, that she step aside as trustee. She should do this, he wrote, to avoid 'what would inevitably be a public dispute'.

The agreement cites the 'potential for (Mr Hancock) to negatively seek exposure with the public or with the media, particularly during periods of negotiation of large commercial projects such as a Hope Downs Project'.

By 2005 a legal truce was settled between John and his mother, in which he guaranteed his silence and agreed to a six-year relinquishment of his rights to income from the trust in return for actual and promised financial benefits, including a settlement of almost $400,000, and a $1 million guarantee if the Hope Downs project was floated to the public. The truce didn't last long. By the last quarter of that year, John legally sought to have his mother removed as trustee. While this legal battle raged, by mid-2006 Bianca, Hope and Ginia signed on to their own settlement, known as the Hope Downs Agreement, which guaranteed them a tidy 25 per cent of any money, to be vested from September 2011. As part of their agreement, they were required to settle any family disputes in confidence and via arbitration. So tight was this agreement that the siblings were not to even divulge details of its very existence. In 2006 Hancock Prospecting signed a joint venture with Rio Tinto to develop the Hope Downs iron ore operation. Under the 2007 deed John Hancock's payments from Hancock Prospecting were increased, provided he worked for the company or Rio Tinto and paid back loans to the family company. John, at war with his mother through the court, refused to sign but for reasons not made public, he and Gina reconciled in 2007, the same year that he lost his three-year battle to have his mother removed as head of the family trust. One of the deeds signed with John that year made it obvious that Gina intended for her children to inherit the whole of her shares in HPPL, providing they show an interest in Hancock Group affairs and could be trusted. In other words, they should work for what they got and toe their mother's line.

'The public will never really know what happened behind closed doors or why John agreed to settle,' an insider tells me. 'The WA Supreme Court nailed it down in suppressions and details of what is in those files will never see the light of day. He signed yet another agreement, this one entitled the Confidential Settlement Deed, a mysterious document in which he pledged to abandon forever any allegations that he had earlier made. This resulted in the Prodigal Son joining the Hope Downs deal.'

'It sounds like something from a secret society,' I comment wryly. 'What allegations had John made that he needed to "forever abandon?"'

'Don't know. They're nailed down as well. What we do know is that he's signed other deeds tying him up in various ways.'

In 2012, Gina's High Court bid to keep the family secrets suppressed failed, and failed spectacularly. With the details of the battle for the billions released to the media with the exposure of documents between Gina and the three children and from her Chief Financial Officer Jay Newby to them, the message was bitter and clear. In return for dropping all unnecessary legal proceedings, Bianca was told she could nominate how much money she would like to receive on a quarterly basis. Hope, too, was warned that if she did not agree to extend the family trust she would 'face the consequences'. The 'consequences' were bankruptcy – financial ruin – if they failed to fall into line.

John, once the firm favourite to lead the House of Hancock, was now clearly out of favour. 'Stop the nonsense,' Gina rebuked him in an email in September 2011. 'You are always saying you want a leadership role, but very sadly in the past you have taken the wrong decisions . . . Please use your intelligence John to good effect, develop a positive leadership role, sign the deed . . .'

With revelations that the family trust would not, after all, be vested on Ginia's twenty-fifth birthday, the siblings, bound as usual by secrecy, also had to promise in the September 11 deed 'not to seek or query or challenge in court proceedings or otherwise any act or omission of Mrs Rinehart in relation to the trust'. With the ghost of Rose Porteous' marriage to Lang clearly alive in Gina's memory, they also had to enter into prenuptial agreements before they married or had children. Then, the clause that broke the camel's back: a demand that they would make no call on Gina to disclose details to them of any accounts relating to the trust.

Once again, the House of Hancock armed the battlements for war, this time by John, Hope and Bianca with allegations of Gina's 'repeated attempts to place emotional, financial and legal pressure' on them to hand over control of the trust. They

sought a determination that their mother is guilty of misconduct as trustee and should be removed.

'We're not talking chicken feed here,' the insider says. 'By the
time the trust vested on 6 September 2011 – the date of Ginia's
twenty-fifth birthday – it was worth around $2.4 billion. With
the incredible rise of Gina's wealth and a successful court action
against Gina, that could translate to a $1 billion each for the
children. But Gina waited until one day before the vesting date
to tell them that if they took the money now, capital gains tax
would ensure that they were bankrupted. It seems that Gina's
advice came from PricewaterhouseCoopers, but none of the
three have been able to see those account details. Unbeknown
to them, Gina had already changed that vesting date to 1 July
2068. John and Bianca would be in their eighties before it vested
again. Gina would be 113 years old.'

With the majority of the correspondence in writing, either
via coldly clinical emails or in court documents, the extent
of the family chasm is impossible to hide. With Ginia in her
corner, Gina, through her lawyers, accused John, Bianca and
Hope of being motivated 'entirely by greed' and added that
if they weren't happy with the income they received through
the trust, they should 'go out and earn for themselves'. They
had all enjoyed 'very privileged lives', McCann wrote. 'All
have enjoyed private schooling, private tutors, private summer
schools, extensive holidays overseas, designer clothes, private
healthcare, expensive jewellery and (or) watches.' Gina hadn't
finished yet. 'Additionally, the plaintiffs have each chosen multi-
million dollar homes with water views, and swimming pools to
enjoy. The trust income after tax was too small to provide the
luxury homes, so these were provided to the three children in
addition to trust dividends and other benefits.' John retaliated
with a salvo of his own, telling *The Weekend Australian* that
he would have loved to have inherited projects and royalties
to work with but instead, he had to rely on his own business

skills to survive. 'What does she (Gina) want me to do – take up her offer of free money if we do as she says? No thanks!' With the gloves off, Gina's lawyers fought hard to explain her extraordinary eleventh-hour attempt to maintain control of the trust. 'None of the plaintiffs has the requisite capacity or skill, nor the knowledge, experience, judgment or responsible work ethic to administer a trust in the nature of the trust in particular as part of the growing HPPL Group,' her defence said in court documents. The children, it continued, had never occupied 'any long-term position of professional or occupational responsibility, either in the resources industry or elsewhere', except short-term positions given to them by her. Ginia joined with her mother in the objections, adding that 'none of the plaintiffs, individually or collectively, are suitable to be appointed as trustees'.

If that is the case, I wonder, had Gina, by her total control of the family business, inadequately prepared them for the heavy mantle that they would one day inherit? Knowing the extreme wealth they would inevitably acquire, why are they, in her opinion, manifestly unsuited to deal with that sort of pressure? Were they uninterested in any long-term position of professional or occupational responsibility – and why, as their mother, could she not have found a way to address the issues with less toxicity and more emotional closeness? But the real concern was laid out in Gina's fear that her children's court bid could jeopardise 'years of work and hundreds of millions of dollars of investment in world-scale projects worth many billions of dollars'.

'There it is, in a nutshell,' the insider comments. 'Gina needs that money to bankroll future projects. She doesn't want it frittered away and she's gone to war with her own flesh and blood to make sure it isn't. For their part, they knew they just needed to wait for that trust to vest, when they would each inherit their dynastic wealth and become overnight billionaires. They are the "trust fund" generation. That is not to say they won't work, but that Gina doesn't think they are equipped to play a meaningful role in the family company. You would have to wonder how this impacts not just on their relationship with their mother, but on their own psyche?' He compares the present situation with Gina's often turbulent relationship with Lang. 'At the height of their war, they exchanged poisonous letters between themselves as well. It was usually about money but it got very bitter, very personal. It was a merry-go-round, and one that Gina's kids are now on. It's the curse that often affects the third generation.'

Warning that bankruptcy is not in the financial interests of the beneficiaries, Gina's lawyers argued that for their own 'personal development' it would be in the best interests of the beneficiaries to force them to go to work and reconsider their holidaying lifestyles and attitudes. Hope, Gina claimed, 'has never undertaken gainful or long-term employment of any substance' and John and Bianca had been unemployed 'for the majority of their lives'. In short: if the kids aren't happy, they should get a job.

To her sister, 'Hopie', Ginia wrote on September 3: 'Hey guys . . . Hope of course I trust you and if you feel up to it and want to take over the mess I support you 100 per cent. But I don't think it's as easy as that, nor do I think it would be an easy task. Really don't want this ripping us all apart . . .' The extent of the sad fracturing of the relationship with her close sibling was never so apparent. 'I'm so lost with all of this, don't know what to do.'

Jay Newby's offer to change the financial arrangements distributed to the beneficiaries was met with a plaintiff plea to her mother to be able to look further at details of the trust. 'I can't sign that,' Hope wrote. 'You're going to cut me off until I move to Perth or Singapore. Or you will make more "loans" to yourself or the company and we'll be forever in debt. I'm never going to be able to provide for my children. Please call me, we need to talk.' The next day Hope made it clear she did not want to instigate legal action. 'I need 6 months extension on divestment to work this shit out and Mem to step down as trustee September 6th. Please do this, I don't want this to tear my family apart and I don't want to get a lawyer.'

On 5 September Gina retaliated with an email of her own. 'If you choose not to extend the Trust you will face the consequences for so doing, yes you will then not "be able to provide for my [your] children" for many years and will have to go to work. From my perspective you have a very easy financial decision to make – you certainly do not need weeks or months to consider. I am sorry if you have been confused by anyone else.'

The three children's response, via their lawyers, was caustic. Their legal action, they wrote, was actuated by the recent 'deceptive, manipulative, hopelessly conflicted and disgraceful conduct' of their mother.

What had started as a fracas between Gina and the children became a war of words between Ginia and her siblings as the pressure was amplified. Rejecting suggestions that his income was derived from 'inherited projects and royalties' from Gina, John asserted that he had called on his 'own set of skills' to earn his money and added that Ginia had a 'Rolls-Royce at 25'. Later, John would retaliate with financial statements proving that his earnings as a day trader were more than sufficient to support him and his family.

Ginia reacted strongly to John's statements. 'I feel great sympathy towards him that he feels the need to create such falsities and spread them globally,' she asserted. 'Addressing each of them would be to no end so let me simply state that while this case has been nothing but a destructive display of greed, jealousy and a selfish sense of entitlement on behalf of my siblings, I stand firmly on my own principles right next to my mother because it is the right and just thing to do.' Calling her siblings' actions 'unjustified', she added that this 'private family matter' should never have been made public. And she went one step further, stating that she did not want her siblings as trustees because they lack 'the perseverance, work ethic, responsibility and dedication . . . to administer the trust'. She would, she wrote to Hope, be outnumbered in a situation whereby John and Bianca have wanted for years to be sole beneficiaries of the trust.

Hope reacted with sadness to Ginia's statements. 'We have been very close our entire lives and I fear she has been used by our mother since at the time when the proceedings commenced, Ginia sent an email saying she supported us 100 per cent,' she wrote. 'We did not want to go to court but were given no option when threatened with bankruptcy if we did not immediately sign a deed to further relinquish our rights as beneficiaries. All we want is to ensure the assets and income of the trust is managed in a proper and lawful fashion. It is deplorable that we are subject to such vitriolic attack, from such coordinated opposition, in taking that stand; the full facts can now be known and the public can judge for themselves.'

NSW Liberal MP Alby Schultz, whose wife is a close friend of Gina's (as noted above), had, it appeared, already made up his mind, wading into the dispute in a letter to Hope aired on the lifting of the suppressions. 'We read with so much sadness of the litigation that you have instigated against your mother. Whilst we do not know all the problems that give rise to this horrific step, because we love and care about you we felt we had to share our experience with you.' Senator Barnaby Joyce, too, wrote to Hope, encouraging her not to go public with her grievances. Later, in Canberra, independent MP Tony Windsor noted that Joyce should 'please explain' why he had written to Hope. 'I think he really does need to answer: Why would he involve himself in a personal family business?' he asked. 'Is he in the business of writing to everybody who has children who might be in some sort of dispute with their parents?' While Schultz declined to comment, Joyce responded he was acting in the capacity of a 'family friend'. John would have none of it, describing the men's interference as 'stressful'. 'Unfortunately the courts are the only forum to remove trustees according to the *Trustees Act* – (Senator Joyce) would know this as an accountant – so the matter was always going to be public,' he told *The Australian*.

Gina, through her lawyer Paul McCann, made no bones about how she felt about the suppressions being lifted. 'Mrs Rinehart and her daughter Ginia are extremely disappointed that three of her children have adopted a course of making public a private matter and jeopardising family security, including that of young dependent and innocent children and can only conclude that they have done so in an attempt to apply public pressure through the media,' he stated. Ginia, too, aired her opinion. 'My siblings and I were blessed with an exceptionally fortunate upbringing,' she said. 'This case is motivated entirely by greed and I have no doubt that one day soon my brother and sisters will regret putting money before family. Unfortunately, this realisation will come too late as the damage to our family and its good reputation will already have been done.'

The feud was to get a lot uglier. Now cut off from the special risk insurance to protect themselves or their children from kidnap or extortion, Gina's company is also scrutinising the very trust fund established by Lang for his grandchildren. Armed with an indignant attitude, the backing of wealthy, well-connected associates and the knowledge that he could not use shares in the family trust as security for any bank loan, nor sell them to anyone outside the family, in mid-March John went to Hong Kong to seek financial help from these backers to keep himself and his two sisters afloat during any court case against their mother. 'And I've a surprise in store for them all,' he enigmatically told *The Weekend Australian*.

Weekend West journalist Steve Pennells, in Hong Kong with John Hancock, noted one gifted transaction from an associate of John's of around A$80,000 – an instalment, he wrote, that followed a previous, smaller one and which answered part of the question as to how, starved of family funds, the three siblings could even consider legal action against their mother which is costing around $100,000 a month. 'The Chinese place high importance on family,' the mystery donor told Pennells, adding that 'A mother usually does all she can to help her children, especially the son,' and that finding support to help John, with no strings attached, would be easy. John, in return, has pledged that if a legal solution is found with his mother, he will repay the debts.

Telling Pennells that the public perception of he, Bianca and Hope as wealthy heirs was incorrect, he added that Bianca and Hope had run out of money after paying the initial few hundred thousand dollars of legal bills and that his funds had run low during his own stoushes with his mother. With a glimpse into his antipathetic relationship with Gina, he cited the example of a business idea he had that was rejected by the Hancock Board – to be paid for iron ore in Chinese yuan, rather than US dollars, and to wait until the yuan reached its appreciation. Instead, he said, Twiggy Forrest, of Fortescue Metals, took the same idea and turned it to a financial advantage. Bianca, too, he said, was forced to sell her house and both she and Hope had, on occasions, resorted to selling jewellery or clothing. 'We are not flying in private jets or driving around in Rolls-Royces, I assure you,' he said. 'Hope is struggling to pay rent from July and Bianca and I are dipping into our limited pockets to help her with kids' school fees . . . The reality is their side has every-thing, as it stands, and we have nothing. I don't think that's fair.' Confirming that his salary from HPPL had been cut off from the commencement of legal action in September, he also indicated that the trust money paid to his two sisters was frozen at the same time. 'Nobody wants to be known to be giving me these personal loans but it's been a few hundred thousand dollars out of Australia already and commitments for much more if needed,' John said. 'They know the risks – they know the limited assets I have now are under my mother's control . . .'

In 2007, John and his partner, Gemma Ludgate, left Perth, which John described to me as something of a 'fishbowl' and moved to the Thai island of Koh Samui, where they built their own tropical luxe home of thatch and bamboo and where they live a low-key existence. Upping the ante in his inimitable fashion, John claimed that he had adequate financial support to keep up the fight and could 'keep going for as long as she wants to resist stepping down from the trust – hopefully before she turns 112, as I'd like to be able to provide adequate security for my children, not just a nice coffin'. Concluding that both he and Bianca want to work in the family company, he added, poignantly, 'Sadly, this has been made impossible.'

Gina, through her spokesperson Tad Watroba, said they were 'perplexed and saddened' by the current events and lack of rationale behind them. 'What further unearned monies or interests are they really after now, given it is through Mrs Rinehart's hard work that so much has been built up?' Watroba said. John retaliated that only a court could remove a trustee, even one who was willing to be removed.

A source who has watched Gina's rise and rise over the past 20 years ponders the latest developments. 'She's undoubtedly a fascinating individual,' he said. 'She has an austere lifestyle; all she does is work. But from the tone of these emails, it doesn't look like her children want to follow suit. The question is, why have the children waited until now to seek a legal challenge to their inheritance by trying to remove Gina as head of the family trust which owns almost a quarter of her company, Hancock Prospecting? The answer, it seems, lies in the vesting date of a trust described by Justice Brereton as holding "no small part" of the family's "immense wealth".'

Shortly after Gina bought into Fairfax, John broke his lengthy silence. 'When my mother buys a few hundred million dollars worth of Fairfax, it's going to draw some attention,' he said in an understatement. 'But she won't share a penny to help protect her grandchildren from the risks she – the trustee of our family trust – is creating by her own actions . . . What more can I do than communicate to any kidnappers out there – over my dead body and you will be wasting your time anyway. If you think you're going to get anything from my mother, good luck.'

'It looks like a catch 22,' my source comments. 'How can her children continue to fight the might of her wealth if they don't have the money to do so?' He speculates on what is behind the latest battle. 'There have been so many shifting loyalties. First John was working for Hancock Prospecting and being groomed for a future senior role, and then he left the stage. Bianca then took the baton and became a director at HPPL, before suddenly exiting and moving with her partner to the Northern Territory. She's still listed as a director but appears not to have any hands-on management role. Next, Hope's husband was appointed to the board but that went by the wayside. What caused anyone's split from the flagship company, who knows, but if the present correspondence between the children and Gina is any indication, it is undoubtedly about Gina wanting to maintain control. She needs to maintain her control over the cash flow she has to fund the development of her next goal, the Roy Hill iron ore project. Gina doesn't want the children to have access to the cash flow, because she needs the money to be available for this project. If she hasn't got that, she has to either sell equity or go to the banks, and the latter is not a good option at this time.'

In *The West Australian* newspaper, Hilda Kickett came out in defence of Gina's children, arguing that that they deserve a share of the family fortune.

'She reckons there's more than enough money to go round and the kids should have been groomed for senior roles in the company,' I comment to the mining source. 'She doesn't understand why Gina is not thinking about the joy of her grandkids. Then again, Gina's friends claim she is deeply hurt by her children's actions, and say she loves them and adores her grandchildren. Is she a happy woman, do you think?'

He grimaces. 'I've been watching her behaviour for 20 years now. Given her objectives, and the fact that she seems to be achieving them, then she should be happy. Her inherited royalty stream pales into insignificance against the profits she gets from her share in the Hope Downs iron ore mine, estimated roughly at A$1 billion per annum after tax. That should make anyone happy. But at a personal level? Who knows? She is not known for a fabulous sense of humour or for enjoying her riches. It's all work.'

'What I'm actually asking,' I press, 'is, is it possible to be happy when you are fighting with your children?'

'Who knows what her definition of happiness is?' he answers.

69

I READ AND RE-READ the emails between Gina, Bianca and Hope. John lives in Thailand; Bianca in Canada; Hope in New York. Did they feel the need to move away from the Perth media fishbowl to escape the intense scrutiny, or was it a desire to put distance between themselves and Gina? And how, I wonder, did Ginia break the news that she was siding with her mother in this latest power play? How did her siblings respond?

I have met John on several occasions – interviewed him, dined with him, talked with him late into the night in Perth and South Africa – and I know his soft side, how he struggled emotionally to reconcile his relationship with the woman he calls 'Mama'; his sense of entitlement, the flash of anger in his blue eyes when he detailed his close relationship with his grandfather, how Lang had *wanted* his grandchildren to inherit and the memorandum in his grandmother Hope's will that her estate, that she left to Lang, be divided later equally among Gina and her children; his fury at Rose Porteous and the

335

humiliation he believed she had heaped on his family name; and his great sense of fun . . . a young man, then 25, who wanted to party as well as work. We had already met in South Africa in 2000; in Perth in 2003 we undertook a lengthy interview and photo shoot for a national magazine that spread over two days. We started at the apartment where he then lived, in the salubrious riverside suburb of Crawley, where Perth's super-rich use the Swan River as their aquatic playground. Below, Mounts Bay Road, clogged with sports cars and BMWs, snaked around the river's edge. John stood on the large balcony overlooking the water and gestured to the road below. 'It really annoys me that the road is so close to us here,' he said. 'I might see if I can do something about that.' I looked at him to see if he was joking. A small smile flickered around his mouth.

The company owned the apartment in which John then lived with his girlfriend, attractive brunette Gemma Ludgate. The Ludgate and Hancock families had known each other for generations and the families lived next door and each owned one half of two large houses at Dalkeith, with views to the Swan River. Gemma's grandmother Tess once joked that when Lang flushed the toilet next door, their bath emptied. Later, Lang bought out their share of the property. Today, cameras stand silent guard above the large, closed front gates, with signs warning *Electric Fence*.

Gina owns two identical apartments at Crawley, one above the other. John's light, spacious home, below the one that Gina owns but no longer lives in, was accessed by tight security and an elevator to each floor and was tastefully decorated: ironbark floors, midnight-blue ceilings, vibrant red walls. John chose the colours, which gave an insight into his relationship with Gina and into his own psyche. 'I wanted the same red as the nail polish I helped my mum choose years ago,' he said. 'I don't think there's anything wrong with having a "feminine side"; it comes from growing up around women. It helps me to understand them.' Photos of Gina cuddling a smiling John showed the pair were very close; a closeness undoubtedly intensified by the lack of a father figure in his early life. 'I remember helping choose dresses for my mother in Milan when I was seven,' he said. His mood became more sombre. 'We were especially close until about that age, but she was careful not to over-mother me and she consciously began to toughen me. She didn't tell me she loved me. I don't think either of us needed to say it. But she always expected me to succeed.' The inference was obvious: the same young boy, once carried on his mother's hip, desperately wanted that motherly attention back. Photos of John's global travels dotted the fridge: sleigh rides at St Moritz; waterskiing at Lake Como; romantic getaways with Gemma. In between the photo shoot, a stylist fussed with Gemma's hair and make-up and the couple sprawled casually on a massive day bed that dominated the lounge room, chatting affably. 'I don't deny I have a lot to be lucky about,' John said, 'but I don't have lots of money myself. My salary is less than most of my friends. I was not brought up thinking I was from a privileged family – there's no red carpet.'

John was charming and cheeky. 'Mama lives up there,' he said, pointing his finger to the ceiling and grinning. 'But I don't see her much.'

'How much is not much?' I asked. He didn't answer the question.

In the late afternoon we moved to Gina's family home at Dalkeith for photographs and the following day decamped to a winery, owned by an old friend of John's, to finish the shoot. It was a sizzling-hot morning, temperatures climbing well into the 30s but no sign of John when we arrived at the agreed time to start. An hour later, while the photographer and I unsuccessfully sought sanctuary from the furnace, he had still not materialised. My patience was thinning, fast. When he finally sauntered in, relaxed and fresh from a swim, he offered no apologies. 'You've kept everyone waiting,' I censured him. He shrugged. 'We've been for a swim.'

'Well, we haven't,' I rejoined, 'and we're running late and it's stinking hot.' His smile disappeared, and in the tense stand-off I knew we were seconds away from him walking out and cancelling the shoot. But just as quickly, he settled down. 'OK. Let's start,' he said. Later, he apologised for keeping us waiting. 'I hate being portrayed as the spoilt, rich heir to my grandfather's fortune,' he said. 'That is not the case. That is not who I am.'

John's adoration for his late grandfather was evident in the soft way he talked about him, his memories of nestling cosily on his mother's lap under a vast outback sky and listening to Lang's stories about the ancient Pilbara, its people, its hidden treasures. But when we spoke, John was 27 and his childhood a long time ago. Over the past decade, he said, he had tried his best to protect his mother from the unwelcome lens of an intrusive media. But as much as he had stood by her side, he was very clear about who was the boss. 'There is only one chief in the tribe and that is Mum,' he told me. 'She is definitely the toughest person I know. She's built of steel. She's never given me handouts and always tried to teach me the importance of hard work and determination. I had a very strict upbringing; lots of chores and no pocket money. She didn't want spoilt brats.' He shared an anecdote of his time at university, when he told Gina he was broke and needed money for food. 'She said to me, "Have you got any tomato sauce in the cupboard? Then make soup!"'

Later, as the wine flowed and we sat under meandering vines lit with soft fairy lights watching the fiery red sun disappear over the vineyard, it became apparent that there were problems in John's relationship with his mother. She did not want to relinquish any company control, he said. She did not wish to give him what his grandfather had wanted him – them – to have. She sometimes belittled him in company and he was tired of it.

They had a complex, often turbulent relationship. He was hurt and angry that it was like this. Shortly after, John changed his name by deed poll to Hancock.

John worked at Hancock Prospecting following our interview but shortly after, around the time that Channel 7 media magnate Kerry Stokes announced the appointment of his son, Ryan, to head its magazine division, John's rift with his mother became public. Ryan was a personal friend of John's and his elevation in his father's company must have irked in comparison to John's own situation. The other major Australian players, the Murdoch and Packer empires, had also invested their sons, Lachlan and James, with more control over the respective companies. In August, John griped to *West Australian* journalist Steve Pennells that his mother had called him a 'gambler' when he made a $50,000 profit on a share-market investment. 'I persuaded her to put $100,000 into an options trading account under the company name,' he said. 'I have since turned this into almost $150,000 – a respectable return for any fund manager.' John complained that for years, he had asked his mother for an increasing role in the commercial direction of the company but that 'the best I have been offered recently was a commission to sell her boat'. John predicted that he would be alienated from any plans concerning the company's future, adding prophetically that, 'All companies, whether family or otherwise, should have a succession plan. My mother refuses to make or discuss such plans. I have three sisters and suspect the youngest has now been earmarked.' Around 2007, John moved to China for work.

John and Gina reconciled later; one photo of them together with Gina's youngest daughter, Ginia, at the Telstra Business Women's Awards in 2009 – all three smiling broadly – appears to show a united, happy family face. John, a moderate thinker, continually entreated Gina to court the press, to allow them to see her warm side, but she refused. He had to defend her, time and time again. She abhors gauche displays of her wealth, he told me. Her private life is her private life. He was her protector, her guardian; her sole male heir. So what has gone so horribly wrong between John and Gina, again? I can't ask him myself; we lost touch years ago.

How difficult would it have been for John to make the decision to blow wide open the very secrecy that Gina so treasures? Was their relationship by now so fractured that he did not care about the public falling-out, about opening the family to further intense media scrutiny? Is he now so alienated from Gina that he feels justified in demanding what he believes is his rightful inheritance? And Bianca? Her email to 'Chum', signed 'Biancs', hints at their former closeness when she was her mother's right-hand girl, the same girl who, in 2005, sat side by side with Gina on a Pilbara rock and who flanked her, smiling at business and social functions.

What is it, I think, about the lives of these dynastic Australian outback families? My first book, *Her Father's Daughter: The Bonnie Henderson Story* – a biography of the daughter of the late, celebrated Sara Henderson of Bullo River station fame – has numerous similarities to the Hancock/Rinehart story. Bonnie strove hard to please her adored, challenging father, Charlie Henderson, and had a difficult, fractured relationship with her mother, resulting in a highly publicised court battle over money until they reconciled late in Sara's life. Bonnie's sister, Marlee, had stood staunchly by Sara's side through years of battles until she, too, had a public and bitter falling-out with Sara over property.

In the foreword to that book, Bonnie wrote, 'I remember my Dad saying, "Bonnie, I just want you to be happy." Well, old mate, I am.' I wonder if Gina, speaking today to her own father, could say that.

'This whole story reads like a Shakespearean melodrama,'

a Perth media source comments to me. 'It's hard for us mere mortals to understand that when someone is richer than Croesus – boasting inestimable wealth – that there needs to be a battle for some part of it. But the spectre of a woman who may become the richest person on earth, wrangling over money with her own flesh and blood, is so unedifying.'

Gina's clout, her reputation for suing those who cross her, and her immense wealth ensures that while many people have much to say about her, they usually do so anonymously. Another source close to Gina's company says that it is understandable that John, Bianca and Hope are seeking what they regard as their fair share of the fortune. 'I suspect that whenever very large sums of money are involved, a lawyer will suggest that they should be going after a bigger share of that money,' he says. 'The value of the trust that was set up by Lang for the children is about 3 billion, so naturally there would be a desire to get hold of it. Her emails indicate that Gina is prepared to pay out to the children, but that she wants to stay in control.' It is, he observes, 'history repeating itself'.

70

PUNDITS PREDICTED THAT GINA would appeal the decision on Rhodes Ridge. They were right: an appeal was lodged and a hearing is to follow. Rio Tinto insiders are concerned that its plans to invest in Rhodes Ridge and to ride the resource boom with China may be adversely affected by the legal stoush. 'Beyond the appeal, there is always the possibility of a High Court hearing,' the mining insider groans. 'You wonder where it all ends.'

Perth mining analyst Peter Strachan, of StockAnalysis, was blunter. 'The original agreement between Hancock and Wright was a handshake deal between a couple of old mates,' he told a newspaper. 'Now you've got these people born with silver spoons in their mouths fighting over it all.'

Speculation that Wright and Bennett's victory in Rhodes Ridge would give them the impetus to sue Rinehart for a share of the Hope Downs royalty proved correct. Wright Prospecting won access in the Western Australia Supreme Court to documents that shed light on the financial agreements between Hancock and Rio Tinto regarding Hope Downs, which was producing 30 million tonnes of iron ore a year in 2012. The action, which began in 2008 not long after judgment in the Rhodes Ridge dispute (but which was not triggered by that success), is now listed for hearing in the Western Australia Supreme Court.

While the outcome of the Wright/Hancock battle was keenly watched by mining insiders, few seemed concerned at Gina's massive loss. One put it into perspective. 'The decision left her with no equity in the Rhodes Ridge Joint Venture,' he told me. 'However, under the terms of the Partnership Agreement, HPPL got the following: McCamey's Monster (sold by Lang to BHP and renamed "Jimblebar"); Hope Downs and East Angelas (the latter areas renamed Hope 4, Hope 5 and Hope 6, Rio Tinto is currently developing Hope 4 which will bring Gina another $500 million a year profit after tax at current prices); Iron Ore (Wittenoom) Agreement areas (Gina still holds four iron ore "scree" areas south of Wittenoom, which were part of this group); all manganese claims; and the 4000 Mount Kevin's Corner steaming coal deposit in Queensland, which Gina sold to GVK of India last year as part of a deal reported to be worth US$1260 million to the Hancock Group. 'Putting it bluntly, she's got the best of the assets from what was always a 50/50 Partnership and yet she is still fighting for more,' the mining source said. 'Her conduct towards people like McCamey, Dalby and Fieldhouse attracted a great deal of criticism. What sort of person is she?'

A common lament is that for all Gina's wealth, she doesn't seem to make much time for herself to enjoy it. 'You see people like Twiggy Forrest, known for his quiet, generous philanthropy, down at the beach with his kids, pushing their swings or just sitting on the sand, talking to them. In comparison, Gina seems to be locked up in her ivory tower, spending all her time thinking about work, building the future,' one person told me.

'What is the point of having all that dough if you can't enjoy it or worse, fight with your kids over it? It's only money. You can't take it with you.' He pauses. 'On the other hand, she has worked incredibly hard to get where she is and needs to keep that wealth intact so she can use it. It is much harder to do that if the empire is broken up into shareholdings; it makes her position much more unpalatable.'

Robert Duffield reported that Gina told him: 'I wish I'd been a boy. I'm not ashamed of being a girl, and since I'm a girl I will do what a boy would have done had I been a boy.' And perhaps that is at the heart of the enigma that is Gina Rinehart. 'Maybe she has spent her entire life trying to live up to the image of what her father wanted – to try harder and harder because she was a girl, not a boy? Who knows? I hope that's not the case for Gina. It is awfully sad if it is.'

71

IN MID-2011, GINA FLEW Nationals Senator Barnaby Joyce, who admits to being a 'mate', Deputy Federal Opposition Leader Julie Bishop and Liberal MP Terese Gambaro to join her and 7000 other special guests in Hyderabad, India for the wedding of GVK's chairman and fellow billionaire, industrialist G.Y. Krishna Reddy's granddaughter. Flying in by private jet, the delegation mixed with Bollywood stars and celebrities at the sumptuous three-day knees up. Gina's invitation to Labor MPs to join her was declined. If the accompanying guests were hoping to enjoy some downtime, they were disappointed. Gambaro later told Jane Kadzow that on the nine-hour flight, Gina 'pretty much' talked coal all the way to India.

GVK, owned by the Reddy family, is negotiating a controlling stake in Queensland coal mines in the Galilee Basin; Hancock Prospecting has held interests in the area since the 1970s. With a reputed price tag of more than $2 billion at stake, Gina and GVK were yet to put their final signatures on the agreement; despite the grandeur of the occasion, no one who knew Gina imagined that her presence at the wedding was purely social. She was there to massage the agreement with GVK to input a near 80 per cent stake in Alpha and Alpha West developments, the thermal coal deposit within the Galilee Basin described as the 'jewel in the crown' of the land-locked Galilee. GVK is also set to fund $1.26 billion for the Kevin's Corner coal project, as well as all of Hancock's rail and port project. The first proposed phase, which will set GVK back $10 billion, will encompass the 500-kilometre rail and port facilities. It should pay off: in full swing, the three mines are projected to produce an annual 84 million tonnes.

Gina's reprisal of her father's cherished dream to dot the north Queensland landscape with railway lines to transport coal trains surprises no one. With coal mining moving further inland, the necessity for a railway that connects mines to ports is critical. Excluding Japan, electricity demand in Asia is expected to triple by 2025 and the proposed railroad will expand opportunities to enable Australia to more than double exports to feed the Chinese and Indian need for supplies. Gina's vision – to build a 500-kilometre railway line to the coast – is in direct competition with that of the fifth-richest Australian Clive Palmer's $6.8 billion plan, backed by the largest coal importer in India, Adani Enterprises, to build in the same area. As with all of Gina's legal stoushes, it will again be a case of 'to the victor the spoils', unless they combine in a joint venture. Unlike Gina, Palmer's fortune was first made in real estate before he turned his attention to the big money to be had from resources. But like Gina, he never gives up and engages in relentless lawsuits, once listing 'litigation' as his hobby in a *Who's Who* entry.

Palmer is indeed a serious litigant: his China First is threatening a massive A$8 billion lawsuit against QR National, the nation's largest coal carrier, for alleged breach of contract relating to the railway proposed for the Hancock Coal operation in central Queensland.

'Gina is very focused, very driven and very tough. When she makes the right decisions it is the result of a combination of intelligence, rat cunning, good advisers and good luck,' a source said. 'There has been a lot of good luck for both her and Lang. He grabbed all the iron ore in sight and then Japan took off. Gina inherited lots of iron ore and just after doing her 50/50 deal with Rio Tinto the iron ore price took off. In the case of Kevin's Corner in Queensland, a deal was initially done with Brian Johnson's Pennant Group back in the 1990s, but one way or another the coal deposit ended up back in Hancock's hands and was recently sold for a fortune. So Gina has a good eye for opportunity, but enjoys good luck, too.'

If you can't get your views across with a megaphone, why not set them in stone? Outside the Coventry Square Markets in the Perth suburb of Morley, a poem is set in a plaque attached to a 30-tonne iron ore boulder donated by Hancock Prospecting from its Roy Hill iron ore project. The poem is entitled 'Our Future'. The poet is Gina Rinehart.

Our Future

The globe is sadly groaning with debt, poverty and strife
And billions now are pleading to enjoy a better life
Their hope lies with resources buried deep within the
    earth
And the enterprise and capital which give each project
    worth
Is our future threatened with massive debts run up by
    political hacks
Who dig themselves out by unleashing rampant tax
The end result is sending Australian investment, growth
    and jobs offshore
This type of direction is harmful to our core

Some envious unthinking people have been conned
To think prosperity is created by waving a magic wand
Through such unfortunate ignorance, too much abuse is
    hurled
Against miners, workers and related industries who
    strive to build the world
Develop North Australia, embrace multiculturalism and
    welcome short term foreign workers to our shores
To benefit from the export of our minerals and ores
The world's poor need our resources: do not leave them
    to their fate
Our nation needs special economic zones and wiser
    government, before it is too late.

The ABC asked Creative Writing lecturer at the University of Western Australia, Professor Dennis Haskell, for his critical opinion of the work. His response was tongue-in-cheek, but less than generous. Questioning the punctuation and grammar, he noted that Gina is 'about as good at poetry as I am at mining', and that she would be 'wise to keep her day job'. 'She won't make as much money out of poetry, that's for sure,' he laughed.

It seems to me that everything she says and does is geared towards ramming home her ideas. First we get Gina the protester; then we get Gina the poet. What's next? Gina, the musical?

Gina's long-time friend Ron Manners would brook no criticism of the poem or the poet; so much so, that for Gina's 58th birthday, he penned a little ditty for her himself. But most comments on the net were less than favourable. One person suggested that 'La Gina' be annointed Australia's Poet Laureate while another wrote that while it is said that money talks and bullshit walks, it is difficult to conceive any greater illustration of this than Gina Rinehart's poem, succeeding as it does to do both.

On Gina's birthday, while deeply embroiled in the feud with her children, an advertising campaign launched by GetUp! – an independent, grass-roots community advocacy organisation which aims, among other credos, to hold politicians accountable on important issues – took a full-page advertisement in *The Age* newspaper, highlighting its perception of how Gina's stake in Fairfax could colour that newspaper's mining coverage. Using a mocked-up newspaper, it had markers pushing for more favourable mining coverage and a request for a headshot of Lord Monckton. The tagline left nothing to the imagination. 'Is this what the mining industry would do to this newspaper?' it asked.

Gina has attracted some respect from her feminist sisters. In an article entitled 'Move over Bill Gates', Adia Spiller blogged on the website Politics & Pumps: 'For all my women with style and grace, I would like to introduce Georgina Rinehart . . .

'In the next decade women should start to transform themselves into real moguls, using Rinehart as an example. Striving to reach and stay in the "millionaire club" should be a thing of the past. It's time to aim for billionaire status. No one said it would be easy, but if one woman can do it, what's stopping the rest of us?'

Plenty. Gina may not like the title 'iron ore heiress' and she has griped that journalists are 'stupid' for not comprehending that she had no inherited funds to dip into for the Hope Downs project. She has also described the term 'inherited', as 'utter nonsense', a description used by people who know little or nothing about the hurdles that need to be jumped to get a project to the start line. But what Gina was given was the golden key to unlock the resources in the Pilbara. Stupid or not, most of us don't have that opportunity.

News of Gina's 'Axe the Tax' chant and her foray into Fairfax and Ten made her a target for bloggers. Most were cynical, commenting that it is gut-wrenching to see the amount of tax this 'poor woman' is asked to bear; no wonder she wants to establish her own fiefdom in northern Western Australia. Another commented on her lack of political moderation and alienation from the common man, posting that it must be sad and lonely at the top of her empire. Some sided with Gina, asking how many people who inherit great wealth go completely off the rails and blow the lot? Some cut to the chase, claiming that the only form of protest against the threat to democracy is to not buy or support Gina's media outlets. Still others accused her of blatant political propaganda and activism, a woman manipulating the big end of town.

Despite Gina being catapulted into the wealth stratosphere, her clout did not deter cartoonists from taking a dig at her right-wing conservatism, her connection with influential talkback hosts and her ballooned weight. In *The Weekend Australian*, 4 February 2012 edition – the same newspaper that headlined Gina in its Business section as a 'reclusive, driven entrepreneur, but a mining pioneer at heart' – a cartoon by Nicholson pulled no punches. Under a spoof of Gina's head, her face as red as the Pilbara earth on which she is sprawled, the caption reads: 'Drilling will start soon on a huge metallic outcrop in the WA desert. Its impenetrable shell is familiar, but its interior unexplored. Prospectors detect talkback with Alan Jones and Ray Hadley deep within its caverns. All we know for sure is it's massive, it's tough, it won't go away and it's worth $20 billion.'

72

GINA'S LAWYER, PAUL MCCANN gave skittish warnings in the NSW Supreme Court that the publicity arising from the fracas could prove 'fatal' to the Roy Hill project by spooking potential investors, delaying the project and resultant loss of 'allocated berths' at Port Hedland for ore export. His client, he said, needed confidentiality. 'Hundreds of millions of dollars have been invested in the project to this date to enable it to have reached the stage of debt financing. Our client accordingly seeks a no-publication order for these proceedings, including their existence in court, and that the hearing be held with the fullest possible protection of confidentiality.'

By mid-March 2012, Gina's dreams looked set to be realised with news that she was on the brink of finalising the structure of a deal to sell 15 per cent of the Roy Hill project: 12.5 per cent to Marubeni, a trading company in Japan, for approximately $1.7 billion and 2.5 per cent – around $300 million – to STX in South Korea. Following that, she will need to source billions of dollars from diverse international banking institutions. With

Posco's planned investment of 11.25 per cent of Roy Hill, the entire project would value around $13.5 billion. Scuttlebutt that the dispute with her children would derail the plans was scotched by Posco representatives who assured a nervous market that the brouhaha would not have any effect.

Then, another bombshell: the news that John Hancock had turned to business friends in Hong Kong and China to bankroll legal action against his mother. This time, the market did react nervously.

'The introduction of the mystery Chinese financiers will cause issues, it will worry the Japanese and Korean partners in Gina Rinehart's Roy Hill project,' journalist Tim Treadgold wrote.

Then Gina, through her lawyers, played another chess move, this time demanding that journalists at *The West Australian* newspaper, controlled by Channel 7 owner Kerry Stokes, disclose any correspondence between themselves and her three oldest children made on or after the start of the September 2011 legal actions had commenced. Her demands were backed by a Supreme Court of Western Australia subpoena that ordered a copy of all recordings or notes of conversations be handed over. At the heart of the demand is a request for discovery to see if the reporters were privy to details before the matter was aired in court, which would in turn be in breach of the confidentiality deed. If so, both parties would be required to retreat behind closed doors into arbitration, a scenario John, Bianca and Hope are fighting to prevent. They want any legal stoush to be aired in open court.

The latest drama came amid news that Gina had requested two board seats at Fairfax, reputedly to give her more clout to influence the board to support the Macquarie Radio Network's investment in Fairfax Media's radio assets. The reports were conflicting: while some commentators claimed the stations were no longer for sale, others linked the push with Gina helping adman John Singleton to expand his radio empire. As the scuttlebutt raged, *The West Australian* newspaper's editor, Brett McCarthy vowed that the paper would do everything in its power to protect any confidential sources.

73

ON MY LAST TRIP to Perth, a city I frequently visit, I was astonished at the visual proof of expansion in the Pilbara by the numbers of workers, male and female, moving in and out of Perth Airport. The taxi queue snaked almost to the terminal and flights to mining bases such as Karratha, Newman and Paraburdoo were frequent. The Qantas Club, previously the quiet, almost sole domain of the corporate set was alive with yellow fluorescent jackets worn by mine workers who lined up for food as if at their workplace canteen. Perth has the hum and buzz of money and expansion; the money and expansion which rains down from those holes in the Pilbara earth.

Many of Lang Hancock's contemporaries are now retired or deceased. Those who are still alive are often prohibited by confidentiality agreements from talking about the man they knew, or have been told by Gina not to talk. Fred Madden was not one. An executive at Robe River for more than 20 years, in 1993 he became Chief Executive Officer at Hancock

354

Prospecting but resigned less than nine months after taking up
the position because he 'wasn't impressed with the organisation'. Madden refused to sign the confidentiality agreement
offered.

Many people express alarm at the sad turn of events following Lang's death. They want him remembered as a nuggety
character, a dinky-di Australian whose visions opened up the
Pilbara for exploration, and as a model for success, despite the
fact that he never owned his own mine. They want him remembered as a man who flew in the face of setbacks and closed
doors, who survived in the cutthroat world of the boardroom
with his gruff humour and bush mannerisms.

Gina bemoans what she describes as the 'red and green tape'
in which Australia drowns and has claimed that she inherited
a company riven by mess, debts and liabilities, a company she
has grown from bankruptcy to billons. Lang's former associates
understand that she inherited an asset-rich, cash-poor company
from her father. They take nothing away from her for her relentless dedication to growing the companies. But Lang's legacy,
they say, should not be clouded by the spectacle that the House
of Hancock has become.

In court case after court case Hancock's fears, encapsulated
in a 1982 letter to his old mate Peter Wright, came to pass. 'We
will both have to do our best to solve the problems right away
rather than pass on the mess to the next generation – a mess
which, if not properly handled, could result in lawyers getting
a large share of the pickings.'

Reading Lang's interviews so long after he died, it is patently
clear that Gina, who surrounds herself with a metaphoric moat,
has inherited her father's deep suspicion of the media and the
need for privacy. In light of the relentless media attention that
she now has, Lang's conversation with journalist Stuart Reid is
eerily prophetic.

REID: 'You've been rather reluctant, even in this interview, to discuss personal matters. Is your privacy very important to you, and why is it so?'

HANCOCK: 'Well, it's more important, I think, to my wife, to my daughter and my grandchildren. I don't want them pestered. So if they can't get something out of me, then they'll rush down to my daughter and then eventually they'll get on to my grandchildren and so on, and I think the best thing to do is to try and guard them as much as possible, because I mean, they could have a real heyday if they . . . they'd sell a whole lot of newspapers.'

After so many years in the media spotlight, her spectacular and titanic battles with Gina, Rose Porteous wants privacy now, too. Her move to the salubrious suburb of Toorak in Melbourne with husband Willie was short-lived; by some accounts she did not like Melbourne, and Melbourne did not like her. Now back in Perth, she has her own business interests and retreats from an intrusive press. She refuses to discuss Gina, even when entreated by me to do so. 'You don't have to say anything nasty,' I say to her.

'I can't think of anything nice,' she replies without rancour. 'We are getting on with our life now. It is the past.'

Willie describes his own successful real estate business in modest terms, acknowledging the market is tough in this difficult economic climate. 'I'm still doing the same thing,' he tells me in modulated tones. 'Still standing on the street corner, flogging real estate.' He will not discuss Gina; will not even mention her name. It is obviously a chapter in their life that they want to put behind them, permanently. But he is happy to narrate why both he and Rose have withdrawn from the media spotlight. 'You know, if you put your head up, somebody knocks it off!' he laughs. 'We're happy. And Johanna, Rose's

daughter, is back living in Perth, very happily married, with two
kids, a boy and a girl.' I try to engage him on the obvious differences between Gina and Rose: the former reserved, guarded;
the latter eccentric, extroverted. He won't be drawn. 'Rose has
sophistication and taste,' he says. 'She has been pilloried since
the day she walked into Australia, some of it racially motivated.
We don't want media attention any more.' He paused to reflect
on the woman he is married to. 'Rose is a robust, mercurial
individual,' he said with remarkable understatement.

There is no arguing with that.

In death, Lang Hancock is back where he started, his resting
place next to his beloved parents facing the mountain ranges
he so loved. Eagles wheel overhead, their wingspans horizontal
as if protecting the headstone, and the ranges are bathed in a
late-afternoon soft burnt-orange glow. There is serenity in the
silence here, a simple dignity; ashes to ashes, dust to dust. It is a
world away from the chaos of Perth, the squabbling of lawyers,
the tawdry scramble over his fortune.

The sun, which earlier in the day had threatened to turn
the ranges into a tinderbox, is retreating and darkness fast
encroaching.

A crow picks at a carcass. A kookaburra laughs.

Epilogue

I AM SITTING AT a Perth cafe, overlooking the Indian Ocean as the Fremantle Doctor brings a welcoming, cool sea breeze to dampen the temperature of this February afternoon and the sun, almost fluorescent, winks as it slides below the horizon. My companion, the mining insider who has watched Gina's personal and professional dealings for 20 years, ruminates on the woman he knows from afar. 'The seeds of her toughness were there all those years ago, albeit disguised somewhat by that irritating and unnerving little-girl voice,' he said. 'She has become such a controversial character, and an unpopular one. When people hear, for example, that she has donated Christmas lights to a Queensland town, they don't think, "That's nice." They think, "She's got enough money to light up the lives of so many desperate children." What's going on in her head and heart? That's the thing people really want to know. What is going on in her head and heart?'

'If this was a soap opera,' I venture, 'producers wouldn't have to invent a thing, would they? It has got the lot: Machiavellian

358

dramas, Shakespearean plots, obscene amounts of money, poor little rich girls, drugs and sex –'

He cuts in. 'And family feuds, the cut and thrust of politics, allegations of murder, witchcraft, bribery, boardroom deals, outback romance, court room dramas . . .' He pauses. 'But how would you end this soap opera? With the reclusive billionaire that Gina is today? You would surely have to ask: who is she doing all this for? Who is going to inherit all her wealth? At what cost her fortune?'

At what cost her fortune?

It is a curious challenge to write about a person one has never met; worse, a woman who does not wish to be written about and who does not wish to meet me. By the time I had finished writing the biography of Lang Hancock, I felt some degree of warmth towards this rogue bull with a cantankerous charm.

Not so Gina. Regarded by some as the most fascinating female of her time, I found trying to get to the heart of the woman as difficult as looking through the changing colours of a kaleidoscope. Robert Duffield's assessment of the adolescent heiress who 'in order to fit herself for her coming roles as matriarch and priestess of the Hancock dynasty . . . has perforce erected around herself a series of armour-plated defence barriers, lest anybody see a little girl inside who could be taken down by the brutal admirals of industry', had found the kernel of the woman. That armour-plated defence barrier is still there. And it is impenetrable. Gina Rinehart is an immovable force; utterly driven, utterly focused. By all accounts she lives alone at the Dalkeith property that her parents owned. Is she the quintessential poor little rich girl?

It must have irked Gina badly to be replaced in her beloved father's affections by a woman she loathed, a woman she once called a 'Filipina prostitute' who had no Pilbara blood in her veins, an outsider who had no interest in growing her father's company. For Gina, who was deeply suspicious of anyone who may try to rumble the family coffers or challenge its status quo, Rose was more than an archenemy; she came to symbolise just how far Gina would go once she raised the battlements for war. The young woman who met her father's heroine, Margaret Thatcher, in the 1970s has in many ways morphed into her. Gina Rinehart: The Iron Lady, Mark II.

A woman who has known Gina all her life, and who knew her parents, ruminates on Gina's fights with her children. 'She certainly adored those kids when they were babies, from what I could see,' she said. 'She would turn up to do things with them, like watching their swimming carnivals. But this battle with them makes me cringe. Lang and Hope would be so sad if they were around to see it. After all, she honoured her mother's name by christening one of her children after her. Her parents wouldn't want the family name dragged through the media like this. They would be very upset.'

'You know Gina,' I venture. 'This obsession to push forward, to carve up the Pilbara – who is she doing it for? Herself? Her children? Or her father?'

'Who knows,' she sighs. 'But it seems to be taking an awful toll.'

'Can you think of why it has come to this, the fight with her own blood?'

'Something has gone horribly, horribly wrong, hasn't it?' she responds. 'It beggars belief.'

Gina was tough before Rose came along. Now, for all her wealth, she cuts not only a tough figure, but a lonely and somewhat tormented one. Her father's warnings to her that, given her vast wealth, she would need to be careful of people have imbued in Gina a sense of paranoia and secrecy; a mistrust of others; a siege mentality.

Lang's prophecy about his daughter was only partly correct. 'As she gets older she'll have a lot of responsibilities ... so it's most necessary to give her a balanced education, balanced outlook, so that she can learn to live with and handle other people.' Despite her demure air, Gina has not perfected the latter. She is respected in some circles for her achievements, but outside her group of friends, not particularly liked. For all that Gina wants – and given her way, doubtless will achieve – the overriding impression in the public eye is of a woman with mind-boggling wealth and the tawdry, unedifying spectacles of her countless court battles.

Deeply distrustful of the media's portrayal of her ideas and actions, privately Gina has expressed a desire to start her own newspaper. Her father and Peter Wright had done so before her, with unprofitable consequences; but profit is not Gina's goal. She wants control over what is written; she wants control over what is said; she wants her ideas disseminated her way.

Her way.

Gina Rinehart meant business when she said: 'Whatever I do, *whatever* I do, the House of Hancock comes first. Nothing will stand in the way of that. Nothing.'

I think back to images of the young Gina who hosted the 'Wake Up Australia!' flight in 1979. She was a slim, pretty brunette then, with lustrous hair worn loose below her shoulders. Her eyes shone with youthful dreams to follow in her father's footsteps; slightly shy, she was poised and forthright with the media as she gushed with innocent praise about this King of the Pilbara who, against all odds, had opened up the outback for exploration.

All those years ago on the 'Wake Up Australia!' flight that young, innocent girl with the world at her feet answered a reporter's final question of her.

'What do you think you might like your children to give you on your seventieth birthday?' he asked.

Debi Marshall

Gina blushed, genuinely taken aback. 'Oh goodness! Goodness me! Well . . .' She gave it a moment's consideration, then smiled.

'How about a kiss?'

Acknowledgements

WORDS CANNOT EXPRESS MY appreciation for the help given to me by the anonymous source quoted herein as the 'mining insider'. Throughout research and writing he checked facts, corrected errors and provided me with a treasure trove of material gleaned from his immense experience in the mining industry and his personal knowledge of the Hancock and Wright families. Heartfelt thanks: I could not have written this book without him.

Special thanks are also due to my co-researcher Wayne Marshall and to the many people who interrupted busy work schedules to flesh out details about Gina Rinehart and Lang Hancock. Many asked to remain anonymous: they know who they are. Thanks also to Michael Wright who pulled out all stops to help, and to Robert Vojakovic, Paul Fitzgerald and Greg Milton.

The late Robert Duffield, author of *Rogue Bull*, was extremely generous in allowing me use of Hancock quotes in his book and of his insights into the man in the 1970s. Acknowledgement

363

is also due to Neill Phillipson, author of *Man of Iron*, and Alan Trengove, *Adventure in Iron: Hamersley's First Decade*. Ben Hill's meticulous research on asbestos for his book *Blue Murder* offered a chilling insight into that story. H.L. (Mick) Kilpatrick's book, *The Hancock Story*, was invaluable. Feature writer David Leser kindly allowed me use of his interviews with Gina Rinehart and Rose Porteous and the late, lovely Matt Price, *The Australian*'s journalist in Western Australia, was also incredibly helpful. Thanks to John McGlue for use of his extensive interviews with Lang Hancock and to the other journalists who have covered the well-worn path of the Hancock/Rinehart sagas, including Jane Kadzow, Tim Treadgold, Adele Ferguson and Alan Kohler. Apologies to the legions of other journalists I have missed.

Rose Porteous and her husband Willie were both very helpful when I was writing *Lang Hancock* in 1999 and their interviews are included herein. For various reasons, they were unable to comment today.

Thanks also to Kerry Faulkner and David Peberdy, who rescued this technophobe through numerous computer disasters, again.

As always, gratitude to my faithful pit crew, my mother Monica Debnam and daughter Louise Hedger, who cheered me, once again from the start to the finish line. I would not have made deadline either without the support of my husband William Neale, who stood staunchly beside me through pre-dawn starts and late-night finishes. Enormous thanks for being a fabulous support.

So, to the legendary 'mining insider' and to Wayne, Michael, Monica, Louise and William: this book is for you. Troopers, all.

Bibliography

'About ANDEV', Australians for Northern Development & Economic Vision, 2011, http://www.andev-project.org/about/

'Asbestos Diseases Society of Australia, Asbestos' (pamphlet), Asbestos Diseases Society of Australia Inc., 1997

Burrell, Andrew, 'Filial Loyalty Pays Off for Gina Rinehart Heir', *The Australian*, 10 January 2012

Dig a Million, Make a Million, BBC, 1966

Duffield, Robert, *Rogue Bull*, William Collins Pty Ltd, 1979

Durie, John, 'Share Raid Makes Gina Rinehart Biggest Stakeholder in Fairfax', *The Australian*, 1 February 2012

Ferguson, Adele, 'Not Enough', *Business Review Weekly*, 29 June–5 July 2006

Hancock, Lang, 'The Great Claim Robbery: The Struggle for Rights. Major Issues of Today' (published address given at the 45th ANZAAS Congress), 1973

Hancock, Rose, *A Rose by Any Other Name*, Argyle-Pacific, 1992

Hewett, Jennifer, 'Rinehart: Reclusive, Driven Entrepreneur, But a Mining Magnate at Heart', *The Weekend Australian*, 4 February 2012

Hills, Ben, *Blue Murderer*, Sun Books/Macmillan, 1989

'House of Hancock', *Australian Story*, ABC, 1998

Kadzow, Jane, 'The Iron Lady', *Saturday Age*, 21 January 2012

Kilpatrick, H.L. (Mick), *The Hancock Story*, Action Press, 1971

Kohler, Alan, 'Rinehart's Fairfax Investment Experiment', *The Drum*, ABC, 1 February 2012

Langley George Hancock Tribute (videotape recorded by Rose Porteous)

Lees, Tish, *Lonely for My Land*, Sid Harta Publishers, 2010

Leser, David, 'Gina Rinehart and Rose Porteous: A Battle of Wills', *Good Weekend*, 4 April 1998

'The Lord Monckton Roadshow' (transcript), Background Briefing, ABC Radio, 19 July 2011

Moyes, John, *Hancock and Wright*, publisher not named, 1972

Newton, Gloria, 'Lang Hancock's Daughter Comes of Age', *The Australian Women's Weekly*, 19 February 1975

Phillipson, Neill, *Man of Iron*, Wren Publishing, 1974

Price, Matt, 'Over My Dead Body', *The Weekend Australian*, 1999

Price, Matt, 'Wars of the Rose', *The Australian Magazine*, May 1999

Readfearn, Graham, 'Australia's Place in the Global Web of Climate Denial', *The Drum*, ABC, 29 June 2011

Reid, Stuart, Hancock interview, 1990, Battye Library tape 9A; NLA tape 18

SISHA, http://www.sisha.org/projects-hope-scholarship-award.html

Thomson, James, 'Gina Rinehart's Now Worth $20 Billion – And Her Hard Work's Just Started', *SmartCompany*, 19 January 2012

Treadgold, Tim, 'Miner's Daughter', *Forbes: Australia's 40 Richest*, 16 February 2011

Trengrove, Alan, *Adventures in Iron: Hamersley's First Decade*, Stockwell Press, 1976

Vincent, John, 'Lust and High Living: Scandal Rocks Hancock Dynasty', *Woman's Day*, 27 Jan 1997

WA Government, *Prospect* magazine, March–May 1998

Thomson, James, "China Kimbar's Now Worth $20 Billion And Her Hard Work Just Started", Smartcompany, 19 January 2012

Treadgold, Tim, "Miner's Daughter", Forbes Australia, 40 Number 16 February 2011

Troupe, Alan, Adventure in Hand Handedship, First People Stockwell Press, 1974

Vincent, John, "Lub and High Lobbys and Platts Laundry", Dynasty Women's Care, 27 Jun 1992

WA Government, Parer magazine, March–May 1995